# MOVEABLE FEASTS

# MOVABLE FEASTS

## The History, Science, and Lore of Food

*Gregory McNamee*

Westport, Connecticut
London

**Library of Congress Cataloging-in-Publication Data**

McNamee, Gregory.
 Moveable feasts : the history, science, and lore of food / by Gregory McNamee.
p. cm.
 Includes bibliographical references and index.
 ISBN 0–275–98931–3 (alk. paper)
1. Food—History. 2. Cookery—History. 3. Plants, Edible—History. I. Title.
TX353.M395    2007
641.3—dc22    2006021049

British Library Cataloguing in Publication Data is available.

Library of Congress Catalog Card Number: 2006021049
ISBN: 0–275–98931–3

First published in 2007

Praeger Publishers, 88 Post Road West, Westport, CT 06881
An imprint of Greenwood Publishing Group, Inc.
www.praeger.com

Printed in the United States of America

∞

The paper used in this book complies with the
Permanent Paper Standard issued by the National
Information Standards Organization (Z39.48–1984).

10 9 8 7 6 5 4 3 2 1

The publisher has done its best to make sure the instructions and/or recipes in this book
are correct. However, users should apply judgment and experience when preparing recipes,
especially parents and teachers working with young people. The publisher accepts no
responsibility for the outcome of any recipe included in this volume.

for Marianne, my favorite chef

# CONTENTS

CONTENTS

# INTRODUCTION

Some years ago, I traveled through China with some doctor friends, studying Tai Chi, walking through countryside and city, and enjoying the endless sights. One of the least scenic of them was the passenger waiting room at the airport in the ancient capital of Xian, a building that seemed to have been built by beginning apprentices sometime in the early years of the T'ang dynasty, encrusted with ancient garbage and coated in generations of nicotine. We were stuck there, fogged in, awaiting a flight that had not yet left its originating airport of Hangzhou, three hours away, and it did not help our collective mood that most of us had the flu. That fact did not stop one of the doctors from brightly saying, "Well, I know a way to pass the time. Let's talk about the best meals we've ever had."

At the moment, I was struggling with the effects of recent meals that I had had, featuring water buffalo stomachs, various other innards, and the inevitable french-fried potatoes that, at least in those days, Chinese chefs seemed to think foreigners required in order to live. Still, I thought hard, and then decided that the single best meal I had ever had came before me at a clifftop restaurant in the southern Italian town of Muro Lucano along about 1978, a meal involving pasta served with fresh peas (does anyone remember what those taste like?), mushrooms, and tuna—yes, tuna surprise, but with a twist—along with *bruschetta* and roast veal and a bottle of good Aglianico wine from the slopes of the ominously named Monte Vulture. I think the pasta may have had the tiniest sprinkling of cheese on it, though perhaps not, since an Italian friend of ours once reeled when

"Flora dispensing her favours on the earth," from Robert J. Thornton, *Temple of Flora* (1799).

my wife asked for a little grated cheese atop her *spaghetti al tonno* and gasped, "Cheese? Weez feesh?" I had doubtless had better meals before, and I have had many exceptional meals in the years since, some in China, some in Italy, some in Mexico, some in my own kitchen. But there, in that smoky Chinese airport, I thought back to that warm evening in 1978. I remembered the meal for several reasons. One was the remarkable freshness of each ingredient; one was the remarkable cheerfulness of the restaurateur, a handsome woman of an indeterminate age. And one, the one that haunted me now, was that as I ate that splendid meal on that magnificent mountaintop, I found myself pondering where all those foods came from. The cheese and the fish were native, more or less; cheese has figured in the Italian diet since the first transhumant herdspeople drove sheep and goats over the Alps, deep in the Neolithic era, and fish of the open sea turned up on Italian plates a moment or two after those Neolithic people launched their boats upon the waves. But the other foods came from farther afield: the peas from Anatolia, the tomatoes and peppers from the foothills of the Andes, the potatoes in my friend's gnocchi from higher up in those mountains, the rice in another friend's risotto from China, the wheat in our bread from the highlands of Syria, the basil from India, the olives from the Black Sea, the coffee from the Horn of Africa.

That meal, just as every other meal you and I have ever eaten, was the product of history, a complicated process of exchange and cultural contact (and sometimes cultural collision). Without that process, our larders would be very much the poorer. Imagine life without pizza or spaghetti. Imagine grilled steak without corn on the cob or green beans to accompany it, a hamburger without french fries, a chili dog without the chili or the slightest hint of catsup. Imagine a world without chocolate ice cream, without steaming hot coffee at breakfast, without pumpkin pie.

It is not that Old World cuisine was bad, to be sure: Henry VIII's girth suggests that the contemporary culinary scene did not want for material. Still, endless processions of suckling pig and roast stag and pickled beets can weary even the heartiest appetite, and gourmands all over Europe

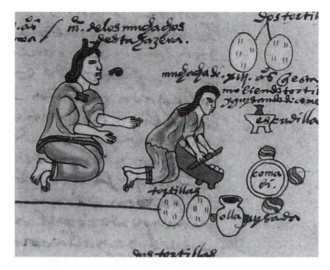

An Aztec mother trains her daughter to make corn tortillas in this scene from the sixteenth-century Codex Tudela.

must have been deliriously grateful when Christopher Columbus returned from his first voyage with a ship's hold full of strange new delicacies from the Indies, among them assorted chiles, avocados, maize, and guavas. A particular treat, at least for southern European palates, was the tomato, which—though not without difficulty—found its way into the cuisine of Italy, where it is called *pomodoro,* or "golden apple," as in France the potato is called *pomme de terre,* or "earth apple." Italian cooks so thoroughly incorporated the tomato into their repertoire that it is almost impossible to conceive of Italian cuisine without it, a wonderfully accidental transformation.

For centuries the peoples of Europe made do without a battery of foods we rely on today, and they developed a culinary tradition that survives in most particulars in every American home: roast meats, boiled vegetables, sturdy breads of all kinds. Fortunately, other highlights of the early European table, such as the late Roman delicacy of parboiled flamingo in rotted-fish sauce, are not much replicated today. Some, though, deserve revival. Consider one Roman recipe, recorded by Apicius in his cookbook *De opsoniis et condimentis sive arte coquinaria* at around the time of Christ, which details ordinary fare that, given the long European memory for such things, Columbus himself might have eaten. The recipe is slightly adapted for the modern kitchen.

Clean and wash assorted vegetables. Shred and boil them; then remove from heat, let cool, and drain. Remove skin from four pounds calf's brains.

Crush ten peppercorns in mortar and wet with beef broth. Rub this mixture on brains. Add the vegetables and puree. Add eight lightly beaten eggs. Add a cup of broth, a cup of red wine, and a cup of raisin wine or juice. Oil baking dish. Put mixture in dish and bake until firm (about twenty minutes at 350°). Sprinkle with pepper and serve warm.

A sixth-century Greek *krater*, or drinking bowl, depicts a figure, possibly the singer Arion or the god Dionysus himself, afloat on a sea full of dolphins—yet with grapes hanging overhead.

Anyone for seconds? Brains are a lovely thing, though we moderns have grown squeamish about eating organs of various kinds, no thanks to spongiform viruses and the like. Even so, until the present, fifteen hundred years after Apicius's day the basic approach to European cooking had changed little. This fourteenth-century English recipe, adapted from Constance Hieatt and Sharon Butler's delightful book *Pleyn Delit*, for a dish called, yes, "Garbage," would have been right at home in Apicius's kitchen, or in Columbus's galley:

Tayke fayre garbages of chykonys, as the head, the fete, the lyverys, and the gysowrys; washe them clene, and caste them in a faire potte, and caste ther-to fresshye brothe of Beef or ellys of moton, and let it boyle; and a-lye it wyth brede, and ley on Pepir and Safroun, Maces, Clowyse, and a little verious and salt, and serue forth in the maner as a Stewe.

In other words, take a pound of chicken "garbage"—that is, feet, liver, and gizzards. Wash it thoroughly, and place in a large saucepan with two cups of beef or mutton stock and simmer slowly for an hour. Add a third of a cup of breadcrumbs, a dash each of ground cloves, ground pepper, mace, and saffron, and a teaspoon of lemon juice. Simmer for five minutes, and you are done. But will you be asked to helm the kitchen again?

Culinary exchange is a two-way street. Europe contributed to the cuisine of the Americas as well, and many of the foods we relish today—pizza, enchiladas, mashed potatoes with gravy—are the happy products of those two far different worlds encountering each other, if so often unhappily.

Because the victor gets to write the histories, we know all too little about the cuisines of the vanquished. Take Native American cuisine, for instance. The first Thanksgiving, in the autumn of 1621, featured only "fowl" and "deer," the pilgrim Edward Winslow wrote; later feasts included succotash, duck, goose, eels, corn bread, wild plums, and other treats from Indian recipes, and we know about them only because grateful New Englanders took the time to learn how to make them *à la indienne*. Pre-Columbian cookbooks will one day be discovered, we can hope; perhaps some Maya hieroglyph will one day turn up with the original recipe for guinea-hen tacos. Until then, ethnobotanist Gary Nabhan suggests that a typical Southwestern Indian culinary concoction of, say, 1300 C.E. might have been something like this:

> Rehydrate 1.5 cups dried venison or antelope in 2 cups water. Drain excess water. Combine with 2 tsp dried red chiltepines or one cup diced hot green chiles and 3 tsp dried wild oregano [Mexican verbena] leaves [oregano can substitute]. Add 1/2 cup venison-suet or sunflower oil; 2 cups amaranth greens; 1 cup prickly-pear pads, well cleaned and cut into 1-inch cubes; and 1 cup tomatoes. Simmer for 10–15 minutes and serve with warm tortillas.

Thanks to fair ocean currents and a swarm of curious adventurers, we need not imagine life without tomato sauce, guacamole, french fries, chili con carne—or, for that matter, sticky rice, watermelon, amaranth, okra, and eggplant.

Most of the foods we eat today, as I have said, are accidents of history. One species of accident is this: a conqueror enters a new land, observes its people eating something strange and wonderful, tries it, and likes it. That new food becomes part of the conqueror's repertoire: Columbus sends chile, Pizarro potatoes, Balboa tomatoes, Cortez maize, and in time all Europe is enjoying meals that would not be out of place at a Hopi table, as if they had been there all along.

Sometimes the process of culinary expansion is gentler. We eat basil, at least in part, because of an ancient idea that to do so brings us closer to the gods. Oranges grace our tables because some ancient traveler on the Central Asian trade routes took to their bitterness and found that they fit easily into a saddlebag; thus transportable, it was an easy matter to trade oranges for other things, doubtless including other foods.

And often the process of culinary expansion involves daring. In the charming, food-centric film *So I Married an Ax Murderer,* Canadian comic Mike Myers, contemplating the strange thing that is haggis (organs again), observes that Scottish cuisine is the only one in the world that is based on a dare. This is not so: the same can be said of nearly every cuisine in the world, at least at some point in its history. What brave Roman was commissioned to determine when the flamingo buried in the back yard was ready to eat? How many Aymara Indians had to die before the potato was finally bred out of its poisonous ways? How many countless humans have fallen before the mushroom? What of the proto-Indo-European steppe dweller who decided that it would be a good idea to raid a beehive for honey? These are our pioneers, explorers of the table, and one day a museum will have to be built in their honor.

History is accidental, but the laws of nature are immutable. Food involves science as well as art, and science can produce some oddities indeed. When, after the Second World War, Americans sought to fill their brand-new refrigerators, they had a product of science par excellence to turn to: colored margarine. Working for Proctor & Gamble, the English scientist Henry Keyser had developed hydrogenated oils as early as 1907, but the dairy industry had long pressed for laws requiring that these oils be colored in order to distinguish them from butter. Fears over the dangers posed by food additives kept margarine a pale white until the war, when hydrogenated-oil manufacturers decided themselves to color their products to distinguish them from then-scarce, heavily rationed dairy products, lest the war effort suffer from unwonted deprivation. The ploy worked; today Americans use far more margarine and vegetable oil than butter, and some dairies even color their butter yellow to attract customers.

Science tells us, too, that merely to look at food causes most of us to experience a significant rise in brain dopamine, the neurotransmitter associated with feelings of pleasure and reward. The response is just that of a drug addict, and a psychiatrist reviewing those findings remarks, "Eating is a highly reinforcing behavior, just like taking illicit drugs. But this is the first time anyone has shown that the dopamine system can be triggered by food when there is no pleasure associated with it since the subjects don't eat the food. This provides us with new clues about the mechanisms that lead people to eat other than just for pleasure, and in this respect may help us understand why some people overeat." If we have come so far unmoored from evolution's cable that merely to see a picture of food can send us slavering, if we are all secret addicts at the table, then we might just as well throw all caution to the wind and enjoy something real: not margarine but butter, not genetically modified ketchup but a real tomato grown in real sun, not hormonally overladen beef but a thin slice of forbidden barnyard veal—the food they eat in France, in other words, where something like civilization still reigns.

Knowing about where our food comes from in history, I think, enhances our understanding of where it comes from today. American taste has shifted, thank the heavens, in the last half-century, toward greater consumption of fresh, organically produced vegetables and other foodstuffs

—at least for those who can afford them in an increasingly class-structured, polarized nation. This pattern will likely continue, so that at least one stratum of society supports a healthy if boutique-like farming culture. Yet, some economists warn, it is likely that as farmland gives way to housing developments and shopping malls, as the world's population grows, and as the supply of fossil fuels declines, the cost of food will rise substantially, perhaps as high as half of net income. If this in fact happens, then grain production, so much of which is given over to livestock feed, will be diverted to human consumption, so that Americans and other first-worlders will in time eat what the rest of the world eats: grains and vegetables, with meat making up only a small portion of our caloric intake.

This, of course, would not be such a bad thing, but it would be a dislocating one for many eaters used to a steady diet of hamburgers and hot links. Hunger has more often than not been a product less of the land's failure to produce food than rapacious politics, as with the potato famine in Ireland and the even more destructive famines in Russia and China in the twentieth century. Yet the near future may well bring hunger of a more generalized sort. In China alone, even with the success of the old one-child policy (and, as Charles Darwin observed, humans are the only animals who have fewer babies the better fed they are), annual grain consumption is estimated to rise dramatically by the year 2030 to 400 kilograms per person, or 641,000,000 tons of grain a year. China will have to import about half that amount; the problem is, even that half is twice the current annual export from all grain-producing countries combined. Someone's bowl will be unfilled, and by the millions.

This book blends goodly quantities of history and food lore, science and nutrition, folktales, and downright trivia to what I hope is a tasty end. As a sometime "nature writer"—I prefer the noted editor Jack Shoemaker's formulation "landscape writer"—I have long been interested in food and its ways, convinced that, just as our making good cities teaches us to protect wilder climes, so learning about what we eat can make us better guardians of the garden and table. That trust may be misplaced, but becoming better consumers is certainly within the sphere of enlightened self-interest, given how many opportunities the present market offers to ingest things that are not good for us, that come from deep in the bowels of dubious labs, that do not much seem like food at all. Think of dessert toppings, or cheese puffs, or most industrial hamburgers—or, for that matter, think of what passes for tomatoes in so many groceries.

I insert this note, in closing, with red flags and klaxons: I like foods that are spicy, pungent, drenched in olive oil, salty, smoky, savory. The recipes in this book, selected for their anthropological and historical interest as well as their capacity to yield good-tasting things, appeal to that sensibility. I have tested all of them at one time or another, but beware: they are adapted to my taste, which is certainly not everyone's—and which may well alarm medically trained or otherwise sensitive readers. Your mileage may vary, so, as with any recipe, you should feel free—indeed, encouraged and exhorted—to experiment so that the taste of the food you make and eat conforms exactly to your idea of what good food should taste like. Similarly, I do not list the number of servings a dish yields, holding, in the words of my much admired friend Jim Harrison, that "small portions are for small and inactive people." Live large until your body tells you otherwise; eat fresh and close to the earth, stick to olive oil and broccoli and wine, stay away from corn syrup in all of its nefarious guises, and—or so I tell myself—you will be all right.

I repeat: this is primarily a book of food history, science, and lore, and not of cookery strictly speaking. Be forewarned, then, that you put a bite of unfamiliar food into your mouth at your own risk. But you knew that, as did the brave men and women who preceded us, generation after generation, to taste and test the foods of the world, bringing them at considerable risk but with great rewards from every corner of the world to our tables. Blessings be upon them, and forgiveness, too.

## FURTHER READING

Jean Anderson and Barbara Deskins, *The Nutrition Bible* (Morrow, 1995).

Don Brothwell and Patricia Brothwell, *Food in Antiquity: A Survey of the Diet of Early Peoples* (Praeger, 1969).

Peter R. Dallman, *Plant Life in the World's Mediterranean Climates* (University of California Press, 1998).

Alan Davidson, *The Oxford Companion to Food* (Oxford University Press, 1999).

Felipe Fernández-Armesto, *Near a Thousand Tables: A History of Food* (Free Press, 2002).

Barbara Gold and John F. Donahue, eds., *Roman Dining* (Johns Hopkins University Press, 2005).

Constance Hieatt and Sharon Butler, *Pleyn Delit: Medieval Cookery for Modern Cooks* (University of Toronto Press, 1976).

Margarita Artschwager Kay, *Healing with Plants in the American and Mexican West* (University of Arizona Press, 1996).

Douglas J. Kennett and Bruce Winterhalder, eds., *Behavioral Ecology and the Transition to Agriculture* (University of California Press, 2006).

Kenneth F. Kiple, *The Cambridge Historical Dictionary of Disease* (Cambridge University Press, 2003).

Richard Manning, *Food's Future: The Next Green Revolution* (North Point Press, 2000).

Sidney W. Mintz, *Tasting Food, Tasting Freedom: Excursions Into Eating, Culture, and the Past* (Beacon Press, 1996).

Marion Nestle, *Food Politics: How the Food Food Industry Influences Nutrition and Health* (University of California Press, 2002).

Giovanni Rebora, *Culture of the Fork: A Brief History of Food in Europe* (Columbia University Press, 2001).

Waverley Root, *Food* (Simon & Schuster, 1980).

Reay Tannahill, *Food in History* (Penguin, 1973).

J.G. Vaughan and C.A. Geissler, *The New Oxford Book of Food Plants* (Oxford University Press, 1997).

Herman Viola and Carolyn Margolis, *Seeds of Change: A Quincentennial Commemoration* (Smithsonian Institution Press, 1991).

# ALMOND

---

If you were a member of the Gilead tribe, back in the Palestine of about 1200 B.C.E., you would have called an ear of wheat a *shibboleth*. If you were from the neighboring and related but rival tribe of Ephraim, you would have called that same ear of wheat *sibboleth,* for your dialect of ancient Hebrew would have been without what is technically called the voiceless postalveolar fricative, the *sh* sound. That lack would have been a source of trouble when Gilead went to war against Ephraim, as the book of Judges 12:1–15 relates:

> Then Jephthah gathered together all the men of Gilead, and fought with Ephraim: and the men of Gilead smote Ephraim, because they said, Ye Gileadites are fugitives of Ephraim among the Ephraimites, and among the Manassites.
>
> And the Gileadites took the passages of Jordan before the Ephraimites: and it was so, that when those Ephraimites which were escaped said, Let me go over; that the men of Gilead said unto him, art thou an Ephraimite? If he say Nay;
>
> Then said they unto him, Say now Shibboleth: and he said Sibboleth: for he could not frame to pronounce it right. Then they took him, and slew him at the passages of Jordan: and there fell at that time of the Ephraimites forty and two thousand.

Thus, the word for a kind of food became the epicene term for those many dividing lines by which families, cliques, interest groups, professions, tribes, and nations distinguish themselves from one another, usually with an eye to expressing superiority in the difference. That *shibboleth*

*Plate 109*

The Almond Tree.
*Eliz. Blackwell delin. sculp. et Pinx.*
1. Blossome
2. Fruit
3. Stone
4. Kernel
*Amygdalus*

Elizabeth Blackwell, "The almond tree/Amygdalus," from *A curious herbal, containing five hundred cuts of the most useful plants, which are now used in the practice of physick* (1739).

should be a shibboleth is most fitting, for food and its treatment can distinguish groups as effectively as costume or language. A potato is a potato is a potato, but *latkes* are not *mickies* are not *pommes frites.* Rice is rice is rice, but it takes on a different quality in *sushi* or *gumbo* or *pilau.* Serve up a dish of corn pone to a Yankee, and you run the risk of being thought an unreconstructed southerner, a habitué of the Virginia truck stop that gave me my first job as a cook in the early 1970s. Call the dish *polenta* and add a sprinkle of parmesan cheese to it, and you can charge four times as much for what is essentially the same foodstuff, now with the added cachet of a foreign pedigree.

This brings us to the almond. Now, the almond has been both familiar and exotic for millennia, or so one would conclude, given its profound antiquity in the Old World. It has been on the Eurasian scene forever, it seems, yet it reveals a pattern of emerging, disappearing, and being reintroduced by one foreign tribe or another, a stranger in an unstrange land. And *Prunus amygdalus,* after all, is a strange sort of thing, a member of the rose family closely related to the peach and plum, whose nut is really an overgrown pit encased in a tiny bit of meat. Botanists surmise that the almond first appeared as a natural hybrid of several species of tree from Central Asia, though it is first attested in the semidesert country of western India. From there, along with the pistachio, it spread rapidly into the Middle East; those two nut trees are the only ones mentioned in the Bible. By the time of the Late Bronze Age, the age of the events of the *Iliad* and the *Odyssey,* the almond had arrived in at least some of the Greek islands, and almonds have been recovered from excavations at the great Palace of Knossos on Crete. The Romans called the almond "the Greek nut," and the tree was grown in southern Italy and Sicily, traditionally Greek areas. The Greeks even developed a fine story about the tree they called *phylla,* "leafy thing," saying that it had been born of a Thracian queen, Phyllis, who so grieved over the loss of her children that the gods took pity on her and changed her into the stately tree.

The Phoenicians and their Carthaginian cousins, though, did more than the Greeks to introduce the almond to the central and western Mediterranean, for they were preeminently people of scientific agriculture and arboriculture, responsible for a vast library of books on growing techniques; one, by the Carthaginian agronomist Mago, was influential throughout the ancient world, and the chapters in Pliny's *Natural History* devoted to fruit- and nut-bearing trees are glosses of the Carthaginian original. Carthage and the Phoenician-colonized coast of eastern Spain and southern France boasted vast groves of almonds, but they took little credit for the innovation; they explained that they had received the tree from the Egyptians, who, according to the book of Genesis, had received it from Israel the patriarch, who had probably received it from the Philistines, cousins of the Phoenicians, who had received it from some unknown source to the east, out beyond the land of the shibboleth.

The almond, then, was planted throughout the Mediterranean long ago, both as a food and as a medicine, for almond potions were traditionally used to treat gastrointestinal disorders. By the time the Roman Empire fell, though, its cultivation was concentrated once again in the eastern Mediterranean, perhaps as a result of agricultural specialization: the best wines came from Campania, the best olives from Miletus, the best wheat from Illyria, the best almonds from the mountain slopes of the Holy Land. And so it was for hundreds of years, as the almond trade inevitably became more and more associated with the Arab world, spreading with the Arab conquests of North Africa and Iberia. It was in the latter place that knights of the Holy Roman Empire encountered the almond, bringing trees back to Charlemagne's court at Aachen, in what is now westernmost Germany. The emperor liked them so much that he ordered them planted at all royal residences, and for some hundreds of years almonds—and pistachios—flourished near Paris and throughout the High Poitou region, Languedoc, and Provence.

Eventually, as Islam and Christianity went to war, two things happened: the Crusaders who went east returned home from Arab lands with a liking for almonds, and vigilant guardians of morals back home denounced the almond as a symbol of the infidel, even though almond milk had served as a convenient substitute for sheep or cow's milk during days of obligation. The result was that many of those ancient groves were uprooted,

[ 3 ]

with the unintended consequence that the almond trade was once more concentrated in Arab hands. That trade was steady, as European palates became accustomed to Arabic tastes; almonds appear in sauces for chicken, pigeons, rabbit, pork, and other meats in the Western recipe books that began to flourish in the thirteenth century, and Richard II of England, that unfortunate victim of the Wars of the Roses, is said to have favored above any other dish a concoction of small birds boiled in almond paste, cinnamon, and rosewater, ingredients that speak to a strong Muslim influence even in England—and even if it may not have been recognized as such.

Exotic and familiar, the almond took its time to arrive in America, for reasons that are unknown but that suggest a touch of clerical suspicion about its fitness for newly Christianized lands. Even so, the founders of the Spanish missions in what is now California planted almonds as they traveled northward in the eighteenth century. The cool, foggy coastal climate proved inhospitable, though, and when commercial growers planted almond groves in the 1850s—with stock reinforced from New York hybrids—they did so in the hot Sacramento and San Joaquin valleys. That area supplies the entire domestic market and about half the world market as well, with Spain and Italy making up much of the rest.

The Middle East contributes little to the international trade today. Now, in Hebrew, an almond tree is called a *shaked*, meaning "the waker," since it is among the very first plants to bloom in spring, bedecked in beautiful white blossoms. In the Arab world, the almond is a symbol of hope, for those blossoms appear overnight on hitherto bare branches. More important in both cultures today is the lemon tree, one of which, as Sandy Tolan writes in his book of that name, now serves as a symbol for efforts to make peace among Arab and Israeli neighbors in the small town of al-Ramla. Their experience suggests that the future of the region need not be tumultuous. I harbor a fond hope that someone will plant an almond alongside that lemon tree, a sometime shibboleth, a traveler among many times and peoples, one that brings good as it wanders.

## BLANCMANGE

Modern blancmange is a sweet, wobbly, generally ghastly dish eaten mostly in the British Isles—and, as fans of Monty Python will remember, an avatar of invaders from outer space. The medieval version of the "white thing to eat" was a much different thing, as this recipe from Richard II's time shows.

> Nym rys and lese hem and wasch hem clene and do thereto god almande mylk and seth hem tyl they al to brest and than let hem kele and nym the lyre of the hennyn or of capouns and grynd hem small kest thereto wite

grese and boyle it. Nym blanchyd almandes and afroun and set hem abowe in the dyshe and serve yt forthe.

In other words:

Cover a cup of jasmine, basmati, or Texmati rice with cold water and let stand overnight. Drain it, rinse it, and allow the rice to dry. In a saucepan, cover the rice in almond milk (see below) and cook over medium heat for five minutes. Add a cup of chopped chicken breast, half a cup of finely chopped almonds, and a little sugar. Cook on low heat for another fifteen minutes, until the rice is done, diluting with chicken stock as needed. Spoon out on a serving dish and dig in.

To make almond milk: add a cup of ground almonds to two cups of boiling water and allow to steep for five minutes. Use a hand blender to smooth the milk out.

## MARZIPAN

Marzipan, a favorite treat throughout Europe, was introduced from the eastern Mediterranean in the fifteenth century. This Venetian recipe is from that time.

Peel the almonds thoroughly. Crush them with a pestle so that they don't have to be put through a grinder. To make the almonds whiter, tastier, and sweeter, soften them in cool water for a couple of days or so. Crush them along with a little rosewater so they don't get oily. If you want to make a good torte put into it equal measures of ground almonds and sugar, and then an ounce or two of good rosewater, and mix them all together very thoroughly. Bathe the bottom of the mixture with rosewater and put some on the bottom of the pan, then cook it in an oven or over a fire like other tortes, taking care to use a gentle flame and to check it often so that the torte doesn't burn. Remember that marzipan tortes should be light and thin, not thick and heavy.

## PANELLETS

In the Tuscany of old, meals began with the serving of a cake made of almonds and pine nuts, served with a strong sweet wine. Today, Catalans enjoy little almond cakes called *panellets*, which, as Patience Gray notes in her lovely book *Honey from a Weed*, are "excellent with a glass of wine."

2 1/4 pounds peeled almonds
2 pounds sugar
1/4 cup vanilla sugar
2–3 potatoes
1/4 cup anise
1/4 cup brandy
1/4 pound grated coconut

[ 5 ]

orange extract
1/2 cup slivered almonds
1/2 cup pine nuts

    With a mortar and pestle or food processor, grind the almonds into powder. Boil, peel, and mash the potatoes, then mix in the almond flour. Add the sugar and vanilla sugar (see below). Divide the flour. Add the coconut and anise to the first part, and the brandy and orange extract to the second. Make each mixture into small cakes, but keep them separate; top the one with slivered almonds, and the other with pine nuts. Cook on a pizza stone or oiled baking sheet for 10 minutes at 350°.

    To make vanilla sugar: crush a vanilla bean with the back of a spoon. Add to sugar and let sit (ideally, refrigerated) for a day or two before using. Vanilla sugar keeps indefinitely, so keep a supply on hand.

## JELLIED APPLES WITH ALMONDS

This recipe comes from a World War I–era collection by apple growers in the Yakima Valley of Washington, perhaps eager to join forces with the almond growers of California.

Pare, core, and quarter Golden Pippins; stew until soft and beat smooth. Make syrup by boiling a pound and a half of sugar and a pint of water for every two pounds of apples. Put the apple pulp and the juice of 3 lemons into the syrup and boil gently until stiff enough to drop heavily from the spoon. Pour into a wet mold and when cold turn onto a serving dish. Stick blanched almonds into the jelly and surround with whipped cream.

## FURTHER READING

Nicholas Basbanes, *A Splendor of Letters: The Permanence of Books in an Impermanent World* (HarperCollins, 2003).

Patience Gray, *Honey from a Weed: Fasting and Feasting in Tuscany, Catalonia, the Cyclades, and Apulia* (North Point Press, 1990).

Alice M. Hodge, *The Encyclopedia of Practical Horticulture* (Yakima Agricultural Association, 1914).

M. E. Postan, *The Cambridge Economic History of Europe,* vol. 1, *The Agrarian Life of the Middle Ages* (Cambridge University Press, 1966).

Odile Redon, Françoise Sabban, and Silvano Serventi, *The Medieval Kitchen: Recipes from France and Italy* (University of Chicago Press, 1998).

Frederick Rosengarten Jr., *The Book of Edible Nuts* (Walker & Company, 1984).

Sandy Tolan, *The Lemon Tree: An Arab, a Jew, and the Heart of the Middle East* (Bloomsbury, 2006).

# AMARANTH

There are not many stories about flowers in the thousands of fables ascribed to the sixth-century Greek storyteller Aesop, animals being better vehicles for imparting lessons to humans about how to behave. One of that handful is about the Mediterranean amaranth, a beautiful flowering plant, and it goes like this: An amaranth, planted in a garden next to a rosebush, said to it, "What a beautiful flower you are. Humans and the gods alike love you. I envy your appearance and your sweet smell." The rosebush replied, "Really, I should envy you. I live for a brief season, while you live forever, blooming each year. No one plucks you from the ground. Take my word for it, you have nothing to envy me for."

Envy not beauty, then, for it is fleeting and dangerous. But the amaranth, in all its many forms, is quite a striking plant; the rose may be more classically beautiful, but the amaranth is nothing to snub, with its bright green, red, and purple flowers atop a tall, slender stalk.

The Mediterranean amaranth, *Amaranthus graecizans,* a symbol of immortality in Egypt and Greece, and its Old World cousins are ecologically similar to but genetically different from the common American amaranth, *Amaranthus cruentus* and its cousins. It is not so, though a lovely tale, that, as one New Age Web site has it, amaranth was brought to the New World by refugees from the Tower of Babel project; but by happy accident, the New World amaranth, in varieties native to Mexico, Central America, and the northern Andes region of South America, was also a symbol of immortality. This was especially true in the worldview of the Aztecs, whose belief system incorporated complex knowledge of plants

"*Amaranthus tricolor,*" from Berthe Hoola van Nooten, *Fleurs, fruits et feuillages choisis de l'ille de Java: Peints d'après nature* (1880).

of all kinds, and who kept huge fields of amaranth in cultivation around their capital of Tenochtitlan. When the Spanish conquistador Pedro de Alvarado arrived there in the 1520s, he discovered that its residents were fond of eating tamales filled with a paste made of amaranth seeds, a treat that honored the agricultural god Huitzilipochtli, granter of eternal life and, in traditional practice, the beneficiary of spectacular human sacrifices. The emperor Montezuma, Huitzilipochtli's earthly representative, received an annual tribute of 200,000 bushels of amaranth grain from the states that made up the Aztec Empire. Alvarado merely puzzled over these strange facts and went about the business of conquest elsewhere, but the Spanish governors who followed him outlawed amaranth cultivation in an effort to uproot this bloody form of worship. Their predecessor, Hernando Cortez, was not so scrupulous; he had sent specimens of the plant back to Spain, where it enjoyed brief popularity as an ornamental but then was largely forgotten.

They had a point, those governors, but their ban, as with any form of prohibition, was hard to enforce. The Aztecs took its cultivation underground, so to speak, and kept the seed stock healthy over the generations, tending out-of-the-way fields away from centers of power. In time the ban faded into history, and today amaranth grows throughout Mexico's temperate zones, as it has for at least seven thousand years as a cultigen. Several Native American tribes on the northern rim of the Aztec Empire—

the Tarahumara of Mexico and the Hopi and Tohono O'odham of present-day Arizona among them—had also taken up amaranth cultivation and incorporated it into their traditional diet.

This was all to the good for those peoples, for amaranth produces protein-rich greens that can be cooked or eaten raw; alfalfa-like sprouts; and fine flour from its milled or ground seeds. It is something of a wonder plant: higher in calcium than beet greens, higher in protein than spinach, amaranth is rich in essential amino acids like threonine, valine, leucine, methionine, and especially lysine, the last of which is absent in other grains. As a source of protein, amaranth grain ranks higher than cow's milk, soybeans, and whole wheat. A half-cup serving of amaranth greens contains only 14 calories, but 138 milligrams of calcium, 47 milligrams of phosphorus, 1.5 milligrams of iron, 423 milligrams of potassium, and 27 milligrams of vitamin C, as well as goodly quantities of vitamin A.

All that is not bad for a plant that Anglo farmers in the Southwest commonly call pigweed, as in food fit only for livestock. But does it taste good? If you like spinach, then its slightly tart leaves are likely to please; if you like sticky rice, then the slightly gelatinous feel of amaranth flour will appeal, too. And if you like caramel popcorn, then you are sure to enjoy the traditional Mexican dish called *alegría* (happiness), a blend of popped amaranth seeds and honey.

Amaranth is drought-resistant, hardy, and adaptable to many environments, so much so that, thanks to green-revolution agronomists, it has been introduced to the Middle East, Africa, and notably India, where it now ranks as a major crop. Indeed, in some places, such as the ecologically sensitive islands of the South Pacific, introduced amaranth has become a pest, overtaking native species. In its travels, it has been somewhat jumbled and hybridized, and even back at home it has defied easy classification. As the definitive *Flora of North America* puts it, "Weedy and introduced species of *Amaranthus* are often neglected or misidentified by collectors. Consequently, some taxa are known only from scattered localities in various regions of the flora, and their actual distribution may be much wider than present data indicate. Some species have been reported for the flora only as rare, casual, non-naturalized aliens, for example, on ballast, or as grain immigrants or wool contaminants, and may not now be present in North America. Because of all these factors, the maps and distribution statements in the treatment show the generalized distribution and may not properly reflect the actual changing distribution patterns of some species, especially those that have expanded their ranges over the decades due to various anthropic factors."

For all its good qualities, however, amaranth has yet to catch on as a food plant in much of the industrialized world, and especially the United States. It continues to be a major foodstuff only in its various Mesoamerican homelands, while only a few thousand acres in North America are under commercial cultivation. The situation is different in China, where amaranth is widely planted, though it has yet to make much of a presence in local cuisines; as here, it seems to be used mostly as fodder.

Private gardens are another matter, and thanks to good public relations work on the part of several botanists and nutritionists in the last quarter-century, amaranth is becoming more common in small holdings. You do not have to have much of a green thumb to grow it (if I can do it, anyone can), which makes it a sure bet for busy gardeners throughout the temperate zones of North America. The light-loving annual, with its long, brightly colored leaves, is both useful and highly ornamental, and it grows well in most types of soil, although it flourishes best in mulched loam. In its early stages, it requires frequent watering, but as it grows it forms a dense canopy of long green, red, and yellow leaves that prevent water loss and keep out weeds.

Drop a scattering of seedlings into a prepared bed along the edge of your garden and watch them grow—amaranth planted in early summer sprouts in under a week. A mature plant can reach heights of five to seven feet. It takes from four to five months from planting to harvest of the seed heads. Hummingbirds seem to like amaranth, too, an added bonus for the bird-watching gardener.

You can purchase amaranth seeds at many organic-gardening outlets, or by mail from Native Seeds/SEARCH, an organization devoted to preserving indigenous Native American crops and promoting their cultivation. A current seed catalog can be found online at www.nativeseeds.org.

## AMARANTH TORTILLAS

Tortillas are fast becoming a staple of world cuisine, having spread from their Mesoamerican homeland to restaurants, grocery stores, and homes in the unlikeliest of places. (I had one of the best tortillas I have ever tasted, accompanied by one of the hottest salsas, at the main railroad station in Zurich, Switzerland.) This recipe, adapted from Beth Hensperger's *Breads of the Southwest*, nicely draws on the old to make something new.

2 cups unbleached all-purpose flour
1 1/2 cups masa harina (found in Latin American markets or online)
1/4 cup whole wheat pastry flour
1/4 cup amaranth flour
4 teaspoons baking powder
1/2 teaspoon salt
1 1/2 cups warm water
1/4 cup cold butter, cut into pieces
    Combine the flours, cornmeal, baking powder, and salt. Cut in the butter and add the hot water to the flour mixture bit by bit, stirring until the dough becomes pasty. Make a soft firm ball of the dough, adding a tablespoon of

water at a time if the dough is dry. Cover the ball with plastic wrap and let rest for an hour.

Divide the dough into twelve equal portions. Shape each into a ball and place on a baking sheet, pizza stone, or marble slab. Then work each ball with your fingers, draping it so that it makes a kind of hood. On a lightly floured surface, flatten the ball with your palm, then press with a tortilla press or roll out with a rolling pin until the tortillas are about a quarter-inch thick.

Cook in a cast-iron skillet, rather in the manner of pancakes or crepes. The tortillas will form dark spots (look for resonant symbols!) and will puff up. Cook until it hardens ever so slightly but is still pliable, then place in a ceramic bowl or basket and cover with a towel. Serve immediately.

## AMARANTH PASTA

Carolyn Niethammer, author of *The Tumbleweed Gourmet: Cooking with Wild Southwestern Plants,* offers this simple recipe for an amaranth pasta that beats other kinds of pasta, nutritionally speaking, hands-down:

Heat 1/3 cup amaranth seeds in an ungreased wok or cast iron pan until it pops, just like popcorn. Grind the popped seeds in an ordinary kitchen blender; the yield should be one cup of meal. Combine the amaranth meal with one cup of all-purpose flour, two eggs, and 5 tbsp water and process as with any other pasta dough. The noodles require only five or six minutes' cooking in boiling water.

Amaranth meal can also be used in corn bread, tamales, granola, and many other dishes.

## ALEGRÍA

Centeotl, one of the principal Aztec agricultural deities, lends his name to an organization in Oaxaca, Mexico, that is working to bring amaranth into general production using organic farming techniques. It offers several recipes on its Web site, including one, adapted here, for what might reasonably be called "happiness bars."

2 pounds popped amaranth seed
2 pounds brown sugar
juice of two limes
2 cups water

Add brown sugar to water and bring to a boil in a large pot. Add lime juice and let boil for twenty minutes. Remove the mixture from heat. Mix in the amaranth cereal. Pour the mixture into a square greased pan, packing it with a wooden spatula. Allow it to cool, then cut into bars with a moist knife blade.

## FURTHER READING

Centro de Desarollo Comunitario Centéotl (http://www.prodigyweb. net.mx/centeotlac/eng/).

Beth Hensperger, *Breads of the Southwest: Recipes in the Native American, Spanish, and Mexican Traditions* (Chronicle Books, 1997).

Robert Kiger et al., *Flora of North America* (Oxford University Press, 1992–).

Carolyn Niethammer, *The Tumbleweed Gourmet: Cooking with Wild Southwestern Plants* (University of Arizona Press, 1987).

G.F. Stallknecht and J.R. Schulz-Schaeffer, "Amaranth Rediscovered," in J. Janick and J.E. Simon, eds., *New Crops* (Wiley, 1993).

C. C. Townsend, "Amaranthaceae," in R.M. Polhill, ed., *Flora of Tropical East Africa* (CRC, 1999).

# APPLE

---

—Shmuel HaNagid (ca. 1020 c.e.)

What was it that Adam and Eve ate in the Garden of Evil, courtesy of the Serpent, that caused them to be cast out into the cruel world? European legend says that the Fruit of Knowledge was the apple, and, though some scholars think the pomegranate—whose name means "apple of Granada"—to be the more likely candidate, the apple may well have been the guilty party. The Garden of Eden, after all, was said to lie between the Tigris and Euphrates rivers, in modern Iraq, where apples have grown since the days of Gilgamesh and the Assyrian kings. But even there, the apple was an outsider. Though there is some disagreement among modern scholars about the matter, a Soviet-era Russian geneticist named Nikolai Vavilov assembled a powerful body of evidence to show that the apple originated in the high Pamir and Tien Shan mountains of Central Asia, in the region where the modern states of Kyrgyzstan, Kazakhstan, and Tajikistan meet near China. Kazakhstan's capital, Almaty, honors this heritage; its Russian name, Alma-Ata, means "father of apples." (In Russian, curiously, *yabloko,* apple, is a feminine noun; in that language, technically, apples are only mothers and daughters and sisters.) From its Central Asian birthplace, apple cultivation spread by swordpoint and trade along the

*The Old Quining.*

"The Old Quining," a variety of cider apple grown by the English pomologist Thomas Andrew Knight (1759–1838). Illustration by Walter Hooker, from Knight's *Pomona Herefordiensis* (London: Agricultural Society of Herefordshire, 1811).

storied Silk Road, by which goods from East Asia were carried as far as North Africa and the Mediterranean. This wide dispersal took place over many hundreds of years; apples are mentioned in Egyptian texts dating to the thirteenth century B.C.E., turn up in Celtic folklore generations before the Christian era, and figure in Icelandic sagas and Chinese poems alike. The number of species increased as the apples traveled farther from their source, adding to diversity and disease resistance, and large orchards throughout the Old World often contained dozens, and even hundreds, of varieties.

Apples probably arrived in southern Europe at about the time the Romans, who did much to advance Silk Route trade westward, began to extend their empire into Asia and northern Europe alike. Apple trees quickly became a staple of European orchards and European folklore. Some scholars, in fact, suggest that the reason the apple was deemed the forbidden fruit was that it had become sacred to the non-Christian peoples of northern Europe. By making the fruit suspect, that theory goes, early missionaries could more easily convert Celts, Germans, and Vikings to Christianity—for who wants to eat poison, spiritual or physical?

The theory has its virtues, but one thing is for certain: the ancients continued to grow and eat apples, and the apple still holds a central place in northern European agriculture and cuisine, having been exonerated through a blending of traditional and Christian beliefs. In Cornwall, for instance, at Christmas, the apple tree was the subject of the honoring ceremony called "wassailing," where cider was poured on its roots and cakes hung from its branches to assure an abundant crop the following year.

The Eurasian apple found a happy home in North America, which had four indigenous crabapple species that humans found unattractive and many animals found inedible. As early as the 1700s, New York and Pennsylvania were providing much of Europe with the fruit. One American grower, the versatile Benjamin Franklin, introduced a variety to England called the Newtown Pippin that proved extraordinarily popular; a barrel went with Captain Cook aboard the *Endeavour,* though apparently the crew chose to make pies of the Pippins rather than plant them on the islands along their course, where they probably would have flourished, the apple tree being an astoundingly versatile plant.

By the end of the Civil War, growers in the East and the Midwest were producing something like eight hundred varieties of the fruit, courtesy, in some instances, of the legendary grower John Chapman (1774–1845), "Johnny Appleseed," who planted orchards just in time to sell fruit to newcomer settlers following his path across Pennsylvania, Ohio, Indiana, and Illinois. By contrast, sadly, nowadays fewer than fifteen varieties are found in most regular grocery stores—including the Granny Smith, that green import from Australia, so important to the production of apple juice. The numbers of commercially available apple types are rising, however, as organic and "boutique" farming and gardening become ever more popular across the country. Just about every pomologist (for that would be the fancy term for an apple grower) with a talent for grafting can produce new varieties, so the prospect of adding more kinds of apples to the 7,500 varieties known to history, the offspring of thirty-five or so distinct species of apple, promises to be bright.

The United States was long the world's leading apple-producing nation, with almost every state growing them in commercial quantities. Some states, such as California, New York, and Virginia, still enjoy significant revenue from exports, while Washington's Wenatchee and Yakima valleys account for more than half of the apples grown in the country. In recent years, China has surpassed the United States, accounting for some 40 percent of the world's production; Italy, Turkey, and France produce most of the remaining apples sold on the world market. Other leading apple producers include Poland, Belgium, Russia, Germany, Argentina, Chile, Australia, and New Zealand.

There is reason to hope that, once they shake off the economic doldrums and political corruption that haunt them, the Central Asian states that border the apple's mountainous birthplace will make their contribution, too—though, Frank Browning reports in his delightful book *Apples,* the speculators who are flocking there seem more interested in ski lodges and gold mines than in orchard keeping. Still, hope must remain: when plant explorers from the U.S. Department of Agriculture first studied Central Asian apples in the early 1990s, they found wild apples of the species *Malus sieversii* that were utterly free of insect damage and had no visible signs of apple scab, a disease that has been epidemic in American orchards. The species is closely related to the domestic apple, *Malus domestica,* which includes most of the commercial varieties that are available today, and researchers are now experimenting with crosses from the wild germplasm that will surely increase the fruit's genetic diversity.

Organic production is making headway wherever apples are sold, in part because of the market demand for chemical-free fruit, and though organic yields are naturally lower than the old factory-in-the-orchard system of the big growers, the energy and environmental costs are so much lower than for conventional methods that it makes good sense for the pocketbook as well as the conscience. Still, growing apples is no way to grow rich, as many a boutique farmer and back-to-the-lander has discovered; in most cases, the advantages still lie with the large producers and packers who can put a sack of apples in a supermarket for a dollar and a half.

Economics aside, is there any reason for us to take seriously the adage, "An apple a day keeps the doctor away"? Indeed there is. For one thing, apples, like their pear cousins, contain plenty of dietary fiber, which is good for the digestive tract. A five-ounce (medium-sized) apple also contains 10 mg of phosphorus and 157 mg of potassium, but no sodium—and nutritionists today caution that Americans eat too much sodium and too little potassium. The anthocyanins found in the skin of red apples are thought, too, to have antioxidant, cancer-fighting properties, delaying the breakdown of LDL—"bad cholesterol"—in the bloodstream, which is thought to contribute to atherosclerosis. An apple's tartaric acids help with digestion, and European folk remedies attribute gout-fighting properties to the fruit as well.

Apple ciders and jellies usually have vitamin C added, but that additional value is sometimes canceled by the introduction of extra sugars, so it is best to look for unsweetened varieties when possible. About the only thing inside an apple to stay away from is the seed, which contains cyanide. Eating a few seeds will not do any harm, but eating several dozen of them can produce a stomachache, and sometimes worse.

Apples are normally picked before they begin to ripen, for, once their polyphenloxidase compounds—the same substances that so quickly blacken bananas and pears—begin to work, the fruit will rot within days. You can slow the action of these compounds somewhat by immersing apples in cold water and then storing them in a cold refrigerator, but, even so, you should eat them within four or five days of purchase. When you shop for them, select apples that are firm, but not woody, to the touch. Do not mind minor dings or mild blemishes on the body; deeper blemishes, however, indicate that the fruit is already ripe and should be eaten immediately.

And do eat them. Americans do not eat nearly enough apples, or so growers lament; as of 2000, we consumed only about twenty pounds apiece each year, a third of the per-capita amount eaten by Italians and Belgians, half the per-person quantity eaten in Germany and England. It is probably not a patriotic duty to add apples to our diets, but every bit helps. So bite into a crisp fruit, and mix up a batch of medieval pudding while you are at it. Enjoy an ancient foodstuff, one of the earliest in the human larder, and enjoy keeping that old doctor a step away.

## APPLE PUDDING

Apples were a staple of the medieval European kitchen, served roasted alongside pork (whence our familiar image of the apple in the pig's mouth) or other meats as a side dish, or treated as a dessert. This recipe, adapted from a fifteenth-century English cookbook, illustrates the latter usage:

> Mix a quarter-cup of rice flour (or cornstarch) with a quarter-cup of ground almonds and two cups of water. Pour this over a pound of cooking apples, pared, cored, and finely diced. Bring to a boil for about five minutes, until pudding is thick. Mix in a quarter-cup of sugar, half a teaspoon of cinnamon, and a dash of ginger. Allow to cool before serving.

The first cookbook published in the United States, Amelia Simmons's *American Cookery* (1796), offers a variant for an "apple pudding dumplin":

> Put into paste, quartered apples, lay in a cloth and boil one hour, serve with sweet sauce. Pears, Plumbs, etc. are done the same way.

## APPLE AND ORANGE TART

*The Good Huswifes Handmaid for Cookerie in Her Kitchen* (1588) offers a recipe that is all the more pleasing for its Elizabethan language:

> For a tarte of apples and orange pilles. Take your orenges and lay them in water a day and a night, then seeth them in faire water and honey and let seeth till they be soft; then let them soak in the sirrop a day and a night: then take forth and cut them small and then make your tart and season your apples with suger, synamon and ginger and put in a piece of butter and lay a course of apples and between the same course of apples a course of orenges, and so, course by course, and season your orenges as you seasoned your apples with somewhat more sugar; then lay on the lid and put it in the oven and when it is almost baked, take Rosewater and sugar and boyle them together till it be somewhat thick, then take out the

Tart and take a feather and spread the rosewater and sugar on the lid and let it not burn.

A modern translation goes something like this:

2 medium (9-inch) pie shells (one for a lid)
4 medium apples, sliced thin
4 medium Valencia oranges, sliced thin
1/2 cup sugar
1/2 cup honey
1/2 teaspoons cinnamon
3 1/2 cups water
1/4 teaspoon finely diced ginger

Soak the oranges in cold water overnight. Dry. Mix water and honey and bring to a simmer. Add oranges and cook on low heat for two hours. Mix apples, sugar, cinnamon, and ginger. Layer apples and oranges in a pre-heated pie shell and bake for an hour at 350°. Remove tart and brush on a light syrup of rosewater and confectioners sugar, then bake for another ten minutes.

## APPLE KUCHEN

*The Settlement Cookbook* (1903), written by a Mrs. Simon Kander and Mrs. Henry Schoenfeld and published in Milwaukee, linked the kosher cooking of the Eastern European *shtetl* with ingredients and kitchen tools found in the New World. Here is their easy recipe for kuchen.

After the pan is heavily greased with nice butter, roll out a piece of dough quite thin. Lift it up with the aid of the rolling pin and lay it in the pan, press a rim out of the dough all around the pan and let it raise for about ten minutes. Then lay on the apples in rows. Pare the apples, core and quarter them, dipping each piece in melted butter, before laying on the cake, sprinkle bountifully with sugar (brown being preferable to white for this purpose) and cinnamon. See that you have nice tart apples. Leave the cake in the pans and cut out the pieces just as you would want to serve them. If they stick to the pan, set the pan on top of the hot stove for a minute and the cake will then come out all right.

## APPLE BUTTER

An 1839 number of *Genesee Farmer,* a rural New York paper, offers this recipe for apple butter. A good cider, the basis of the recipe, is not so easy to find in these days of mandatory pasteurization, but with a little sleuthing a bottle will turn up somewhere.

Take a quart of cider and boil until it is reduced to half its original volume. Meanwhile, quarter, pare and core a large bowl of apples. Boil the prepared apples in the reduced cider stirring frequently so that it does not stick to the sides or the bottom of the pot. Stir and boil until the mixture is as thick as hasty pudding.

## FURTHER READING

Frank Browning, *Apples* (North Point Press, 1998).

W. D. Haley, "Johnny Appleseed, A Pioneer Hero," *Harper's New Monthly Magazine* 43 (1871): 830–836.

Shmuel HaNagid, *Selected Poems of Shmuel HaNagid,* translated by Peter Cole (Princeton University Press, 1996).

Gervase Markham, *The English Housewife: Containing the Inward and Outward Virtues Which Ought to Be in a Complete Woman; As Her Skill in Physic, Cookery, Banqueting-Stuff, Distillation, Perfumes, Wool, Hemp, Flax, Dairies, Brewing, Baking, and All Other Things...,* ed. Michael R. Best (McGill-Queen's University Press, 1986).

# ARTICHOKE

Did the ancient Greeks know the artichoke, that thistle kin gone six feet tall and extra-prickly? More than a few food historians think not, arguing that *Cynara scolymus* was bred from its cousin, the cardoon, at the hands of Arab traders in the Middle Ages. There are virtues to their arguments, but then comes a passage from the poet Hesiod, who lived around 700 B.C.E. and knew his way around farms, gardens, and wild places alike:

> But when the artichoke flowers, and the chirping grasshopper sits in a tree and pours down his shrill song continually from under his wings in the season of wearisome heat, then goats are plumpest and wine sweetest; women are most wanton, but men are feeblest, because Sirius parches head and knees and the skin is dry through heat. But at that time let me have a shady rock and wine of Biblis, a clot of curds and milk of drained goats with the flesh of a heifer fed in the woods, that has never calved, and of firstling kids; then also let me drink bright wine, sitting in the shade, when my heart is satisfied with food, and so, turning my head to face the fresh Zephyr, from the ever-flowing spring which pours down unfouled, thrice pour an offering of water, but make a fourth libation of wine.

In other words, when the artichoke flowers, then the weather is on the verge of turning hot—and hot as it can be only in the islands of the south-central Mediterranean, where great winds pour northward from the Sahara and sandblast everything they encounter, making of Sicily, the artichoke's probable place of origin, a semidesert with more than a few African connections.

The Greeks certainly knew the artichoke, for they colonized Sicily thousands of years ago. The Romans knew it, too, their elite having developed a fondness for eating the leaves. Charlemagne knew it; he ordered that it be grown in the gardens of his many palaces, but though he loved artichokes, he could never get the citizens of the Holy Roman Empire to share his enthusiasm, and it was left to Catherine de' Medici to reintroduce their cultivation to France in the sixteenth century, thus assuring her reputation as a harlot—for only a woman of loose virtues, the courtiers of Paris whispered, would eat a food well known to have aphrodisiacal properties.

"Fructa artitchochi," by Basil Besler (1561–1629), who published his *Hortus Eystettensis* from his workshop in the southeastern German city of Eichstatt, where his patron, Bishop Johann Conrad von Gemmingen, kept a large garden.

The word must have gotten around, and the artichoke became the pep pill of the Renaissance. The Italian food historian Giovanni Rebora notes that in a Genoese market of the late sixteenth century, three hundred grams of meat could be had for two *soldis*, whereas a single artichoke cost two and a half *soldis* and a single cabbage top cost a *soldi*. Now, greens are often thought of as poor people's food, but cooked greens tend to be expensive, since they yield comparatively little bulk or protein; even so, the disparity can be explained only by some extracurricular demand, which explains why tongues went wagging when Catherine filled her stomach to bursting with the first artichokes of the new harvest.

Though Arabs were also known to savor artichokes, further clouding its reputation in certain quarters of Europe, knowledge of the artichoke eventually spread north and west, and by the Georgian era the upper crust in Germany and England made it a point to enjoy artichokes, even though the frost-sensitive things had to be imported at considerable expense.

The advent of quicker transport in the nineteenth century reduced those costs somewhat, but even so, the plant was associated with gentlemen and well-groomed country houses, where, as this scene from Thomas Love Peacock's *Gryll Grange* (1860) hints, it was likely to be mixed up with the wholly unrelated Jerusalem artichoke, a kin of the sunflower native not to Palestine but North America:

> "Palestine soup!" said the Reverend Doctor Opimian, dining with his friend Squire Gryll; "a curiously complicated misnomer. We have an excellent old vegetable, the artichoke, of which we eat the head; we have another of subsequent introduction, of which we eat the root, and which we also call artichoke, because it resembles the first in flavour, although, *me judice,* a very inferior affair. This last is a species of the helianthus, or sunflower genus of the *Syungenesia frustranea* class of plants. It is therefore a girasol, or turn-to-the-sun. From this girasol we have made Jerusalem, and from the Jerusalem artichoke we make Palestine soup."

A misnomer piled on a misunderstanding: some English speaker misheard *girasole,* the Italian word for sunflower, as Jerusalem, and the two species were confounded.

In the United States, *Cynara scolymus* was barely known outside Mediterranean immigrant communities in California until the 1960s, when California growers made a push to introduce it to the larger market. It worked, if slowly, and if only to an extent; even now, the entire industry generates only some $50 million annually, less than a single Hollywood film with the right lead. Almost all of the artichokes grown in the United States come from California, and almost all of those come from the Salinas and Monterey areas, where the warm days and cool, foggy nights appeal to the artichoke's core—that is, the flower bud, the heart that artichoke aficionados prize so dearly, scraping away at leaf after leaf until they finally unwrap the prize. It is a small payoff for all that work, some might say, but there are good reasons to eat artichokes, provided they are well cooked. They are fat-free, cholesterol-free, and low in calories, though this will depend on the age of the artichoke; a freshly picked one is low in inulin, an indigestible starch that the body converts to sugar, while one that has been on the shelf for a while will contain much more. Artichokes also provide goodly doses of vitamin C, dietary fiber, magnesium, and folate. Cynarin, a compound extracted from artichokes, has anti-inflammatory and cholesterol-lowering properties and helps lower blood sugar, all useful qualities in this pudgy, sugary age. And who knows? They might just have the qualities Catherine de' Medici sought—after all, Marilyn Monroe herself was California's first Miss Artichoke, which must mean something. All of which would make the artichoke, though ever expensive, a lot cheaper than other remedies on the current market.

# ARTICHOKE STEW

This recipe, from medieval Seville, is very probably Arabic in origin, although somewhat reversed, inasmuch as classical Arabic cuisine favors stuffing vegetables with meat, not scattering them atop a stew. Whatever the case, the recipe is inexact; I have experimented with ground turkey and ground beef, and both hold up nicely.

Cut meat and put it into a pot with water, salt, a spoonful of vinegar, a spoonful of olive oil, and some dry coriander. Put the pot on the fire. When the meat is cooked, clean some artichokes, cut them into little pieces, and sprinkle them atop the meat. Heat the mixture, then add one or two chopped hardboiled eggs and a cup of breadcrumbs, cover, and let stand for a few minutes.

# CARCIOFI ALLA GIUDEA

Whenever we are in Rome, my wife and I make it a point to call on Giorgio Sermoneta, a much-admired couturier, businessman, and bon vivant who knows where the best restaurants are tucked away—and who serves a fine gelato himself, as visitors to his shops along the Piazza di Spagna will discover. Most of those restaurants serve some variation of a local favorite, once confined to the Jewish Ghetto. "Jewish artichokes," as they are called, resemble flowers once they are cooked, and they are altogether delicious.

2 lemons, cut in half
1 cup water
salt and pepper
8 fresh globe artichokes
1 cup olive oil

Cut each artichoke so that only a short stem protrudes from the bottom. Cut the top of the head off flat and remove the outer leaves. Blanch for 20–30 seconds in boiling salted water, then allow the artichokes to cool and drain on paper towels. Smack the bottom of the artichokes on a wooden cutting board or pizza stone so that the "flowers" open up a little. Sprinkle salt and pepper inside the leaves. Heat olive oil in a deep skillet and cook the artichokes, stalk upward at first, then turning so that all sides are cooked. Serve with lemon wedges.

Mariangela Rinaldi and Mariangela Vicini, social historians and gastronomes from the fabled city of Parma, add this twist: cook the artichokes in a heat-proof earthenware dish. Then "bring a bowlful of water close to the earthenware dish, dip a hand in, and then sprinkle a few drops of water into the oil. This is the secret for giving the artichokes that final extra crispness."

## GREEK ARTICHOKES

M.F.K. Fisher, the great California food writer, favored artichokes in all forms, from whole artichokes dipped in rough salt to this easily prepared but elegant side dish, adapted from her *With Bold Knife and Fork:*

1 lb artichoke hearts (available frozen in specialty markets)
1 cup black currants or raisins
1 cup white wine
1/2 cup olive oil
1/4 cup balsamic vinegar
    Mix ingredients in a saucepan and cook until the artichokes are tender to the fork, about fifteen minutes. Let cool, then drain in a colander. Refrigerate until cold. Serve with rice pilaf or stuffed grape leaves.

## FURTHER READING

M.F.K. Fisher, *With Bold Knife and Fork* (Putnam, 1968).
Mariangela Rinaldi and Mariangela Vicini, *Buon Appetito, Your Holiness: The Secrets of the Papal Table* (Arcade, 2000).

# ASPARAGUS

---

"The cooking of a vegetable is the transformation of a given object without consciousness into another object equally devoid of consciousness. And it is the taking over of the thing by the human world. If it is cooked, a vegetable stops being a vegetable and becomes a thick soup or a cooked salad. Rawness sets it farther apart from us."

Thus intoned Jean-Paul Sartre, existential luminary, who, in a moment to win an American president's heart, admitted to not much liking vegetables. Those who are inclined to ponder the alienating effects of vegetables in their natural form may well find agreement with his sentiment; few pondering a turnip would find much kinship there, and a world of difference between them. But, ethereal as his conversations with Simone de Beauvoir might have been, Sartre had at least one big branch of the argument right: in the matter of asparagus, even a little cooking transforms the raw object into something quite different, and a little more cooking transforms it into a slimy mass.

Regrettably, for whatever reason, that is the way asparagus first came into the consciousness of American consumers of a certain age. I can well remember, in the glory days of the 1960s and TV dinners over *Gilligan's Island* and *I Dream of Jeannie,* confronting the horror of canned asparagus with the consistency of a blend of okra and cottage cheese gone bad; suffice it to say that I did not clamor for it. Even when fresh asparagus became widely available in this country in that decade, it was all too often boiled or steamed into a submissive pulp, its chewy straw-like fiber turned into a stringy mess, its nutrients gone, its flavor now suspiciously like that

Kurt Stüber, "Triticum vulgaris," from Otto Wilhelm Thomé, *Flora von Deutschland, Österreich und die Schweiz* (1885).

of the mold growing in the stony corners of our swampy Virginia basement.

To this day, and to the trauma of many a child, Washington State leads the nation in the production of canned asparagus, which permits lesser cuts, so to speak, than the fresh stuff. It has traveled far to get there, for *Asparagus officinalis,* a member of the vast lily family, is a native of the plains of eastern Europe, thriving in the salt marshes and slow-moving rivers of what is now Bulgaria, Hungary, and southern Poland. It grows prolifically in the wild in the sandy soils of west-central Russia and the Crimea, and travelers attest to passing mile after mile, verst after verst, of unbroken asparagus fields. Asparagus prefers the cool weather of such places, but it has adapted to a slightly broader range of climes over the years, nursed along by geneticists and breeders.

Perhaps by way of the Thracians, the Greeks knew of asparagus—a Greek word meaning "stalk"—but seem not to have taken to it much. Instead, they passed it on to their rivals across the western sea, the Romans, who adored asparagus both for its taste and for its medicinal properties, both of which the historian Cato praised, advocating that his fellow citizens raise asparagus in every garden. He offered these instructions:

> Break up thoroughly ground that is moist, or is heavy soil. When it has been broken, lay off beds, so that you may hoe and weed them in both directions without trampling the beds. In laying off the beds,

leave a path a half-foot wide between the beds on each side. Plant along a line, dropping two or three seeds together in a hole made with a stick, and cover with the same stick. After planting, cover the beds thickly with manure; plant after the vernal equinox. When the shoots push up, weed often, being careful not to uproot the asparagus with the weed. The year it is planted, cover the bed with straw through the winter, so that it will not be frostbitten. Then in the early spring uncover, hoe, and weed. The third year after planting burn it over in the early spring; after this do not work it before the shoots appear, so as not to injure the roots by hoeing. In the third or fourth year you may pull asparagus from the roots; for if you break it off, sprouts will start and die off. You may continue pulling until you see it going to seed. The seed ripens in autumn; when you have gathered it, burn over the bed, and when the asparagus begins to grow, hoe and manure. After eight or nine years, when it is now old, dig it up, after having thoroughly worked and manured the ground to which you are to transplant it, and made small ditches to receive the roots. The interval between the roots of the asparagus should be not less than a foot. In digging, loosen the earth around the roots so that you can dig them easily, and be careful not to break them. Cover them very deep with sheep dung; this is the best for this purpose, as other manure produces weeds.

Where Romans went, asparagus followed; it was introduced to France and England at the moment the Roman Empire came knocking. As with all foods, the French eventually made an art form of asparagus, while the English, who called it "sparrowgrass," established all sorts of rules about who was entitled to grow it, how much of the crop had to be delivered to the lord of the manor, and where the royal plateful had to come from —namely, the Vale of Evesham and the Cornish coast around The Lizard. Such regulations must have been an affront to English civil liberties, for today, between April and June, some of the tastiest asparagus in the world is grown in all parts of England, and the people have learned to appreciate their stalks al dente rather than boiled to death.

Just so, gardens in the French and English settlements of North America saw asparagus from the start; Thomas Jefferson grew several varieties in his gardens at Monticello, and apparently it was his favorite vegetable. The presidential seal of approval notwithstanding, asparagus would not be cultivated commercially until waves of Italian and Eastern European settlers began to settle in California, then as now America's leading producer. It is also grown extensively as a winter crop in southwestern Arizona and northwestern Mexico, where a February day can be as warm as a Crimean June.

But not too warm, for asparagus is really something of a shrinking violet, extremely sensitive to warmth. Plucked from a home garden, it will keep for only a few days unrefrigerated, and its qualities decrease rapidly as its sugars and vitamin C begin to burn up, leading to a loss in both taste and nutrient value. Asparagus is also sensitive to light, which means that, put in the cooler, it needs to be hidden away in the crisper or put far back on the bottom shelf. Even if refrigerated, asparagus has to be kept near the freezing point, or it will develop those dread fibrous threads throughout the stalks that make eating an exercise in textural terror. Still, properly attended to, and with its cut stalks wrapped in a wet paper towel, asparagus can keep for ten days or so, but, all things considered, it is best just to eat it fresh and quickly.

Another terror, at least for some, is a curious and much remarked phenomenon: the effect a diet of asparagus has on—there is no way to put it nicely—the odor of one's urine. English medical researcher S.C. Mitchell, a scientist in the best tradition, one unafraid of dealing with life's unpleasantries, observes that that phenomenon does not turn up in the literature before the eighteenth century, when observers linked asparagus to "graveolent" urine; Queen Anne's physician, John Arbuthnot, noted that asparagus "affects the urine with a foetid smell...and therefore have been suspected by some physicians as not friendly to the kidneys." Mitchell further remarks the coincidence of the smell problem's arrival in the literature with the introduction of sulfate and organic sulfur compounds as fertilizers; onions, garlic, and asparagus alike produce stronger flavors the greater the sulfur in the ground. It may have something to do with the metabolism, too, and even something down at the mitochondrial level; something yet to be discovered is going on between our plumbing and asparagusic acid. Whatever the case, the smell seems to increase with one's age, which is yet another of the indignities of getting older.

Call it one of life's little ironies: smelly asparagus is also a diuretic and laxative, prescribed by ancient and medieval doctors just for those qualities. One physician added that asparagus "is good to clear the sight, and being held in the mouth easeth the toothache"—and, for good measure, relieves cramps and sciatica. Certainly it is good for edema, and asparagus extract is used in preparations for urinary tract health. Moreover, asparagine, an essential amino acid, is important in the metabolism of toxic ammonia in the body; science buffs may be interested to know that it was the first amino acid to be isolated from its natural source, purified from asparagus juice in 1806.

There are other good reasons to eat plenty of asparagus, and never mind the olfactory consequences. It contains glutathione and folic acid, the first helpful in fighting cancer, the second of extreme importance in fighting neural defects such as spina bifida. Asparagus is a ready source of potassium, dietary fiber, vitamins A, D, B6, and thiamin. Add its absence of fat and low levels of sodium, and asparagus begins to look like a perfect health food. Just do not overcook it, I implore you.

## ASPARAGUS WITH MEAT SAUCE

Although it is by no means rare, asparagus does not much figure in the cuisine of Iberia. That may be a holdover from the days of Moorish rule, for the Muslim nobility of Andalusia certainly enjoyed asparagus, as this recipe adapted from the *Kitab al Tibakah,* a medieval Andalusian cookbook, suggests. The ingredients are learned guesses at modern equivalents, but the instructions are authentic.

1 pound asparagus
3/4 pounds ground lamb
salt and black pepper to taste
1 teaspoon caraway seed
2 tablespoons coriander
1 tablespoon olive oil
1 egg white
murri
3 eggs
1 cup breadcrumbs

Take asparagus, the largest you have, clean and boil, after taking tender meat and pounding fine; throw in pepper, caraway, coriander seed, cilantro juice, some oil and egg white; take the boiled asparagus, one after another, and dress with this ground meat, and do so carefully. Put an earthenware pot on the fire, after putting in it water, salt, a spoon of murri and another of oil, cilantro juice, pepper, caraway and coriander seed; little by little while the pot boils, throw in it the asparagus wrapped in meat. Boil in the pot and throw in it meatballs of this ground meat, and when it is all evenly cooked, cover with egg, breadcrumbs and some of the stuffed meat already mentioned and decorate with egg, God willing.

Murri is a kind of Arabic seasoning with many elaborate recipes; in most instances, it ends up tasting so much like soy sauce that a dash of soy sauce will do just fine as a substitute. If you insist on authenticity, a recipe recorded in a Byzantine cookbook might encourage the simpler solution.

There is taken, upon the name of God the Most High, of honey scorched in naqrah, three ratls, pounded scorched oven bread, ten loaves; starch, half a ratl; roasted anise, fennel and nigella, two uqiyahs of each; Byzantine saffron, an uqiya; celery seed, an uqiyah; Syrian carob, half a ratl; fifty peeled walnuts, as much as half a ratl; split quinces, five; salt, half makkauk dissolved in honey; thirty ratls water; and the rest of the ingredients are thrown in it, and it is boiled on a slow flame until a third of the water is absorbed. Then it is strained well in a clean nosebag of hair. It is taken up in a greased glass or pottery vessel with a narrow top. A little lemon from

Takranjiya is thrown on it, and if it suits that a little water is thrown on the dough and it is boiled upon it and strained, it would be a second [infusion]. The weights and measurements that are given are Antiochan and Zahiri.

## ASPARAGUS WITH TRUFFLE BROTH

Gourmets and gourmands prize truffles, which have a taste rich enough to overpower many other flavors—save for asparagus, which holds up very well to it. This magnificently rich preparation comes, of course, from France.

1/2 cup chicken broth
1/4 cup olive oil
1 cup truffles, chopped fine
2 cups water
1/2 teaspoon salt
2 pounds asparagus
1 tablespoon unsalted butter
   Blend chicken broth, oil, and truffles in a ceramic bowl, using a wooden spoon. In a skillet, bring salted water to a boil. Lower heat, then add asparagus and simmer for 4–5 minutes. Toss in the dressing and serve immediately.

## BOILED ASPARAGUS

It may be that overcooking asparagus is an American tradition, though Amelia Simmons's *American Cookery* (1796)—the first cookbook known to have been published in the United States—makes it plain that asparagus should be cooked "quick." The sliced orange is a wonderful touch.

First cut the white heads off about six inches from the head, and scrape them from the green part downward very clean, as you scrape them, throw them into a pan of clear water, and after a little soaking, tie them up in small even bundles, when your water boils, put them in, and boil them up quick; but by overboiling they will lose their heads; cut a slice of bread for a toast, and toast it brown on both sides; when your asparagus is done, take it up carefully; dip the toast in the asparagus water, and lay it in the bottom of your dish; then lay the heads of the asparagus on it, with the white ends outwards; pour a little melted butter over the heads; cut an orange into small pieces, and stick them between for garnish.

## FURTHER READING

Marcus Cato, *De Agricultura* (Loeb Classical Library, 1934).
Simone de Beauvoir, *Adieux: A Farewell to Sartre* (Pantheon Books, 1981).

F.M. Hexamer, *Asparagus: Its Culture for Home Use and for Market* (Orange Judd Company, 1914).

S.C. Mitchell, "Food Idiosyncrasies: Beetroot and Asparagus," *Drug Metabolism and Disposition* 29 (April 2001): 539–543.

Amelia Simmons, *American Cookery* (Oxford University Press, 1958).

# BANANA

---

A thousand years ago, a Christian missionary whose name we do not know happened upon a curious fruit in a North African marketplace. It tasted wonderful and strange, he wrote to his bishop in Rome, and the fruit, which the natives called *anana,* was perfect. For, he continued, if you slice it horizontally, you will see in each segment a reminder of the Christian faith: a cross, a sure sign of the grace of God.

Cut a banana open, and sure enough, you will find in the tiny black seeds a cross—or, if you prefer, a Zuni or Tibetan sun symbol. For that reason, the banana often turns up in religious imagery wherever it has traveled. In its homeland of Southeast Asia, where it ranks as a major food-stuff on a par with rice, millet, and wheat, the banana appears in many Buddhist scriptures as an example of the world's generosity, for it grows abundantly and feeds millions. As it spread eastward to the Arab nations and Africa and westward to Polynesia, it took on significance in other beliefs. Some Muslim and Christian traditions hold that the forbidden fruit that Adam and Eve so briefly enjoyed in the Garden of Eden was not the apple, which is not native to the Persian Gulf region, but the banana, which has grown there since antiquity. Paintings from those traditions show the first man and woman wearing not fig or apple leaves, as medieval European iconography would have it, but banana leaves to hide their nakedness.

Our missionary and his brethren knew a good thing when they saw it. They returned to Italy with banana plants, and soon farmers were busily exporting fruit, and then plants, to Spain, where, under Moorish rule, banana cultivation was widespread. Following the *reconquista,* perhaps associating bananas with the departed Muslim rulers, Iberia's Catholic rulers did nothing to encourage production, which moved offshore; the Canary Islands, under Portuguese rule, became one important center of banana cultivation. From there, plants were taken to the New World, to be planted on the island of Hispaniola, from which banana cultivation fanned out across the Caribbean and into South America. Few Europeans at

"Banana," from Johann Wilhelm Weinmann et al., *Phytanthoza iconographia, sive, Conspectus aliquot millium* (1737–1745).

home could enjoy that particular treasure of their colonies, however: until refrigeration systems were developed in the mid-nineteenth century, the fruit could not survive the ocean crossing.

When refrigeration did arrive, bananas became big business. In 1885, the Boston Fruit Company—later known as the United Fruit Company —began importing the banana to the United States, mostly by way of New Orleans via "banana boats" that brought along with their cargo the tarantulas and boa constrictors that now thrive in the bayous of the Mississippi Delta. Until the Dole Company set up shop in Hawaii, the Massachusetts importer protected its monopoly by supporting a series of Central and South American strongman governments. One was Nicaragua, which a clever journalist dubbed a "banana republic," giving us a new term for a dictatorship. The system of political patronage had at least one desired effect, as far as the corporations were concerned: bananas became so common an element in the American diet that by 1911 the *Boy Scout Handbook* suggested that a particularly good deed—given how lethal the things apparently were in those days—would be to clear the streets of banana peels. (Apart from its role in comedic pratfalls, has a banana peel ever killed anyone? That is a question demanding further research, though we do have on record a few fatalities due to allergic reactions and choking.)

Banana republicanism has haunted many other shores. But unless you are a close reader of international journals such as *The Economist* or the *Asian Wall Street Journal,* while we are considering dangers and politics alike, you likely missed hearing the news of a trade war that raged unchecked for nearly a decade: a war to make Europe safe for American bananas.

At issue, as far as the United States was concerned, was the European Union's selfish view that Europeans should eat bananas grown in former European colonies and distributed by European firms. American banana firms such as Chiquita and Dole took a different view, holding that the world should gobble bananas brought to them courtesy of the world's sole superpower—bananas, that is, produced by American client states in Latin America and Southeast Asia.

The war took serious turns. In 1999, American soldiers landed on St. Vincent, a former British colony that lies southeast of Puerto Rico, to destroy the island's thriving marijuana crop. In the inevitable ensuing collateral damage, those troops torched a few banana groves as well, just to press the point. One small irony, a well-heeled St. Vincent grower told the *New York Times,* is that many islanders turned to growing pot only because they were tired of playing banana politics with trade representatives from Washington and Paris. In the meanwhile, *The Economist* grumbled, "America's bully-boy tactics will stiffen European resolve in disputes over beef and much else." Those tactics included the United States government's slapping retaliatory import tariffs on a range of European goods ranging from Italian prosciutto to French handbags to Scottish wool sweaters. There was also talk of extending the tariff to cultural imports such as films, objets d'art, books, and magazines—which meant that it might have cost just that much more to read about the banana wars in the first place, since for the most part the American media studiously ignored the absurd and embarrassing story. Bananas here, other fruit there: though the banana war ended in Pyrrhic victory, China recently acceded to American citrus growers' demands that its markets be opened to gwailo oranges—and this in a country where citrus fruit has been grown in abundance for thousands of years.

Whatever its tangled political and religious history, the banana has long been recognized as a rich food source. Buried in the scientific description of the banana that most often graces our tables, *Musa sapientum,* is quiet homage to its presumed wonders: the Latin means "muse of the wise person." Potassium, which the banana contains in abundance, has been likewise called "the salt of the intelligence," perhaps because it figures prominently in most so-called brain food. The banana holds a heavy concentration of natural sugars, almost 20 percent by weight. This makes it a convenient source of energy, and thus a favored treat of athletes and outdoors enthusiasts—to say nothing of dieters, who benefit greatly from the banana's low fat (half a gram in a medium-sized fruit of about 110 grams) and total lack of cholesterol.

Thanks to its high pectin content, in fact, bananas are known to reduce blood cholesterol significantly. Bananas also have goodly quantities of phosphorus, iron, thiamin, calcium, and vitamin A. About the only black mark on their record, so to speak, is their tendency to spoil quickly, thanks to the high presence of the enzyme polyphenoloxide, the same substance that causes human skin to tan in sunlight. To slow this spoilage, you can either keep your store of bananas in a cold refrigerator or hang them from a rack so that the fruit dangles in air. It is best, however, simply to eat a banana quickly and be done with the problem of storage—or, as the lads of Monty Python proposed in a memorable skit, get rid of a murder weapon—once and for all.

Botanically, the banana is a strange thing: the plant itself is an herb, related to coriander, and in its wild state it is thin and grassy, reaching a height of twenty-five feet. Its fruit is technically a berry, born of and containing many seeds, and the wild banana is even seedier than its domesticated counterpart. The peel of both the wild and cultivated varieties is full of latex, making it an easy source of gum. The peel also contains serotonin and dopamine, natural mood-elevating sedatives, which gave rise in the sixties to a near-canard: that smoking dried banana peels will get a person high. It is likelier just to yield a headache, though that did not stop the banana from appearing, iconically, on the covers of albums by the Rolling Stones and Velvet Underground and inspiring Donovan's ditty ''Mellow Yellow,'' which has mood-elevating powers on its own. The latex yields another benefit of the banana and, more specifically, of its less sugary variety, the plantain—namely, its ability to stimulate the production of mucus lining in the stomach wall. This, in turn, retards the formation of stomach ulcers and provides some relief for those who suffer from them. The greener the plantain, it is said, the better the protection against the ravages of digestive acids. While the medical jury is still out, even common dessert bananas seem to have some value in this respect as well, and many pediatricians suggest their use for children suffering from gastritis.

Whatever their benefits, people eat bananas because they taste good, and bananas have thus become the world's most popular fruit by a commanding margin. Though Americans may identify themselves symbolically with the apple and the pies made from it, for instance, they eat a third more bananas than apples—nearly twenty-eight pounds per person as of the dawn of the millennium. (This is well below the count in Uganda, the world's leading consumer of bananas, where, as of 2003, each person ate 772 pounds a year.) Today bananas are grown across the world, not only in the tropics but also in greenhouses in temperate climates—and even in Iceland, outdoors, on geyser-studded volcanic soils. Growers face many challenges, though. Much of the world's production takes place on small farms of often poor soil quality, and cultivation and harvest practices are often ecologically destructive, often involving the use of slash-and-burn agriculture. The fact that the banana is, technically, a clone makes it highly susceptible to both pests and disease, which can devastate a harvest, and which has historically meant that bananas are heavily treated with pesticides to bring them to market, though large growers such as Dole, Del Monte, and Chiquita have taken steps to reduce pesticide spraying in favor of environmentally sustainable methods.

Defying those grim odds, in the mid-1990s, following decades of experimentation, Honduran plant breeder Franklin Rosales and American geneticist Philip Rowe announced the development of a new banana variety, FHIA-01, popularly called the Goldfinger, that is resistant to the suite of pests and diseases—especially the dreaded black sigatoka, or black leaf streak, caused by a fungus—that now afflict the Cavendish variety, which dominates today's markets, accounting for 99 percent of sales in Europe and North America. (The Cavendish emerged as the world winner mostly by virtue of its large size, durability in shipping, and happy habit of ripening almost exactly three weeks after being harvested. It helped its fortunes, though, that Panama disease wiped out the former leader, the Gros Michel, in 1959.) With genetic tinkering, too, ethylene releases can be better timed so that a banana can take even longer to mature, affording it an expanded shelf life that the average book might envy. The Goldfinger and other so-called super-ripe bananas may well turn out to be the perfect version of what has long been considered the perfect fruit.

## SENEGALESE BANANA GLACE

12 bananas
1 pint heavy cream
1/2 cup sugar
   Blend four bananas until pulpy. Add cream and sugar, then place mixture in a glass bowl and freeze for two hours, or until firm but not frozen. Halve the remaining bananas lengthwise and crosswise. Set four pieces on a small plate or saucer and spread the banana mixture over the banana segments just before serving. Add slivered almonds, roasted peanuts, and raisins to taste.

## FRIED BANANAS

A favorite of many South American and Caribbean cuisines, fried bananas are the matter of a moment's work to make. Simply take a peeled banana, halve it lengthwise, and sauté the segments in butter until brown on both sides. Coat with sugar and cinnamon.

# BANANAS IN SILK THREAD

This Chinese recipe, adapted from Gloria Bley Miller's delightful *Thousand Recipe Chinese Cookbook* (Grosset & Dunlap, 1970), makes an elegant, only slightly more complicated variation on the earlier recipe for fried bananas.

4 bananas
4 tablespoons vegetable oil
1/2 tablespoon wine vinegar
2 cups sugar
1 1/2 cups water
   Peel bananas and slice lengthwise. Heat oil and fry bananas until brown. In a saucepan, combine vinegar, sugar, and water and boil. Coat bananas in hot syrup, then briefly immerse them in ice water to crystallize the coating.

# SULAWESI BANANA PANCAKES

1 teaspoon active dry yeast
2 tablespoon sugar
1/4 teaspoon salt
1 cup water
3 bananas
1/2 cup rice flour
1 teaspoon vegetable oil
   Put water into a mixing bowl and add the yeast, sugar, and salt. Stir until the dry ingredients dissolve. Mash peeled bananas and add to the mixture. Mix thoroughly to form a batter. Allow this to rest for an hour. Pour batter in portions into a nonstick frying pan in which vegetable oil has been heated. Fry on medium heat until golden.

# FURTHER READING

Lawrence S. Grossman, *The Political Ecology of Bananas: Contract Farming, Peasants, and Agrarian Change in the Eastern Caribbean* (University of North Carolina Press, 1998).

Virginia Scott Jenkins, *Bananas: An American History* (Smithsonian Institution Press, 2000).

D. R. Jones, *Diseases of Banana, Abaca and Enset* (Oxford University Press, 1999).

William O. Lessard, *The Complete Book of Bananas* (Lessard Farms, 1992).

Julie Morton, ed., *Fruits of Warm Climates* (Florida Flair Books, 1987).

J. C. Robinson, *Bananas and Plantains* (CAB International, 1995).

# BASIL

If wishes were horses and herbs lived in an organized society, then basil
would be its king. So, apparently, thought the ancient Greeks, who prized
good food and the pleasures it brought, and who gave *Ocimium basilicum*
its name: *basilikos,* befitting a *basileus,* a king.

Certainly basil distinguishes itself from the ordinary run of labiate
herbs—that is, herbs of the mint family, Labiatae—by being a mysterious
outsider. Most labiate herbs are native to and grow profusely in and
around the Mediterranean, where the sea air caresses the plants of the
*maquis,* the scrubby coast, with a fine nourishing mist. Like its kin, basil
grows profusely in Mediterranean gardens, has done so for two millennia
and more; yet it evolved far away from its cousins, first emerging in semi-
tropical India and migrating westward along the trade networks that flourished on land and sea throughout the ancient world.

It may have been faith, rather than any terrestrial utility, that sent basil
on its way. In India, basil enjoyed a role as a protector, a plant sacred to
the Hindu gods Vishnu and Krishna. Ayurvedic physicians used juice
pressed from basil leaves to treat snakebite, a common occurrence in that
snake-rich land, and as a tonic for the treatment of malarial fever, arthritis,
and gastrointestinal disorders. If the patient was too far gone, a sprig of
basil went into his or her hands and into the grave; just so, plantings of
basil surrounded temples and hospitals, as if to ward off evil and illness.

Yet evil and illness accompany another set of beliefs associated with *Ocimium basilicum,* which portray the plant as a magnet for, even a fellow
traveler with, the *basiliskos,* "the little king," a kind of reptile resembling

the Gila monster. A medieval Catholic bestiary describes it as "frequenting desert places and before people can get to the river it gives them hydrophobia and makes them mad....It can kill with its noise and burn people up, as it were, before it decides to bite them"; the Roman naturalist Pliny records that "once a basilisk was killed with a spear by a man on horseback, the venom passing up through the spear killed not only the rider but the horse as well"; and in William Shakespeare's tragedy *Cymbeline*, Posthumus says of the ring given to him as evidence that his wife has been unfaithful,

> It is a basilisk unto mine eye,
> Kills me to look on't.

A dangerous critter, then, that made our blameless labiate herb guilty by association. There is more: Dioscorides, the first-century Greek physician and author of the original *Materia Medica*, records that the nomads of North Africa used basil in poultices to treat scorpion stings, an observation that would be echoed in medieval southern European beliefs that scorpions grew under pots planted with basil.

That belief is not so far-fetched: in the hot lands of the Mediterranean, the cool underside of a well-watered pot would well serve as the paradise of scuttling creatures. In all events, a cluster of beliefs traveled with basil, which, by the time Dioscorides and the bestiary compilers came along, had enjoyed pride of place in plantings in the Hanging Gardens of

"Basilicum," from a seventeenth-century German herbal.

Babylon, adorned Assyrian and Hittite palaces, and found a most welcome reception in the land whose cuisine we most readily associate with basil to-day—namely, Italy, where the frost-intolerant plant flourishes, often grown in several varieties, chief among them the sublime *nano verde,* or "green dwarf."

From the Mediterranean, and from India, basil has now spread throughout the world. In North America, it has long been grown commercially in California—but also in Mexico, where it is traditionally planted in dooryards to ward off any evil that happens to be abroad. Basil is now reckoned to be the fifth most commonly used medicinal plant in Mexico today, used to combat earache and other pains, as well as to ward off those less tangible woes.

Siamese cuisine adapted basil early on, and many ethnic groceries in North America and Europe offer *krapao,* a peppery-tasting favorite of Thai chefs. Other basils from New Guinea, Africa, and the Middle East add hints of citrus, cinnamon, and fennel to basil's slightly bitter, slightly minty base. Indeed, more than sixty varieties of basil are grown worldwide today.

Notwithstanding the prospect of raising a harvest of scorpions along with it, basil is an uncomplaining presence grown in pots or in a summertime garden in most climes; it asks only for abundant sunlight and adequate water. In return, if eaten fresh, it yields small but meaningful quantities of vitamins A, D, and B2 and of calcium, iron, and phosphorus—to say nothing of a pungent, pleasing flavor. All of these things diminish somewhat if basil is dried, which, regrettably, is how it is found in too many households, old, forgotten, tucked away in the back of a cabinet. Basil is better frozen than dried, although it has an unfortunate tendency to turn black in the process; one novel way to freeze it without that blemish comes from the good cultivators of Iowa State University's Reiman Gardens, who suggest finely chopping a quantity of basil leaves, mixing them with water, and freezing them in ice-cube trays. Thaw the cubes and, presto, you have near-fresh basil.

Modern researchers give basil marks for more than flavor, having recently discovered that methyl chavicol and linaool, abundantly present in basil, retard the growth of lethal bacteria, including *E. coli* and *listeria,* that are responsible for so many food-related deaths and so much discomfort throughout the world. Departing from this observation, scientists working at the Technion–Israel Institute of Technology have developed a packaging material that blends plastic and basil leaves; the chemical compounds ooze from the wrapping, extending the shelf life of such things as cheese, fish, meat, vegetables, fruits, and even baked goods.

Fear not food poisoning, scorpions, Gila monsters, or snakebites, then. The royal herb is there to protect.

# BRUSCHETTA

A specialty of central Italy, bruschetta (which comes from the word for "toast") is the simplest of pleasures to prepare and, as regional cuisines leave their borders thanks to television and increased travel, has become a favorite treat throughout the nation. I adapt this recipe from the splendid kitchen of the Villa Cheta, in Acquafredda di Maratea, far in the country's south.

6 ripe Roma tomatoes
4 leaves fresh basil
1/4 cup extra virgin olive oil
1 tablespoon sea salt
freshly ground black pepper to taste
1 small baguette or loaf of ciabatta or pane rustica

Chop the tomatoes into small pieces. Scrape away the seeds with a knife and discard them. Chop the basil leaves coarsely; they should fill about a quarter of a cup once the chopping is done. Toss the tomatoes and basil in a bowl with olive oil, salt, and pepper. Refrigerate, wrapped, for up to two days to blend flavors (this step is entirely optional). Allow the mixture to sit at room temperature for an hour. Cut bread into slices, two or three per person, and toast slightly. Spoon the tomato-basil mixture over the bread and serve as a snack, first course, or accompaniment.

# PESTO

So nutritious is pesto, a blend of basil, olive oil, and pine nuts, that, in 1998, scientists working for NASA determined that basil should be among thirty plants hydroponically grown at an experimental space station then scheduled to be put into the sky. Alas, funding cuts have assured that we may never know, but the compliment paid to basil is good reason to eat it here on Earth.

In strictest terms, pesto is a product of the Italian province of Liguria and a culinary specialty of Genoa, though, like bruschetta, it has long since spread to other provinces and nations. "The soul of pesto is basil," writes Waverley Root in *The Food of Italy*, and lots of it. But not just pesto leaves; there is more to it than all that.

First, take two cups basil leaves. With a sharp knife, remove the larger veins and stems, and discard them. Place the deveined leaves in a marble mortar or large ceramic bowl, and, using a wooden or marble pestle, grind them against a tablespoon of sea salt and a clove of garlic. Add grated parmesan or pecorino cheese to the mix, taking care not to dilute the dark-green color of the mixture. (If you do, add more basil leaves.) Add to the mixture olive oil, splash by splash, and ground pine nuts, which are abundant on the pine-rich Ligurian coast and available in most groceries (but walnuts are a perfectly acceptable substitute). In the end, the consistency should be somewhere between condensed soup and salad dressing, too thin to stand up by itself, too thick to flow off the countertop if spilled.

This is one of those your-mileage-may-vary dishes, and it is notoriously fattening. Experiment, and you'll get it just right—meaning just right for your taste. If you are worried about the high-octane variety, a blend of cottage cheese and chicken broth can substitute for some of the olive oil and cheese. Fat or non-fat, pesto can be frozen indefinitely, a good way to preserve basil until the next season's batch is ready.

## FURTHER READING

American Technion Society, "Wrap Mine in Basil" (press release, June 27, 2003).

Cornell University, "Extraterrestrial Cuisine Cooking in Cornell Lab" (press release, January 20, 1998).

Iowa State University Reiman Gardens, "Growing and Using Basil" (pamphlet, 2005).

Waverley Root, *The Food of Italy* (Atheneum, 1971).

Frederick Rosengarten Jr., *The Book of Spices* (Livingston, 1969).

# BROCCOLI

George H.W. Bush, the forty-first president of the United States, famously hated a certain cruciferous vegetable. "I do not like broccoli," he said, defiantly, in 1990. "And I haven't liked it since I was a little kid and my mother made me eat it. And I'm president of the United States and I'm not going to eat any more broccoli." The passages of fifteen years did nothing to temper Bush's dislike; his personal chef, a former Navy cook named Ariel De Guzman, remarked in 2005, "It's not only broccoli, but we are also talking about brussels sprouts, alfalfa, and cabbage and anything that does not have a good smell."

Now, in fairness, Bush's distant predecessor and presumed nemesis, Franklin Delano Roosevelt, also detested broccoli, refusing to allow it to be served in the White House. And Bush's successor, William Jefferson Clinton, was once rumored not to care much for broccoli undisguised by heavy cheese or cream sauces, though his attitude toward the stuff seems to have changed after quadruple bypass surgery, to judge by his subsequent stint as a spokesperson for the cause of healthy diets for young people. Indeed, lots and lots of people of all ages dislike broccoli, a healthy specimen of which looks like a tree topped with brains and whose name embodies the Latin word for "arm," honoring the plant's appearance and not, like Popeye's spinach, the curative, restorative, and preventative powers of *Brassica oleracea,* a broad species that includes cabbage, cauliflower, rutabaga, kale, and brussels sprouts, all variations on a grand theme, and all much dishonored by the undiscerning.

"Broccoli," from a late-nineteenth-century British gardening catalog.

The species' *italica* variety, the one Western diners know and love (and hate), has been in cultivation for at least three thousand years, and it is one of the few food plants to have been domesticated away from the better-known food centers of Central Asia, the Levant, East Asia, and Mesoamerica. But not too far away: the best available evidence at this date suggests that the plant was first cultivated on the island of Crete, in the eastern Mediterranean. This best evidence, as all prehistorians know, may well be superseded tomorrow, and contending scholars assign broccoli a birthplace either somewhere on the Anatolian Plateau or in northwestern Europe, where kin of *Brassica* grow wild on the shores of the North Sea. Whatever its origin, broccoli was showing up on tables in ancient Greece and Italy more than twenty-five hundred years ago, and it was especially prized by the luxury-loving sophisticates of Etruria, who knew a good food when they saw it. The Etruscan kings of Rome introduced the plant to that city, and soon it was spreading throughout temperate Europe, carried afield by legionaries and colonists. Broccoli came to figure prominently in the cuisines of what are now Germany, Switzerland, and France, though it never seems to have caught on in Iberia—though both Spain and Portugal now produce quantities of the vegetable for the European export market.

So, too, does China, which has its own varieties of *Brassica*, probably introduced from Central Asia about two thousand years ago. Chinese cuisine makes abundant use of these several broccolis, but only one of them has penetrated the West thus far, if in disguise: *Brassica campestris* turns out rapeseed oil, which, owing to its unattractive name, was rechristened "canola oil" by some enterprising marketer, perhaps the same one who renamed Chinese gooseberry so that New Zealand growers could profit from it—whence "kiwi fruit."

Broccoli took its time arriving in England, too, a place notoriously suspicious of any food plant that French or Italian speakers might conceivably enjoy. When it first appeared in the eighteenth century, it bore the agreeable name "Italian asparagus," and long afterward it was regarded as an exotic thing that only a bohemian would eat. Just so, though growers in America knew of the plant, and though Thomas Jefferson enjoyed broccoli at Monticello, it did not occur to his compatriots to rush to consume the stuff. And therein, a conspiracy theory–minded observer might conclude, lies the rub: American blue bloods, Protestant stalwarts, and others likely as a matter of class upbringing to shun the things of southern Europe never acquired a taste for *Brassica* and would not know it from Brasso.

Vegetable lovers on these shores may thus want to thank the unknowable forces of history for the great southern Italian migrations of the late nineteenth and early twentieth centuries, for it was the children of Basilicata, Calabria, and Sicily who taught Americans how to hold broccoli in proper esteem. The Johnny Appleseeds among them were many, but the brothers D'Arrigo, Stefano and Andrea, who brought seeds from Messina when they arrived in the United States in 1924, take top honors both for their skills as growers and experimenters and for their knack for promotion: they made it seem as if they had invented broccoli on American soil, which appealed to the patriots in the audience. Thanks to the D'Arrigo brothers and like-minded immigrants, California, with its Mediterranean climate, swiftly became the nation's leading producer of broccoli and its hybrid kin the cauliflower, which *really* looks like brains and which even some broccoli lovers disdain to eat without much disguising with sauces and other vegetables. However, take a lesson from the Italians: they eat as much cauliflower as broccoli, though the former is generally treated as a summer dish and many more varieties of it are available to them than the sickly white "snowball" stuff grown in America.

On its native soil and elsewhere, the commercially predominant varieties of broccoli—Calabrese, sprouting, and Romanesco—enjoy a nice overlap of growing seasons, allowing harvests as late as December in temperate climates. A variety long known in the Mediterranean, called *rabe* or rape, looks much like Chinese broccoli; its thin stalks and small flower head give it a delicate appearance much favored by gourmets, though its taste is a touch more bitter than that of its larger cousins.

California being a famously health-conscious place, it is fitting that broccoli should have become known as one of the most healthful of all food plants. Broccoli (and other *Brassica* varieties) contains some thirty antioxidant and cancer-fighting compounds, while a single medium-sized stalk contains as much vitamin C as two pounds of oranges. Its stores of phytochemicals such as sulforaphane, as well as beta-carotene, can be instrumental in combating heart disease as well as cancer; one synthetic compound that models sulforaphane—which can be toxic in high concentrations—has been shown to reduce breast-tumor formation, while the plant's ability to block the movement of so-called free radicals means, at least potentially, that broccoli can be useful in battling arthritis, cataracts, and Alzheimer's disease as well. (The presence of so much sulforaphane, incidentally, explains why overcooked broccoli smells so sulfurous, a powerful argument for cooking it *al dente,* which preserves nutrients.) Broccoli's load of folic acid and dietary fiber assures a good scrub of the bowels and helps keep cholesterol levels down. Its store of chromium may even fight diabetes, and there is at least some evidence to suggest that other broccoli compounds may undo some of the damage caused by cigarette smoking (though not so much, of course, as quitting). According to a joint study conducted in 1999 by Harvard and Ohio State universities, men who ate a single cup of broccoli each week had a 44-percent lower incidence of bladder cancer than did their counterparts who shunned the green. And cruciferous vegetables of all kinds even seem to detoxify carcinogens that are already present in the body, which means that once a cancer starts to flourish, compounds derived from broccoli and its kin may be useful in slowing its spread.

There is no downside to eating broccoli, then, and plenty of reasons to do so, even if it tastes strange and looks funny and has dangerous associations with licentious lands of sunshine and shadow—which, come to think of it, makes it seem more attractive than not.

## SPARACEDDI

A favorite on traditional Sicilian tables, this dish is also called "drowned broccoli," so called because of its ample use of red wine and olive oil.

2 pounds broccoli, cut lengthwise and across in 2-inch pieces
1/2 cup extra-virgin olive oil
2 yellow onions, chopped fine
3 tablespoons chopped fresh basil
1/2 cup coarsely chopped black olives (pitted)
anchovy fillets to taste
1 cup red wine
sea salt and black pepper to taste

Heat olive oil in a heavy skillet. Sauté onions and broccoli over medium heat for about ten minutes, until the onions are translucent. Mix in the chopped olives, basil, and anchovy fillets. (The last ingredient is wholly optional, but the correct choice to make is yes. Use about a dozen, chopped up coarsely.) Cook over medium heat for just a couple of minutes. Then add red wine, reduce heat to just a whisper of flame, cover the skillet, and cook for an hour. Finish by cooking off any remaining wine over medium heat, then serve.

# ORECCHIETTE AND BROCCOLI

Giovanni Grano, a classical guitarist and accomplished cook who hails from Rionero in Vulture, a small town in the southern Italian province of Basilicata, once revealed to me that, while the best food in Italy is generally reckoned to come from Emilia-Romagna, knowing gourmets look to another southern province, Puglia, for hidden culinary treasure. Located opposite Greece and culturally much similar to it, Puglia has a long tradition of cooking with the freshest of pastas and vegetables. This dish, which features the pasta type whose name means "little ears," is a standout.

1 pound broccoli florets, cut into small pieces
3 cloves chopped fresh garlic
3 tablespoons anchovy paste
1/4 cup olive oil
1 pound orecchiette
ground black pepper to taste
grated parmesan or pecorino cheese to taste

Bring a gallon and a half of salted water to a boil and cook the broccoli al dente, about four minutes. Add the pasta and cook until it, too, is done al dente, about twelve minutes for dried pasta, just a minute or two for fresh. While the pasta is cooking, heat the olive oil in a large pan, then cook the garlic on low heat until it begins to glow. (Do not let it brown.) Add the anchovy paste, stirring frequently. When the pasta is done, add a cup of the water in which it has cooked. Then add the pasta and broccoli, stirring to coat them with the sauce. Serve immediately.

# BROCCOLI WITH GINGER

Broccoli is a familiar dish on Chinese tables. This recipe exemplifies the principle of binary opposition called *yin* and *yang,* the cool, feminine, *yin* vegetable meeting the warm, masculine ginger to produce a perfectly balanced treat.

1 pound Chinese broccoli (or other variety with slender stalks), cut into 2-inch pieces
1/2 cup chicken stock or broth
2 teaspoon sake or dry sherry
1 teaspoon ginger juice
1/2 teaspoon cornstarch
3 thin slices of ginger
2 tablespoons sesame or peanut oil

Combine chicken stock or broth, sake or sherry, ginger juice, and cornstarch with a dash of salt. Set this sauce aside. Heat a medium-sized wok or skillet, then add oil and ginger, stir-frying it for ten to fifteen seconds (reduce the heat at once if the oil becomes smoky). Add the broccoli pieces

[ 47 ]

and stir-fry on medium heat for a minute, then add the sauce and cook for another minute.

# PRESIDENT CLINTON'S CHICKEN AND BROCCOLI ENCHILADAS

William Jefferson Clinton is renowned for knowing a good meal when he sees one. While in office, he contributed this recipe to some good cause or another, and it has since proliferated on the World Wide Web. As it happens, it is quite heart-healthy.

6 small corn tortillas
12 ounces broccoli
2 teaspoons olive oil
1 medium red onion, chopped fine
2 medium cloves garlic, minced
1/2 jalapeno pepper, minced
1 teaspoon ground cumin
1/2 teaspoon chili powder
1/4 teaspoon ground cinnamon
8 ounces cooked, skinless, boneless chicken breast, shredded
1/4 teaspoon salt (optional)
1 15-ounce can no-salt-added whole tomatoes
2 tablespoons minced fresh cilantro
1/2 cup evaporated skim milk
3/4 cup shredded, reduced-fat Monterey Jack cheese
2 cups cooked brown rice
1 cup nonfat yogurt

Preheat oven to 350 degrees F. Remove tough stems from broccoli and break into florets. Steam broccoli until crisp but tender, and set aside. In a large nonstick pan, heat the oil; sauté the onion for 3 or 4 minutes to soften. Add the garlic, jalapeno, cumin, chili powder, cinnamon and chicken. Stir and cook to mix well and heat through. Season with salt, if desired. Remove from heat and stir in broccoli; divide into 6 equal portions, and set aside.

In blender or food processor combine tomatoes, cilantro and evaporated milk; blend well. Pour into pot and heat just to boiling. Remove from heat and dip each tortilla into the hot mixture to soften slightly. Fill each tortilla with 1/6 of the chicken mixture; roll up, and place seam side down in a baking dish large enough to hold all the enchiladas in a single layer. Repeat the process and pour the remaining tomato-milk mixture over enchiladas; sprinkle cheese over the top. Bake 15 to 20 minutes, or until sauce is bubbly, and serve with brown rice and a dollop of yogurt.

# FURTHER READING

American Chemical Society, "New Broccoli Compound Appears Promising Against Breast Cancer" (press release, August 14, 2002).

American Dietetics Association, *Handbook of Clinical Dietetics* (Yale University Press, 1992).

Barbara Haspel and Tamar Haspel, *The Dreaded Broccoli Cookbook* (Scribner, 1999).

Deborah Madison, *The Savory Way* (Broadway Books, 1998).

# CANTALOUPE

There are few things quite so refreshing as a slice of chilled cantaloupe on a hot summer day, few arts so precise as judging when one of those rough-skinned fruits is exactly right for the table. In season, vast quantities of this delicious fruit await their turn at the table, in such abundance that it is hard to imagine that not so many years ago the cantaloupe was reserved for the mouths of the nobility and the very wealthy.

Those of us who live beyond the shadow of the high mountains of southern Asia owe the pleasure of its taste to one accident of history after another. The wild ancestors of *Cucumis melo cantalupensis* sprouted eons ago in what is now the highlands of Persia, Pakistan, and India, and there is archaeological evidence that people there had begun to domesticate them by 5000 B.C.E., during the time of the great worldwide "agricultural revolution." Melons of various kinds spread in antiquity to the Levant— there are several references in the Old Testament to them—and eventually graced the table of sophisticated Greeks and Romans. During the so-called Dark Ages after the collapse of the Roman Empire, the trade in melons from the Near East to Europe dried up, and half a millennium would pass before the Crusaders found cantaloupes in Arab markets. Still, none seems to have thought to tuck away a few seeds to cultivate back home, and Europe's table remained the poorer.

In 1273 the Venetian traveler Marco Polo, making his way to China, wandered into the plaza of Shibarghan, a dusty city in the Persian desert, where he tasted the strange fruit and pronounced the local cantaloupes to be "excellent, a good of trade that is deservingly widely sold throughout the countries alongside." His fellow Italians were not impressed; they called him *il milione*, after all, "the teller of thousands of lies." Nonetheless, later Italian traders brought cantaloupe seeds back with them from the great markets in Armenia, and the first large-scale crop was grown in about 1620 in the papal gardens of Cantalupo—the name means "wolf howl"—outside Rome. Armenian immigrants would cultivate a hybridized cantaloupe in California nearly three centuries later, the fruit that we enjoy today, drawing on materials from both their homeland and the Italian hills. This cantaloupe is technically a muskmelon, which is quite different from the Eurasian model in both structure and taste, but the terminological imprecision has provoked no effort at reform on this side of the pond—so cantaloupe it remains, sad though that may make purists.

"Melo," an engraving by Nikolaus Friedrich Eisenberger, from Elizabeth Blackwell's *Herbarium Blackwellianum* (Nuremberg: Christian de Launoy, 1757–1773).

Introduced to the aristocracy, the cantaloupe was an instant hit. The French writer François Voltaire (1694–1778) complained that the decadent rich of this time were slavishly addicted to the delicacy, but his argument that cantaloupe "turns bad too easily in the stomach" did nothing to dissuade them from their devotion to the fruit. Neither did it keep the cantaloupe from making its way into humbler gardens, and today it graces tables throughout the world.

To choose a cantaloupe, have a look at its meshed rind, which should be consistent across the fruit; if it is slick or flattened, then the fruit has begun to spoil. There should be a small indentation at the stem end, while the blossom end should give off a heady fragrance. The fruit can be a little sunbleached—it has been in desert climes, after all, since much of the American harvest is produced in arid California and Arizona—but should roll easily; if it is flattened or squishy, the chances are it will not keep long enough to enjoy. Think of Ogden Nash's poem:

> One cantaloupe is ripe and lush,
> Another's green, another's mush
> I'd buy a lot more cantaloupe
> If I possessed a fluoroscope.

Like the banana, cantaloupe contains pleasing quantities of potassium, essential brain food. A cup of cut cantaloupe contains only 56 calories (there is a nice tongue twister), half a gram of fat, and no cholesterol, along with a gram of protein, 68 milligrams of vitamin C, and 494 milligrams of the aforementioned potassium. Moreover, that cup contains 100 percent of the recommended daily allowance of vitamin A, which is essential for eye health; a long-term study reported in the *Journal of Ophthalmology* suggests that those who eat cantaloupe regularly have a far lower chance of developing cataracts and age-related macular degeneration than do their fruitless counterparts. Cantaloupe also contains a blood-thinning anticoagulant, adenosine, which makes it of interest to those with heart conditions, and, thanks to its high beta-carotene content, is believed to have anticarcinogenic properties as well.

The best way to eat cantaloupe, I think, is the Italian model: wrap a slice of prosciutto or other dried ham around a wedge of melon and use it to fend off hunger on a hot summer afternoon. These days, as it happens, what Italians call *prosciutto e melone* uses the cantaloupe Americans know; true cantaloupe is becoming harder to find, a kind of sideways imperialism of the fork, or another illustration, as if one were needed, of the tyranny of the marketplace. Whatever the case, just about any way you can think of to serve cantaloupe is likely to be correct—and good for a person as well.

## CHILLED CANTALOUPE SOUP

1 cantaloupe, peeled, seeded, and cubed
2 cups orange juice
1 tablespoon lime juice
1/4 teaspoon ground cinnamon

    Peel, seed, and cube the cantaloupe. Place cantaloupe and ½ cup orange juice in a blender or food processor; cover, and process until smooth. Transfer to large bowl. Stir in lime juice, cinnamon, and remaining orange juice. Cover, and refrigerate for at least one hour. Garnish with mint if desired.

## CANTALOUPE SALSA

1/2 large ripe cantaloupe
3/4 cup diced red bell pepper
1/4 cup finely chopped cilantro
3 tablespoon chopped green onions
Juice of 1 lime
1/2 teaspoon salt
1/2 teaspoon red pepper flakes (or to taste)

Remove seeds and rind from cantaloupe and dice the fruit. Add diced red bell pepper, cilantro, onion, and lime juice. Stir. Add salt and red pepper flakes. Chill and serve with grilled fish or chicken.

## INSALATA DI MELONE

A favorite summertime dish in the mountains of northern Italy, cantaloupe salad sounds a little improbable. Give it a try, and its virtues will soon become apparent.

1–2 lbs cantaloupe, cut into small pieces
Endive, aragula, or other lettuce leaves, 2–3 per diner
Salt and freshly ground black pepper
2 teaspoons extra-virgin olive oil
2 teaspoons white wine or balsamic vinegar
prosciutto, soppresatta, or Serrano ham

Scoop cantaloupe with a melon baller onto a serving plate. Surround with lettuce leaves. Add salt and pepper to taste, then sprinkle on oil and vinegar and serve.

## FURTHER READING

John William Lloyd, *Muskmelon Production* (Orange Judd, 1928).

# CARROT

The famed animator Chuck Jones had no intention of changing America's food habits when, half a century ago, he stuck a carrot in Bugs Bunny's hand as talisman, protector, and object of desire. Rabbits like carrots, Jones must have figured: after all, did not Peter Cottontail always head first for Farmer Brown's carrot patch when out raiding for food?

Now, insofar as rabbit culinary preferences go, any old weed would have done nicely for Bugs. Put a carrot in a pile of assorted vegetables and greens and set it before a hungry bunny, and the cute rodent will show no special preference for *Daucus carota sativa*. But Bugs Bunny is a more influential rabbit than most. Call it the purest of coincidence, but Bugs's life span has coincided very nicely with a marked upsurge in the last few decades of carrot consumption in this country.

That it took a cartoon to make the carrot popular is a strange matter. Still, you cannot really blame Americans for not valuing the bright-orange vegetable more highly than they do. As a food item, it is notably limited: you cannot do much more with a carrot than boil it or gnaw on it raw, and most cookbooks skip by it with only a nod. Although it was one of the first food plants brought from England to North America by the colonists, the carrot remained almost an afterthought for centuries, something to add to stews and casseroles—but more often to animal fodder. Strange to say, but one of the carrot's most popular manifestations— that is, in the form of cake—seems to be an innovation that dates only to the early 1960s, traced to a bake sale in Texas. Indeed, in the American culinary past, its closest relatives enjoyed wider use than the carrot itself, they being plants used almost exclusively as spices: anise, cumin, caraway, dill, chervil, parsley, coriander, and fennel. Just so, even today we do not much use an even closer relative, the plant known as Queen Anne's lace, which is, in fact, a carrot that escaped from some New England garden long ago and reverted to wild form.

Even with the influence of Bugs, American consumption of carrots falls far short of that in Europe, where purple, white, and red varieties of carrots are sold alongside the carrot we know. That bright-orange vegetable is a hybrid cultivated in Holland—governed by the House of Orange, which makes the carrot a patriotic thing—in the seventeenth century from varieties common in Europe since ancient times, brought there from the

*Woman Peeling Carrot,* oil painting by the Flemish painter Gerrit Dou (1613–1675).

carrot's original home of Afghanistan. Although there is no clear chronology on which to draw, historians suppose that trade by way of Mesopotamia brought the carrot first to Egypt, where it is depicted in papyrus scrolls. The expansion of international trade networks under the Roman Empire introduced the Egyptian carrot, a purple variety, to Europe; it was reintroduced, now in yellow form, to southern Europe by Muslim invaders in the 1100s, and a century later it was being cultivated extensively in Germany and the Low Countries.

The carrot has long been a staple in the British Isles as well, where it has been associated with the diet of poverty. As the actress Joyce Green recalls in her 1947 memoir *Salmagundi,* her well-to-do mother was horror-stricken at the thought of having to endure a nightly meal of cooked carrots with a little boiled cabbage during World War II, although such a diet kept millions of Britons from starving.

Two decades before, the American automobile maker Henry Ford tried to impress upon his business associates the value of a vegetable-based diet. He held a banquet in a Detroit hotel that highlighted carrots in all their splendor, complete with a master of ceremonies dressed in a carrot suit who proclaimed, "I am King Carrota! I am full of vitamins, full of iron, full of iodine, full of bottled sunshine. I have no enemy but a bad cook. I am a friend of flappers and the bald-headed, the spindly baby and three-chinned monsters, but who shall mix me with canned peas shall be consigned to outer darkness." After a twelve-course meal consisting entirely of carrots—carrot soup, carrot loaf, carrot au gratin, carrot torte—washed down with carrot juice, a doctor remarked that he had seen children who ate too many carrots turn yellow, which certainly dampened the festivities, at least at his table.

Eat a few dozen carrots a day, indeed, and you run the risk of developing jaundice, for the body can take only so much of a good thing. And—every child knows the horrifying phrase—carrots are surely a good thing, good for a person. Low in calories (about 50 to a cup of raw carrots, and 70 to a cup of cooked carrots), fat-free, and high in fiber, they make for a nutritional and filling side dish or snack; if you eat only a couple a day, you can do much to reduce your blood cholesterol. They are also rich in potassium, a mineral in which too many Americans are deficient. Carrots contain other metallic minerals as well, such as iron, magnesium, and selenium, which explains why sparks sometimes fly when they are cooked in a microwave. As the microwaves deflect from the metals, they produce an arc. Whole carrots can be difficult to cook evenly in a microwave, and they have a strange tendency to burn at their tips.

Carrots also abound in natural sugars; of vegetables, only beets contain more. Their healthful sweetness makes carrots a recommended substitute for sugar in cakes, dressings, and puddings. Shredded carrots atop breakfast cereal has yet to catch on, but adding some to fresh or canned tomatoes in sauces, however, helps cut acidity and thus reduce the risk of heartburn. They have other effects digestive and otherwise, as the seventeenth-century English herbalist Nicholas Culpeper noted:

Wild carrots belong to Mercury, and expel wind and remove stitches in the side, promote the flow of urine and women's courses, and break and expel the stone; the seed has the same effect and is good for dropsy, and those whose bowels are swollen with wind: It cures colic, stone, and rising of the mother; being taken in wine or boiled in wine and taken, it helpeth conception. The leaves being applied with honey to running sores or ulcers cleanse them; I suppose the seeds of them perform this better than the roots: and though Galen recommended garden carrots highly to expel wind, yet they breed it first, and we may thank nature for expelling it, not they; for the seeds of them expel wind and so mend what the root marreth.


Wild and domesticated, carrots are shot through with beta-carotenes, the chemical precursor to vitamin A, the precursor of the pigment retinal, so important in animal vision. Another component, zeaxanthin, helps prevent age-related macular degeneration, which can lead to blindness. The heightened carotene content of our supermarket variety, the descendant of those Dutch hybrids of centuries past, is what makes the carrot orange to begin with. Carotene also gives color to egg yolks, mangoes, sweet potatoes, apricots, and grapefruit—and, thanks to the addition of carrot juice, to most yellow cheeses. Carotene is released with cooking, and a single cup of cooked carrots contains more than four times the federally recommended daily allowance. Although scientists have yet to agree conclusively on the matter, too, those carotenes are thought to inhibit—and perhaps even prevent—the growth of many kinds of cancers, especially those of the lungs, pancreas, and spleen. For that reason, many doctors suggest that smokers especially add carrots to their diets.

The first-century Greek doctor Dioscorides, who served in Nero's legions as a surgeon, wrote of carrots in this connection in his manual *De materia medica,* a sort of *Physician's Desk Reference* used until the early modern age. He observed that several peoples throughout Europe and North Africa employed carrot leaves as a poultice with which to treat tumors, among other ailments. Dioscorides describes the carrot as "sweet-smelling and edible after being boiled.... It is good for the bites and stings of venomous beasts, and it is said that those who eat it beforehand will not come to harm by wild animals. It helps with conception, and it also helps expel poisons, and the leaves, minced with honey, rapidly clean the spreading destructive ulceration of soft tissues."

Carrots have also been supposed, over the years, to have certain aphrodisiacal qualities—another connection to our friend the rabbit. Henry Ford, a recent biographer tells us, was an unlearned man who dated the Revolutionary War to 1812 and who once remarked, "I don't like to read books; they muss up my mind," so he may not have heard the tale of how Caligula, the mad Roman emperor, once ordered the Senate to convene and then fed the assembled dignitaries a banquet of carrot dishes, hoping that it would produce a delightful orgy for his viewing pleasure. History does not record whether Caligula got his jollies that day, but we do know that Ford carried on a long affair with a much younger secretary of his, and we can surmise that carrots played their part in it—yet another reason, for the likeminded, to enjoy a specimen of *Daucus carota* or two a day.

Scientists, too, have yet to figure out why carrots and apples cannot coexist side by side in the icebox. Yet there the mystery remains: put a carrot next to an apple, and both will turn bitter overnight. Not even the mighty Chuck Jones knows why.

## CARROT PUDDING

John Evelyn, a gentleman scholar and founder of the Royal Society, published a learned treatise in 1699 called *Acetaria, a discourse on Sallets,* in which he lauded the virtues of vegetarianism and observed that Adam and Eve did not eat meat until after they fell from grace. Here, with some modification for the modern kitchen, is his recipe for carrot pudding—which is surely less healthful than a purist might wish for today.

2 cups white bread
4 cups grated carrot
1/2 pint fresh cream or whole milk
1 cup butter
3 egg yolks
3 eggs whole
1 cup sugar
dash each salt, nutmeg, and cinnamon
   Grate the bread and carrot. Mix the remaining ingredients. Pour into a buttered dish or pan and bake 45 minutes at 350°.

Amelia Simmons's *American Cookery* (1796), the first known American cookbook, offers an elegantly simple recipe that requires some guesswork and estimation; fortunately, nothing in it can hurt a person, so that there is room for experimenting.

A coffee cup full of boiled and strained carrots, 5 eggs, sugar and butter of each 2 oz. cinnamon and rose water to your taste, baked in a deep dish without paste, 1 hour.

## ROAST CARROTS

The medieval Italian chef Bartolomeo Platina offers this recipe for carrots roasted in a comfortable hearth:

Roast carrots in the coals, then peel them, cleaning off the ashes, and cut them up. Put in a dish with oil, vinegar and a bit of wine; scatter a few mild herbs on the top.

Nowadays, carrots are usually roasted in glass or enamel cookware, although a barbecue works well, too. As for the "mild herbs," oregano, basil, thyme, tarragon, and dill all accompany carrots nicely.

# CARROT JAM

Maud Grieve, an English horticulturalist, took great pride in her Buckinghamshire gardens, which yielded great quantities of vegetables. Here is her recipe for a sturdy carrot jam:

> Wash and grate some carrots; boil until reduced to a thick pulp. To 1 lb. of this pulp add 9 oz. sugar, the juice and grated rind of 2 lemons, and 3 oz. margarine. Boil the mixture well for 45 minutes to 1 hour. The result is a useful and inexpensive jam, which can be made for 6d. to 8d. a lb. (according to the price of the lemons), if all materials have to be bought, and for considerably less by those who have home-grown carrots available.

Lemons are less expensive these days than in Ms. Grieve's time, but even so, she was looking at a per-pound cost of about ten cents—not a bad deal, then and now.

## FURTHER READING

Maud Grieve, *A Modern Herbal: The Medicinal, Culinary, Cosmetic and Economic Properties, Cultivation and Folk-Lore of Herbs, Grasses, Fungi, Shrubs & Trees with Their Modern Scientific Uses* (Harcourt, Brace & Company, 1931).

Chuck Jones, *Chuck Amuck: The Life and Times of an Animated Cartoonist* (Farrar, Straus & Giroux, 1989).

Steven Watts, *The People's Tycoon: Henry Ford and the American Century* (Knopf, 2005).

# CHILE

Five hundred–odd years ago, Christopher Columbus set sail for America in search of gold and precious gems. He found a bit of each, though surely less than he wanted, and on his return trip to Spain in 1493, his ships were full not of rare metals and jewels but of the exotic plants and foods he had found in the Indies: tomatoes, cacao, chocolate, tobacco, and chile peppers of all kinds.

The new plants spread quickly throughout the Old World, especially the chiles, which grew well in many climates. Soon Hungarians began to enjoy stews rich with dark-red paprika, Italians their smoldering chile-based arrabbiata sauces. Asian Indians soon developed a series of mouth-ravaging chile curries, substituting so-called capsaicin chiles for their native *Piper nigrum,* or black pepper, while daring Japanese chefs invented fiery santaka and tagarashi sauces and garnishes.

Chiles, which were probably first cultivated in the temperate country between the northern Andes and the semiarid plains of northeastern Brazil, thrived in North America as well. Thomas Jefferson grew several mild varieties in his gardens at Monticello. Travelers to the newly opening West brought back seed stock from the upper Rio Grande Valley and along the Mexican border, introducing now-customary sweet pepper relishes and hot sauces to Southern cuisine. Wherever they went, from their origins in the lowland jungles of Peru to the finest restaurants of Peoria, Paris, and Peking, the peppers enjoyed a spectacular success for both their culinary and medicinal qualities.

The culinary qualities are obvious: peppers can add zest to even the most bland of foodstuffs—jicama, say, a tuberous plant that, without a dash of chile powder and a squeeze of lemon juice tastes, at least to my tender sensibilities, pretty much like wet cardboard. The nutritional and medicinal qualities are perhaps less obvious, but no less real. Chile peppers are rich in vitamins A and C (a single sweet pepper can pack as much vitamin C as an orange), in riboflavins and natural fibers. Hot peppers can stimulate digestion, tone the cardiovascular system, reduce cholesterol, and burn off excess calories. A Mexican cowboy I know swears that they can cure ulcers and relieve earaches (they unclog the eustachian tubes, to be sure). They can also dull pain. Latino healers, or *curanderos,* have known this for countless generations, concocting many kinds of analgesics from chiles. Modern medi-

This scene from the sixteenth-century "Drake manuscript," reputedly kept by a member of one of Sir Francis Drake's expeditions to the West Indies, depicts an Arawak Indian of the Lesser Antilles working a garden. Among the plants in it are maize, squash, and chile peppers.

cine has just begun to catch up with this ancient knowledge: a recent Mayo Clinic study suggests that pepper ointment can bring relief to patients who have undergone invasive surgery, because the pepper short-circuits nerves that would otherwise transmit agonizing pain.

They are also downright fun to eat, though I am put to mind here of the night I took a distinguished poet from Northern Ireland to a meal in South Tucson. Though I asked the chef to prepare the blandest possible version of a salsa, something that would not frighten, say, a group of elderly Scandinavian churchgoers from Wisconsin, my visitor took a few bites and immediately broke out into the most profound, and possibly clammiest, sweat that I have ever seen. He went to bed soon thereafter, bravely insisting that he had enjoyed the meal. I keep waiting for chiles to turn up in his poems, which abound in references to such plants as valerian, loosestrife, twayblade, angelica, mountain avens, and stitchwort, but I have yet to spot any mention of them.

Even old-time chile eaters have a healthy respect for the stuff, of course. Writing in his charming book *A Bowl of Red*, Frank Tolbert calls the chile-laden concoction called son-of-a-bitch stew "Texas' greatest contribution to civilization." Why the name? Well, the heat probably has something to do with it; the phrase may have escaped the mouth of the tenderfoot diner, along with a cascade of steam and fire. Tolbert theorizes, too, that the name may owe to a cowboy's telling said tenderfoot, when asked what went into the stew, "I'll be a son-of-a-bitch if I know all that goes into it. Different cooks put in different things, but it's sure good."

Dozens of varieties of chiles are commercially grown today. A good Mexican or Central American market will boast whole aisles full of different kinds and brands. Anglo-American markets offer fewer choices, but even in the far reaches of New England shoppers can easily find the ever-present jalapeño and ancho varieties grown in the Southwest, and sometimes even the intensely hot pico de gallo, serrano, and moreno peppers used in the cuisine of Mexico.

Just how hot is hot? Commercial growers rate peppers on an intensity scale that runs from 1 to 120, gauging the heat factor of capsaicin, the chief active ingredient. A bell pepper, its fire bred out over the generations, barely earns a point, while the average jalapeño weighs in at 25, which most American palates find plenty hot. Habañero, Bahamian, and chiltepin peppers rank in the triple digits. Whether anyone has survived eating a pepper at the very top of the scale is not known, although science has established that drinking a quart and a half of tabasco sauce can kill the average human. (I implore you: do not try this test at home. Neither should you take a bar bet, as I once did, over how many habañeros a person can down. I won, but alas, did I also lose.)

The growers' rating system owes to Wilbur Scoville, an American pharmacologist who was fascinated by the tongue-warming power of capsaicin. In 1912, he devised a system to measure the number of parts of water that are required to dilute a measure of capsaicin extracted from a pepper; refining this, his Scoville scale measures the heat of chiles, rated by ranking the number of grams of water that a gram of chile needs to be dissolved into until the heat is no longer detectable. Humans can detect capsaicin in dilutions of one part chile to a whopping 15 million parts water. These are the dilutions needed for the taste of these chiles to become scarcely perceptible:

| Anaheim | 1:50–250 |
|---|---|
| Jalapeño | 1:1,000 |
| Serrano | 1:5,000 |
| Habanero | 1:5,925 |
| Chile de arbol | 1:8,000 |
| Red chile | 1:10,000 |
| Chiltepin | 1:13,300 |

Trusting such measures of chile intensity, try adding them to taste to your diet. And if you have a jicama lying around, chop it up and give it a healthy dash of chile powder, which you can make for yourself: dry one dozen red peppers in the sun (or in an oven on low heat) until brittle; cut the peppers open in a well-ventilated area and remove seeds. Slowly put peppers in a blender on high setting. Store the powder in a labeled jar; it will keep well indefinitely.

The hottest peppers can now be found in ethnic markets around the world, and also in the mailbags of just about every postal carrier in the land, it having long been known that dogs dislike chiles but no one having made a dog-warding concoction from them until the 1980s. One of the hottest commonly available iterations comes from Louisiana, to which a soldier in the war against Mexico returned with chile seeds and gave a handful to the prominent banker Edmund McIlhenny. The banker in turn grew the seeds out on his plantation on Avery Island—which, to complicate matters, is not an island—and developed the scathing, mouth-melting hot sauce that bears his name.

There are hotter sauces on the market, but McIlhenny's remains the gold standard for those who prize hot food, as all right-thinking people do. To see some of those sauces at work, make a pilgrimage to Java Junction, a coffee shop in the little hippified town of Madrid, New Mexico, that doubles as a salsa museum. One of my favorite salsas, a blistering concoction of papaya and habanero, is called Bad Girls in Heat, its bottle proclaiming, in perfect noir speak, "You should have stayed on the Interstate. These buxom beauties won't settle for just a lift, they wanna take you for a ride, guaranteed to overheat more than just your engine." That's a natural fact—and there are many worse ways to melt down.

## GREEN CHILE SALSA

Place six fresh jalapeño chiles under the oven broiler for about three minutes, or until the skins are slightly charred. Then put the chiles in a paper bag and steam for ten minutes. Wearing rubber gloves to protect hands from acid, remove the chiles from the bag and let cool. Peel the skin and remove seeds. Combine with one diced yellow onion or, better, 1 cup of tomatillos (available in Caribbean and Mexican specialty markets). Heat

1 tbsp olive oil in pan. Sauté one clove minced garlic until soft. Add to vegetables with 1 tsp flour and simmer for ten minutes. Add 1 tbsp each coriander and minced fresh parsley, a pinch of oregano, and 1 cup vegetable stock or water and cook until the sauce has thickened. Add a squeeze of lemon or lime juice.

## TAM SOM

Green papaya salad is a staple of Lao and Thai restaurants worldwide, though its familiarity makes it no less potent to the unwary diner—and, in its traditional form, it is hotter than blazes, so much so that chefs will sometimes make a dare of it. This not very painful recipe can be adjusted to bank the fire or set it higher.

3 cups shredded green papaya
12 cooked shrimp, chilled
5 serrano chiles, red or green
3 cloves garlic, skinned
2 cups string beans, cut into small pieces
10 cherry tomatoes, halved
Cabbage leaves
1/3 cup fresh lime juice
1/4 cup nuoc mam (fish sauce)
1/4 cup sugar
　　Combine lime juice, nuoc mam, and sugar and let rest. Grind or food-process chiles and garlic into a rough blend. Add papaya, beans, and tomatoes and continue to blend. Add dressing and mix. Distribute over cabbage leaves and garnish with chilled shrimp. The salad makes a fine accompaniment to barbecued meats or vegetables.

## PAPRIKASH

Paprikash, or paprikás in Hungarian, is traditionally made of bits of chicken cooked with a local pepper that is both intensely hot and sweet. Ground paprika works fine, so long as it is not too old; the Mexican variety, however, has the heat but not the sweetness, so look for the genuine article.

4 chicken breasts, boned and cubed
2 cups finely chopped onion
3 tablespoons olive oil
2 tablespoons bacon fat (optional)
2 tablespoons Hungarian paprika
1/2 cup dry white wine
1/2 cup chicken broth
2/3 cup sour cream
Sea salt and pepper to taste

Heat olive oil and bacon fat in a large cast iron skillet and brown the chicken on all sides. Season with sea salt and black pepper. Remove the chicken and set aside in a baking dish. Add the onion to the skillet and cook until it is translucent. Stir in paprika to coat the onion. Return the chicken to the skillet and mix thoroughly, adding wine and broth. Bring to a boil; then cover and simmer for 1 hour, adding broth as needed. Remove the chicken and return it to the baking dish. Then bring the skillet drippings to a boil and add sour cream. Pour the mixture over the chicken and serve over egg noodles, Spätzle, or orzo.

## FURTHER READING

Jean Andrews, *The Pepper Trail: History and Recipes from Around the World* (Texas A&M University Press, 2001).

R.W. Apple Jr., "Following the Pepper Grinder All the Way to Its Source," *New York Times*, October 29, 2003.

Ronald Johnson, *Southwestern Cooking New & Old* (University of New Mexico Press, 1985).

Frank X. Tolbert, *A Bowl of Red* (Texas A&M University Press, 1953).

# CORN

---

Thousands of years ago, by some cosmic intuition that modern historians have yet to explain, nomadic peoples around the world came to understand that they could extract a basic diet from the grasses around them. In East Asia, that grass was rice. In Eurasia, it was wheat. In North America, it was corn. All three were domesticated at roughly the same time; all three provided the agricultural basis for the urban civilizations that would soon rise around fertile grain fields and paddies; all three became staples of the world, spread far beyond their original homelands.

First domesticated in the Valley of Mexico, *Zea mays* originated from *Zea mexicana*, a wild grass commonly called teosinte. This floury-kerneled maize required a growing period of only ninety to one hundred days (varieties grown today mature in anywhere from sixty to three hundred days), making it a relatively quick source of nourishment. Its adaptation also allowed the native peoples of Mexico—and, thanks to its rapid spread across the two continents, indigenous cultures elsewhere in the Americas—to escape the cycles of feast and famine that had governed their lives.

An Aztec etiological myth, one that explains the origin of things, ascribes the discovery of maize to the ant, busily working the slopes of the volcano Tonacatepetl; when the god Quetzalcoatl asked him where he had gotten the grain that he was rolling into his anthill, the little fellow at first did not want to say, then owned up to it, for which the assembled gods rewarded the ant and his fellows with varieties of blue, red, yellow, and white corn and threw in beans in the bargain. A hardy, low-maintenance plant, maize also allowed its first cultivators to do other things than chase up food—that is, to build pyramids, ball courts, palaces, and empires. The last, arguably, owes directly to corn, for among the greatest innovations in world military technology, the Mesoamerican prehistorian Ross Hassig argues, was the tortilla, the thin, dried corn cake that graces tables in Mexican restaurants around the world. So commonplace an item that we scarcely give it a thought today, the tortilla, Hassig has demonstrated, was developed so that Aztec armies on the march could have a quick source of nourishment, a kind of New World proto–C ration. It enabled Aztec troops to travel quickly through much of Mexico, bringing the light of their civilization to their usually unwilling neighbors at the obsidian point of a spear.

"Epi à Grains de Diverses Variétés," engraving by Anga Bottione-Rossi, from Matthieu Bonafous, *Histoire naturelle, agricole et economique du maïs* (Paris: Madame Huzard, 1836).

Christopher Columbus, a military-minded man, probably never saw the tortilla in action. He nonetheless brought back an abundance of corn to Spain from his first voyage to the Caribbean, ranging from dwarf varieties to giant strains that grew eighteen feet high. Some of these varieties flourished in Spain, but most others did not. Those varieties that survived were soon exported across the world, and corn (known as maize in all English-speaking countries save for the United States and Canada) has become a staple foodstuff in places as far afield as Central Asia, the Philippines, Romania, and Senegal.

Other European travelers to the New World quickly adopted corn in their diets as well, most famously the Pilgrims who endured that first Massachusetts winter thanks to corn provided by local Indians. So welcome was this gift of corn in time of need that, as a Puritan leader noted in his journal, "a few ears were thought as good as a feast." For his part, one of the first things Robinson Crusoe did on being shipwrecked, Daniel Defoe relates in his 1719 novel, was to plant corn, an act that kept him alive for long years of exile.

Corn, those Europeans discovered, grew so quickly and so well in so many climates that it was often the first crop planted in new territories, especially on the Great Plains. In her memoir *Little House in the Big Woods*, Laura Ingalls Wilder writes of a particular treat of the Kansas prairie: hulled corn and milk. To hull the corn, Wilder recalls, her mother would boil ears of corn for so long that "they swelled and swelled until their skins split open and began to peel off." Then her mother would soak the boiled corn in cold water and scrub it, ear by ear, until the hulls separated from the corn, whereupon it was ready to eat with a dish of fresh milk.

With all respect to Laura Ingalls Wilder, family loyalty precludes me from admitting that there could be any sweet corn better than what my grandfather grew in his Virginia garden. Still, I have had some sublime meals of corn in my travels: delicate, lightly boiled white corn on a quiet lakefront in Ontario and in the marshes of Delaware; just-picked, grilled blue and red maize on the Hopi mesas; lovely polentas throughout Italy; memorable *sopa de elote* in southern Mexico, where, in folk belief, each stage of the corn's growth is governed by a different god. Only in Germany have I failed to encounter some culinary use of maize; my redoubtable childhood housekeeper once remarked in horror, on seeing me eat it, "That is food for pigs, not people."

The good Frau had a point. On its own, corn is a poor source of fuel for humans, because its protein and niacin are bound up in molecules that the human digestive tract cannot wholly metabolize. For that reason, commercially processed corn is washed in a mild solution of lime, which breaks up those molecules—a trick nutritionists first learned from latter-day Aztecs while seeking a cure for pellagra, a disease brought on by eating too much untreated corn, as the poor of Europe and the American South once had to do in the absence of other food.

Thus treated, but only thus treated, yellow corn is a good source of vitamin A, and it contains moderate quantities of vitamin C, iron, and some of the B vitamins. Low in sodium, one medium-sized ear contains about 82 calories, with one gram of fat, 19 grams of carbohydrates, and 190 milligrams of potassium. Because of its fiber content, corn also gives the illusion of being far more filling than it really is, making it a good choice for dieters. Popcorn in particular is a good bet for dieters, and Americans consume 17 billion quarts of the stuff every year—more than fifty quarts per capita, that is. But that is popcorn plain, with perhaps a touch of salt, and decidedly not the greasy, palm oil–laden popcorn of the local cineplex, an offense to popcorn lovers and corn admirers every-where.

Indeed, ironically, one of the ruinations of the American diet has been—well, corn. Heavily subsidized in the domestic market, corn is widely used in cereals and snack foods, where it is at least somewhat easy to eat in controlled portions. Less visibly, corn syrup, produced by a highly complex enzymatic technique (for the technically inclined, the enzymes involved are alpha-amylase, glucoamylase, and glucose-isomerase), is a component of all sorts of processed foods, from soft drinks to ketchup, macaroni and cheese, smoked meats, peanut butter, and even beer. According to the U.S. Department of Agriculture, the average American consumed only half a pound of high fructose corn syrup in 1970, when the product first became widely available. Thirty years later, the figure stood at 62 pounds. Fructose appears to behave more like fat than a sugar within the body, and overconsumption thus directly contributes to weight gain and type 2 diabetes, as well as heart disease produced by elevated tri-glycerides and bone loss produced by lowered levels of magnesium in the body. (Strangely, bovine trypsin, an enzyme derived from corn, is now being used to manufacture insulin for those very diabetics.) Just so, some genetically modified corn is difficult to break down in the human gut; intended for animal feed, some of this has found its way over the years into such fast-food favorites as taco shells. Donella Meadows, the late food activist, wisely counsels, "If you want to be a creative irritant, just ask every time you buy a product or order a meal containing potatoes, corn, canola, or soy, 'Is there anything genetically modified in here?' If you want to play it absolutely safe, buy certified organic."

Ironically, too, the use of high fructose corn syrup is rising in Mexico, where the ever-restless Aztecs first arrived upon the idea of the tortilla. Every street in the nation today, it seems, has at least one *tortilleria*, where fresh tortillas are rolled out by hand and baked on a griddle or steel barrel, and anyone who has eaten one knows that by comparison the mass-produced variety would not please even the hungriest of Aztec grunts. Yet tortillas are a big business—the *Wall Street Journal* reckoned the world market a decade ago at $5 billion, and it has almost certainly jumped in the succeeding years—and industrial production has become ever more commonplace in Mexico and Central America. One difference that can be immediately perceived is that factory tortillas do not hold up well to freezing, unlike handmade ones, and their high oil content—of, yes, corn oil—yields a slightly sour taste that becomes stronger as the tor-tilla ages, indicating rancidity.

To grill corn or to microwave it, leave the husk and silk on until after the corn is cooked; this makes the corn all the more succulent. You should eat sweet corn just as soon as you pick it or buy it at market, for corn's sugars begin to convert almost immediately into starch, and overripe corn is a gummy mess. And remember, if you are one of those who believes that corn silk was put on earth to test the patience of the eater, that corn germinates, kernel by kernel, from that very silk.

Now the world's most plentiful grain after wheat, used to produce food for machines as well as people and animals, the corn we have today is the result of hybrids crossbred from maize's five principal types: pop, flint, dent, flour, and sweet. We may soon be seeing even more kinds of corn. A few years ago Rafael Guzmán, a plant scientist at the University of Guadalajara, who had spent years looking for the ancestor of domesticated corn, eventually turned up what he thought might have been the world's last remaining stand of *Zea diploperennis,* a variety of maize powerfully resistant to the blights that now beset *Zea mays.* Hybridized with commercially grown corn, *Zea diploperennis* is now yielding new varieties of maize—and, potentially, billions of dollars for its cultivators.

## WHERE THE CORN GOES

| | |
|---|---|
| Feed/Residual | 5.8 billion (56.8 percent) |
| Exports* | 1.9 billion (18.6 percent) |
| Ethanol (fuel) | 1.2 billion (11.7 percent) |
| High fructose corn syrup | 530 million (5.1 percent) |
| Corn starch | 228 million (2.2 percent) |
| Cereal/Other | 187 million (1.8 percent) |
| Beverage alcohol | 132 million (1.2 percent) |

*The ten leading export markets for U.S. corn are Japan, Mexico, Taiwan, South Korea, Egypt, Colombia, Algeria, Canada, Israel, and the Dominican Republic. The statistics, from the U.S. Department of Agriculture, are for 2003–2004.

## HUSH PUPPIES

Every Southerner knows the wonders of hush puppies, which take their name from their job: throw one to a restless dog while you are out fishing, and it will quiet down and eat. A Yankee variant, without onion, is called "corn oysters."

2 cups white cornmeal
1 tablespoon sugar
3/4 tablespoons baking soda
2 teaspoons salt
1 tablespoon minced white or yellow onion
1 egg
1 cup buttermilk
4–5 tablespoons cold water

Blend cornmeal, sugar, baking soda, and salt in a bowl. Put the onion in another bowl, add egg and buttermilk, and beat until froth forms on the surface. Pour the liquid into the meal and stir lightly to mix. Add a little cold water to give the dough a consistency like pancake batter. Drop dough balls into hot oil and fry until brown on all sides.

# CORN TORTILLAS

An experienced tortilla maker requires no flat surfaces other than her hands (and in Mexico, tortilla makers are almost always women). Those of us with less experience can make use of a tortilla press and this traditional recipe, which requires skill even so—so much so that the packaged thing may seem in order. Prepared *masa*, or corn flour, can be found in most grocery stores, and in all events, persevere. This recipe from the University of Puebla, a leading researcher in corn, yields fine-tasting tortillas—which are now so ubiquitous that they can be found at supermarkets almost everywhere in the United States.

1 bushel white corn
3.5 ounces powdered limestone
 Cook corn in water and limestone on low heat overnight. When the corn can be shelled, add more water and steam for an hour. Rinse the corn and grind it with a stone mortar and pestle. Make small balls of dough and press between two heavy plastic sheets in a tortilla press. Then cook the tortillas on a griddle, removing them from the heat when they puff up on both sides.

# POLENTA

I have a theory that when Americans die, if they have been good, they are reborn as Italians. This Italian favorite, polenta, will make a Southerner think that hush puppies can enjoy the same fate.

1 cup medium-coarse stone-ground cornmeal
3–6 cups water (the more water, the more pudding-like the polenta will be)
1 tablespoon olive oil
1 teaspoon salt
 Preheat oven to 350°F. Grease a medium cast-iron skillet. Pour in the ingredients and stir with a fork or whisk until blended. Bake uncovered for 30–40 minutes. Stir the polenta and bake for an additional 10 minutes. Remove from the oven and let the polenta rest in the pan for 10 minutes, then remove to a bowl lightly greased with butter or olive oil.

## SUCCOTASH

This is my own recipe for succotash, a dish of American Indian origin that, it is supposed, made its way to Puritan tables on those first feasts of thanksgiving.

2 cups lima beans
4 cups corn
6 cups water
4 slices cured bacon
salt
black pepper

   Soak the lima beans in water overnight. (Even if they're frozen, they'll cook a little more thoroughly once they've been soaked.) Cook the beans in fresh water until tender, then cook with corn. Drain, place in a bowl, and stir in diced, cooked bacon. (This is decidedly optional.) Add salt and pepper to taste.

## FURTHER READING

Vance Bourjaily, "The Corn of Coxcatlán," *Horizon,* July 1973.

Malcolm Gladwell, "The Pima Paradox: Can We Learn How to Lose Weight From One of the Most Obese People in the World?" *The New Yorker,* February 2, 1998.

Ross Hassig, *War and Society in Ancient Mesoamerica* (University of California Press, 1991).

Charles C. Mann, *1491: New Revelations of the Americas Before Columbus* (Knopf, 2005).

Gary Paul Nabhan, *Songbirds, Truffles, and Wolves: An American Naturalist in Italy* (North Point Press, 1994).

*Recetario de Maíz* (CEICADAR/University of Puebla, 1990).

John B. Rehder, *Appalachian Folkways* (Johns Hopkins University Press, 2004).

Sally Squires, "Sweet But Not So Innocent? High-Fructose Corn Syrup May Act More Like Fat Than Sugar in the Body," *Washington Post,* March 11, 2003.

# CRANBERRY

Do you want to see a bear? If so, you can go to your local zoo, or switch on the Discovery Channel, or head out the door to Yellowstone or Glacier national parks. Or, if you live in northern Canada or Alaska, you can just step outside, though the bears are getting ever skinnier there: to begin with a digression, scientists have confirmed that North America's largest terrestrial carnivores have shrunk about 10 percent since 1980, and they hypothesize that global warming keeps ice from forming on the Hudson Bay and other hunting locales until comparatively late in the season, depriving the animals of food they might have taken in that time.

But a century ago, if you lived pretty much anywhere in temperate, forested parts of the United States, you would need only to have made for the nearest cranberry bog—quintessentially American country, celebrated in the works of Henry David Thoreau and Aldo Leopold—in order to find a bear. Bears revel in the presence of cranberries, seeking them out for a convenient snack and making their dens near supplies of this favorite treat. Hunters knew this, and they positioned their blinds accordingly, a bummer for the bears. Other settlers knew this, too, and they took pains to build their cabins as far away from cranberry bogs as they could.

By all rights, then, cranberries should be called bearberries. Instead, they are named for another denizen of the bogs—cranes, those graceful, long-necked waterfowl. Some etymologists suggest that the cranberry, originally the "crane berry," is named not because the bird itself had any special fondness for *Vaccinium macrocarpon,* but because the plant's slender pistil suggested the crane's narrow neck. The Pilgrims associated the

"Cranberry Bog, Ocean County—Pickers at Work," *Harper's Weekly,* November 10, 1878.

cranberry—with the blueberry and the Concord grape, the only fruit native to North America—not with bears or cranes but Indians, and for good reason: the Massapequody people who saved their narrow necks that first winter at Plymouth made extensive use of the berry, especially as one of the principal ingredients in pemmican, a mixture of berries, nuts, dried meat (often, in fact, dried bear meat), and tallow. The Pilgrims followed suit, cultivating the plant in quantity. Wrote one English visitor to the Pilgrim colony in 1639, "The Indians and English use [cranberries] much, boyling them with Sugar for Sauce to eat with their Meat, and it is a delicious Sauce." Half a century later, a resident of New England recorded that the cranberry had become a staple:

> We have from the time called May until Michaelmas [that is, about the time of the autumn equinox] a great store of very good wild fruits as strawberries, cranberries and hurtleberries. The cranberries, much like cherries for colour and bigness, may be kept until fruit comes in again. An excellent sauce is made of them for venison, turkeys and other great fowl and they are better to make tarts than either gooseberries or cherries. We have them brought to our homes by the Indians in great plenty.

The Indians' kindness and the Pilgrims' remembrance is what brings cranberry sauce to our tables at Thanksgiving and Christmas dinner; North Americans tend not to consume much solid *Vaccinium macrocarpon* outside of the end-of-year holiday season. Perhaps this is because cranberry sauce and tarts, like candied yams, are so closely associated with the holidays that they seem out of place in other seasons. The rest of the year, most Americans forget all about *Vaccinium macrocarpon*, except as an ingredient in mixed-fruit juices. Cranberry growers would like to change all that, but they seem to be fighting a lost cause; in 1910, one New Jersey cultivator alone developed fifteen cranberry varieties, but only a few are grown commercially today in the leading cranberry-producing states: Wisconsin, Massachusetts, Oregon, New Jersey, and Washington, in that order. Lately, specialty growers have also developed a sun-dried, sweetened "craisin," but these have yet to become a popular item in the pantry.

Perhaps that is because the cranberry is a bitter little pill to swallow. Perhaps it is because Americans believe somehow that, like candied yams, cranberries are meant to grace only the holiday groaning board. Even Henry Thoreau, who championed its regular consumption, had to admit that the berry took some getting used to. "Perhaps the prettiest berry, certainly the most novel and interesting to me, was the mountain cranberry," he wrote in his journal of 1860, "now grown but yet hard and with only its upper cheek red....They were very easy to collect, for you only made incessant dabs at them with all your fingers together and the twigs and leaves were so rigid that you brought away only berries and no leaves.... We stewed these berries for our breakfast, and thought them the best berry on the mountain, though...a little bitterish."

Those bitterish cranberries are, folk wisdom has it, great tonics for the human urinary tract. (How they influence bears, I do not know. The biological literature is full of mentions of bearish toothaches, ursine teeth evidently being on the delicate side, but it says nothing about the bear's susceptibility to kidney troubles.) In 1830, Constantine Samuel Rafinesque, an American herbalist, recommended the cranberry for its "refrigerant, laxative, anti-bilious, anti-putrid, diuretic, sub-astringent, etc." properties and prescribed it against diarrhea, dropsy, and scurvy, adding that cranberry "juice mixed with sugar or alcohol keeps a long while, and forms a fine acidulous drink with sugar, allaying thirst, and lessening the heat of the body." Nineteenth-century doctors prescribed cranberry extract for a variety of digestive complaints, and for fevers generally. Yet all that hardwon wisdom was discounted and discarded for much of the twentieth century, when it was assumed that something had to be pharmaceutical in order to be effective. Thus, until recently, medical doctors scoffed at the notion of drinking cranberry juice as a preventative for urinary tract disorders, ranging from relatively minor discomforts to more serious ailments like kidney stones and interstitial cystitis.

The folk and premodern medical remedies have a solid basis in fact. We now know that plants of the *Vaccinium* genus—in North America, the cranberry and blueberry foremost among them—contain enzymes that keep certain kinds of inflammation-inducing acids from bonding to our sensitive plumbing. These polymeric compounds, called condensed tannins (or, more formally, proanthocyanidins), keep microorganisms such as *Escherichia coli* from bonding to the epithelial cells that line the urinary tract. Because they cannot attach to the cell walls, these harmful bacteria cannot stay within the urinary tract long enough to reproduce and cause infections. The antibacterial qualities of *Vaccinium* are of particular benefit to the countless millions of women who suffer from urinary tract infections. It is not yet known whether the effect is primarily preventive or curative, but doctors now commonly suggest that women who suffer from this all too common ailment consume cranberry juice or extract daily. This regime reduces the need for antibiotics and lessens overall healthcare costs, which, for urinary tract infections alone, have been reckoned to exceed $1 billion annually in the United States.

Recent research suggests that the "antistick" effect may also prevent *H. pylori,* a bacterium believed to cause certain kinds of stomach ulcers, and reduce the prevalence of other harmful bacteria on the teeth and gums, which can cause infection and decay. And cranberries have been shown to help combat herpes virus type II (HSV-2) infection, one of the most common viral infections in humans. For good measure, too, cranberries also contain high concentrations of potassium, phosphorus, iron, calcium, vitamin A, vitamin E, and vitamin C, as well as natural antioxidants that are believed to protect the body against cancer.

All this is good news not only for the health-minded, but also for cranberry producers, who, after all, managed to find a market for 600 million pounds of cranberries in 2004 in the United States alone. And, although it is true that Americans stay away from solid cranberries for so much of the year, they still consume more than 400 million pounds of cranberries in the form of juice in all seasons—a figure that may well rise as the medicinal qualities of *Vaccinium macrocarpon* become more widely known. The popularity of cranberry juice–based cocktails is growing elsewhere in the world, too, and the cranberry, once confined to sandy bogs throughout northeastern North America, is now grown as far afield as Scandinavia, Japan, and Chile.

Strangely, sadly, and altogether predictably, though, the fastest growing segment of the cranberry market, as *The Economist* notes, "is for cranberries that do not taste like cranberries," particularly in the United States, where, as the great food writer A. J. Liebling once grumbled, many people seem not to like food that tastes like food. The largest producers are turning out flavored juices that taste like oranges, cherries, raspberries, or other sweet-but-not-sour fruits, apparently in the belief that the world is increasingly not ready for bitterish reality. The producers have learned that they can fill cranberry hulls, being tough little customers, with the juices of other fruits, the better to bake with, and that, impregnated with gelatin, the hulls can be made to stay chewy for years, the better to lace an unsuspecting breakfast cereal with at least a hint of something that might be good for a person, or a dog or cat: cranberries are increasingly being used in pet food, a $17 billion market in this country, for the same reasons that they are recommended for the human diet.

In our national cuisine, cranberries figure prominently in muffins, cakes, and puddings, and, of course, in sauces: jellied, smooth, or lumpy, as you prefer. Although you will not usually see much variation in the sauce from table to table, National Public Radio (NPR) commentator Susan

Stamberg offers a family recipe for an idiosyncratic garnish that mixes standard-issue cranberries with sour cream, onion, horseradish, and sugar. If you are adventurous, give it a try, using whatever proportions suit your taste; you can find the recipe on the NPR Web site in season.

Dolly Madison, the wife of President James Madison, was more adventurous still. At her husband's second inauguration, she served a cranberry sherbet that made news; a reporter for the *National Intelligencer* could not get over how delicious it was. (That reporter was less fascinated by Dolly's bitter cranberry chutney, which made mouth-puckeringly liberal use of green peppers, vinegar, crabapples, cayenne, and lemon juice.) The First Lady's sherbet recipe goes like this:

Mix 1½ cups cranberry jelly with the juice and grated rind of one lemon and the juice of one orange. Freeze for one-half hour. Add ½ pint whipped cream. Pour into a mold and freeze until solid.

Whip up a batch of Dolly's cranberry sherbet, carve off a sliver of jellied cranberry sauce, or pour yourself a tall glass of cranberry-juice cocktail, which lends itself very nicely to a discreet quantity of vodka. Then settle in with a good book—I recommend something on bears, or perhaps better, Peter Matthiessen's lively *Birds of Heaven: Travels with Cranes*—and enjoy.

## CRANBERRY-NUT MUFFINS

Many of the good residents of Whitman Mission, now a national historic site in Washington, did not live long in their new home, owing to an Indian attack of 1847. But, as luck would have it, they at least had a chance to discover cranberries nearby before departing the territory, and this recipe honors their find.

1/4 cup butter
1/2 cup honey
2 beaten eggs
1/2 cup orange juice
1 1/2 cups flour
1 teaspoon grated orange rind
1 teaspoon baking powder
1 1/2 teaspoons salt
3/4 cup chopped cranberries
1/2 cup chopped walnuts
Whip butter and honey into a cream. Add eggs, orange juice, and orange rind. Mix in the flour, baking powder, and salt. Add cranberries and walnuts. Bake in oiled muffin tin at 350°F for 30–35 minutes.

## CRANBERRY FRITTERS

The Wisconsin State Cranberry Growers' Association offers this tasty recipe for cranberry fritters, which, though perhaps not the healthiest thing, surely hit the spot of a wintry North Woods morning.

1 cup cranberries
1/4 cup sugar
1/2 cup water
2 cups all-purpose flour
3/4 cup sugar
1 teaspoon baking powder
2 eggs
1/4 cup ice water
1 apple, peeled and diced
confectioner's sugar
raspberry jam
oil for frying

In a saucepan, combine cranberries, sugar and water. Over high heat, cook until berries begin to burst. Remove from heat and chill. Sift together flour, sugar and baking powder. Separate eggs. Beat egg yolks with ice water. Add the sifted dry ingredients, apple, cranberries and any liquid in the pan used to cook them. In a separate bowl, beat egg whites until soft peaks form. Fold into cranberry mixture. In a deep skillet or deep fat fryer, heat an inch or two of oil to 350°. For each fritter, drip two tablespoons of batter into the oil. Cook for one minute, flip the fritters over, and continue frying until golden. This may have to be done in batches; be sure oil returns to 350° between batches. Drain fritters on paper towels and dust with confectioners' sugar. Serve with raspberry jam.

## FURTHER READING

A. B. Howell et al., "Inhibition of the adherence of P-fimbriated Escherichia coli to uroepithelial-cell surfaces by proanthocyanidin extracts from cranberries," *New England Journal of Medicine* 339 (15): 1085–1086.

Peter Matthiessen, *The Birds of Heaven: Travels with Cranes* (North Point Press, 2001).

C.S. Rafinesque, *Medical Flora, or Manual of Medical Botany of the United States of North America* (Samuel Atkinson, 1830).

# EGGPLANT

In the Middle Ages, the world's biggest city was not London or Paris or even Tokyo, then collections of small villages alongside major roads and rivers, but Baghdad, a great walled metropolis of 900,000 inhabitants, 360 towers, and countless minarets. The Frankish Empire kept an embassy there. So, too, did the Jewish Khazars, the Kievan conquerors of Russia, and several Chinese dynasties, anxious to keep in touch with developments in the West. To all those places went the learning of Islam, the sciences and arts long lost during the European Dark Ages, kept alive by the great Caliphate of Baghdad, which considered itself to be at the very center of the world.

And to all those places, along with algebra, alchemy, and astronomy, went a local delicacy: the eggplant.

The good residents of Baghdad called *Solanum melongena* by its Persian name, *badinjan,* for they had come to know the perennial shrub and its delicious elongated fruit through the courtesy of traders from the Hindu Kush. It had come to the foothills of those imposing mountains much earlier from its source in the tropical gardens of Southeast Asia, where today hundreds of varieties of eggplant are grown, and it already played a central role in the cuisines of northern India and Persia. But in Baghdad it reached its culinary apex, joined to rare and exotic spices that sharpened the eggplant's flavor and made it a highly prized treat fit for a king—or, better, a sheik.

The Iraqi eggplant, *al-badingan,* traveled to Charlemagne's court with a French accent, bearing the altered name *aubergine.* Its name saw

"Aubergine," from A.W. Sythoff, *Flore des Jardins du Royame des Pays-Bas* (1860).

other permutations in other tongues; in the opening pages of his grand novel *Don Quixote,* Miguel de Cervantes writes that he recovered the history of the knight of woeful countenance from a Toledo marketplace in the form of a heap of notebooks and loose papers in Arabic, all penned by Cide Hamete Benengeli, "an Arab historian" whose exotic name means "eggplant." Whatever it was called, the eggplant found a welcome home in gardens throughout temperate Europe, though the papal botanists of Rome received *Solanum melongena* with more suspicion; they called the strangely shaped plant *mala insana,* "evil unhealthy thing"—an ironic designation, given that the recommended diet of the day included little more than red meat and high-octane wine. The botanists' disapproval did not keep Italians from wholeheartedly embracing the plant, name and all—*mala insana* became *melanzana* in their language—into their cuisine, where it now appears in a variety of soups, stews, and other dishes.

But why the unlikely name *eggplant?* Upper-crust English diners of the Middle Ages spoke French, and they called the plant as Charlemagne and their Norman forebears did, *aubergine,* the name by which it appears on London menus today. The Anglo-Saxon cooks who prepared the exotic new dish for their rulers, though, knew no French. Confronted with this strange thing, which looked vaguely like a cucumber but tasted altogether different, they likened its translucent, pale flesh to the shell of an egg, and eggplant it became.

Commercial varieties of eggplant, bearing names like Black Beauty, Santana, and Casper, are generally easy to grow in a range of climates—and especially the temperate South, where, as with so many things, Thomas

Jefferson proved a pioneer of eggplant cultivation. The seeds can be germinated and raised indoors ten to twelve weeks before transplantation outside after the last frost of spring. Many growing guides suggest that young eggplants be planted first in containers and moved indoors at night, the idea being to acclimate them gradually to the outdoors; in all events, the young plants should not be exposed to temperatures below 60°F. Under good conditions in warm climates with daytime temperatures of 80° to 90°F, eggplants can be grown for half the year, and even in colder climates they can be grown in hothouses.

Eggplant is best grown in well-drained, sandy, slightly acidic (pH 5.5–6.5) loam that usually needs to be worked to introduce good supplies of nitrogen, phosphorus, and potassium. Eggplant also needs room to grow: set the plants two feet apart along the vertical axis and three feet apart on the horizontal axis, and watch them go. The plants can be staked like their tomato cousins to keep the leaves from mildew and to allow good air circulation around the fruit. Eggplant requires regular but light watering, and it definitely prefers to be dry at night, so it is best to water your plants in the morning.

Eggplant is ready to harvest when the skin takes on a highly glossy shine. Press the skin with your finger, and if it does not spring back to the touch, it is ready to use. Because eggplant does not keep particularly well, it is best to eat it within a few days after picking. It can be refrigerated, though it should be stored apart from plants that produce ethylene gas: cut flowers, apples, avocados, bananas, pears, peaches, plums, cantaloupes, honeydew melons, and tomatoes.

When you first cut into an eggplant, have a look at the seeds. If they are large, remove them, because they can be bitter. If they have turned dark brown, then the plant is decidedly past its prime and probably needs to be discarded.

Eggplant, a fleshy and substantial vegetable, makes a fine substitute for meat in casseroles and stews. Like okra, asparagus, and other fleshy vegetables, however, eggplant can lose its form quickly under cooking, turning from delicacy to soggy mess in no time at all; I have found that most people who claim not to like eggplant in fact like it just fine, so long as it has not been cooked to death. To avoid this common catastrophe, take care to cook eggplant only lightly. In a baked casserole, for instance, such as eggplant parmesan or ratatouille, add eggplant raw and allow it to cook slowly. Rather than sauté slices of eggplant for an omelet, lay them on top of the cooking egg and let the rising steam permeate the vegetable, which will then retain its crispness. Deep-frying eggplant in seasoned batter helps it keep its shape, too, though if you are watching the calories you will want to use olive or canola oil. If, on the other hand, you follow the tenets of Lucio Sforza, the masterful chef of L'Asino d'Oro, a wonderful restaurant in Orvieto, Italy, then you will cook eggplant in a careful quantity of olive oil—and then cover it in bitter chocolate, yielding a strange but very pleasing taste.

And why bother? Well, a well-cooked eggplant—that is, without fat— acts as a kind of drain opener of the cardiovascular system, thanks to its abundant store of chlorogenic acid and related esters that eat up mutagens and microbes and apparently have antiviral properties as well; these things are among the strongest free radical scavengers found naturally in any food anywhere. Furthermore, the eggplant's bioflavonoids are now thought to help prevent strokes and hemorrhages and impede the development of heart disease and tumor formation. If it is innocent of introduced fats, too, eggplant is a low-calorie proposition, about 25 calories for a three-ounce serving. The same serving contains about 2 grams of dietary fiber and 1 gram of protein, as well as small amounts of vitamin C and iron.

Match an eggplant with an excellent olive oil, though, and you have something truly special. A Turkish folktale tells us as much: an imam, or Muslim holy man, marries the lovely daughter of an olive oil merchant. Her dowry includes a dozen jars of the finest olive oil, and for the first twelve nights of their marriage the bride prepares a meal of eggplant cooked in it and mixed with tomatoes and onions. On the thirteenth night, no eggplant graces the imam's plate; informed that they have run out of olive oil, he faints. The Turkish dish is still called Imam Bayildi, "The Imam Fainted."

All the evidence therefore argues that eggplant is one of the world's good things. As long as you do not overcook it to oblivion, condemn it to the shameful victimhood of steam table or heat lamp, it will repay attention: it is a fine kind of bitter, and it may well cure what ails.

## IMAM BAYILDI

4 medium eggplants
1 1/2 cups olive oil
2 onions, chopped fine
4 large Roma or plum tomatoes, skinned and chopped fine
1 garlic clove, crushed
Juice of 1 lemon
Salt and black pepper to taste
Fresh parsley or cilantro as garnish

Cut eggplants in half. With a spoon, scoop out the pulp, leaving only a thin wall of flesh inside the eggplant shell. Set the pulp aside. Sprinkle the inside of shell with sea salt. Heat oil in a skillet on medium heat. Add the eggplant pulp, onions, and garlic, mix well, and sauté until the onions are soft, about ten minutes. Reduce heat to simmer, stir in tomatoes, add salt and pepper to taste, mix well, and simmer for another five or ten minutes.

Rinse the eggplant shells, fill them with the eggplant mixture, and arrange them in a baking dish. Bake at 325° for an hour.

## BADINJAN MUHASSA

Ibrahim Ibn al-Mahdi, half-brother of the Abbasid Caliph Harun al-Rashid, compiled an influential cookbook in the tenth century. Here, as translated by Charles Perry, is one of his recipes for eggplant:

Cook eggplants until soft by baking, boiling, or grilling over the fire, leaving them whole. When they are cool, remove the loose skin, drain the bitter liquor, and chop the flesh fine. It should be coarser than a true purée. Grind walnuts fine and make into a dough with vinegar and salt. Form into a patty and fry on both sides until the taste of raw walnut is gone; the vinegar is to delay scorching of the nuts. Mix the cooked walnuts into the chopped eggplant and season to taste with vinegar and ground caraway seed, salt and pepper. Serve with a topping of chopped raw or fried onion.

A modern adaptation follows.

3/4 pound eggplant
1 cup walnuts
2 tablespoons vinegar (for nut dough)
1/2 teaspoon salt (for nut dough)
1/8 teaspoon each pepper and salt
1 teaspoon caraway seed, ground
1 1/2 tablespoon vinegar
1/4 cup chopped raw onion

Simmer the eggplant 20 to 30 minutes in salted water. Let it cool, then peel. Slice the eggplant and drain in a colander or on a cloth for an hour. Grind the walnuts and add vinegar and salt to make a dough. Make dough patties about half an inch thick and put them on a frying pan at medium heat, without oil. When the bottom side has browned, turn the patty over and squash it flat with a spatula. Repeat until both sides are brown and crispy; the patties will begin to break up. Chop the eggplant, mix in the bits of nut patties, add pepper, salt, caraway seed, and vinegar and top with raw onion.

## EGGPLANT WITH LENTILS

Eggplant is a staple of Thai cuisine, though most chefs prefer the smaller Asian eggplants to the larger European variety. This recipe makes a delicious blend of eggplant and lentil.

1/4 pound lentils
1/2 teaspoon salt
1/2 pound eggplant
4 cloves garlic
1 small hot pepper (jalapeño or Scotch bonnet)

2 tablespoons vegetable oil
1 tablespoon fish sauce
4 tablespoons water
1/4 cup mint leaves

Cover the lentils with boiling water and let stand for two hours. Drain, cover with cool water, add salt, bring to a boil, and cook, covered, for thirty minutes. Drain. Cut the eggplant into two-inch cubes. Pound the garlic and pepper into a paste and fry in vegetable oil until golden. Add the lentils, fish sauce, eggplant pieces, and water to the paste. Continue frying for two or three minutes, until the eggplant is cooked. Add mint leaves and remove from heat.

## EGGPLANT PARMESAN

A classic eggplant parmesan can be a diet-killing, fatty concoction. This version lands on the lighter side of the spectrum, though it can be modified even further with nonfat cheese, slightly less olive oil, and so forth.

1 1/2 pounds eggplant, peeled and cut in half-inch slices
1/3 cup olive oil
2 tablespoons garlic, finely chopped
6 Roma or plum tomatoes, skinned and finely chopped
1/4 cup water
sea salt to taste
2 sprigs fresh basil, or 1 tbsp dried basil
2 sprigs fresh oregano, or 1 tbsp dried oregano
2 cups grated mozzarella cheese
1/2 cup freshly grated imported Parmesan cheese

Brush eggplant slices with oil and grill on barbecue on medium heat, about four minutes per side or until lightly brown. In a saucepan, lightly cook the chopped garlic in the remaining olive oil for just a minute. Stir in tomatoes, water, salt, basil, and oregano and cook on low heat for five minutes. Layer eggplant slices in a glass or ceramic baking dish, sprinkling cheese and dollops of tomato sauce between layers. Cook under a broiler (or put on the top rack of a covered outdoor grill) for just a minute or two, until the cheese is melted.

## FURTHER READING

Nina Kehayan, *Essentially Eggplant* (Da Capo Press, 1996).
M.M. Parker, *Eggplant Culture* (Virginia Truck Experimental Station, 1926).

# GARLIC

It is the mid-eighteenth century. A Spanish officer, magnificent on horse-back, comes trotting up to a Hia-Ced O'odham, one of the Sand People of the formidable desert of southwestern Arizona, produces a map-in-progress, and demands to know where he is. The Indian woman, shrugging her shoulders—for she does not speak Spanish, nor he O'odham—guesses what he is after, and says something like "*aw'a-ho*," pointing to the jagged mountains nearby. Aha, the conquistador thinks; there must be a garlic field at their base, for that is just what *ajo* means in his language.

Thus Ajo, Arizona, it has ever been, and though a native member of the lily family, *Hesperocallis undulata,* grows nearby and tastes a little like garlic, the woman was really saying, "The place where the red clay for paint comes from," a different thing altogether. Still, our hypothetical soldier can be forgiven for longing for garlic, long a staple of the Spanish diet and other cuisines of the Mediterranean region. Indeed, without garlic, those foodways would be very different indeed.

Garlic, *Allium sativum,* has been a presence in the Mediterranean for at least five thousand years. It was almost certainly brought in from Mesopotamia, though its origins lie farther to the east, in Central Asia; its closest wild counterpart comes from the mountains of eastern Iran, Afghanistan, and Turkistan. A cousin to onions, leeks, and shallots, it is different from other *Allium* species in growing entirely underground, its presence signaled by thin green stalks with a whitish, pleasant-looking flower. It is like many other *Allium* kin, though, in taking a long time to grow. The poet laureate of garlic, New Mexico writer and farmer Stanley Crawford,

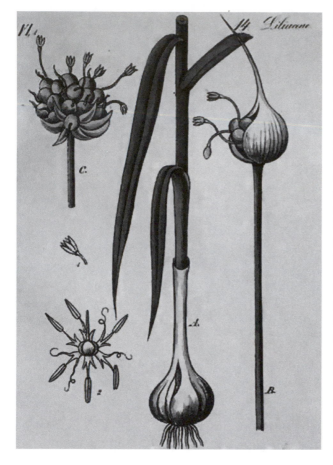

"Allium sativum," from D.F.L. von Schlechtendahl, *Flora von Deutschland* (1885–1886).

observes, "One of the singular characteristics of garlic is that it makes you wait. For radishes and spinach, you need to wait only a month or so. For lettuce or carrots or summer squash or green beans you can begin to taste the results of your plantings in two months. Tomatoes and eggplants and peppers and winter squash take another month. But for garlic you must wait seven to nine months from the time you plant to the time you harvest, and during perhaps half of the growing cycle there is little to look at besides a few shoots sticking up here and there in a row."

It is well worth waiting for, of course. Garlic has a certain hard-to-express deliciousness that makes it a highly prized commodity among the cognoscenti, even though it is repellent to vampires and the olfactorily squeamish. In the last category, we can count the ancient Greek physician Hippocrates, who warned that not only did garlic smell on its own, but it also produced some supercharged flatulence. We can count, too, the Roman poet Horace, who, though born in the garlic-loving Italian province of Lucania, seems not to have had a taste for the plant. His Epode III proclaims,

> Parentis olim siquis impia manu
> senile guttur fregerit,
> edit cicutis alium nocentius.

That is to say, "If there were ever a case where a boy throttled his old dad to death, I'd sentence him to eat garlic, far more noxious than hemlock," and which goes on to add that the fire of a good dose of garlic feels in his stomach very much like a viper's poison, and which concludes that anyone who eats the stuff will have to sleep on the opposite side of the bed and be content to live without the poet's kisses. The Roman aristocracy seems to have shared some of Horace's ideas, including the thought that anyone who smelled of garlic was a victim of poor breeding and therefore not really a candidate for mixing with the ancient jet set, who had plenty of prejudices but perhaps not much self-control when it came to putting things into their bodies.

Those hedonists would probably have been unimpressed by the fact that garlic packs a great deal of punch, nutritionally speaking: a bulb of raw garlic, even the rather insipid white-skinned elephant garlic now making inroads into the world market, contains goodly quantities of vitamin C and potassium, as well as a small but meaningful amount of protein, about 8 percent of the bulb by weight. Moreover, many of its compounds, some not yet fully described, suggest that garlic is a singular pharmacopoeia. It has demonstrated medicinal uses as an antiseptic, antifungal, and antibiotic agent, for instance, for which reason field doctors in the classical world treated wounded soldiers with poultices laced with chunks of garlic. A group of those compounds, called disulfides, offers an effective treatment for malaria; one series of medical tests conducted in 2003 showed that most of the individual disulfides were effective against *Plasmodium falciparum*, the malaria parasite, and were also effective in killing cancer cells, which opens the door to a whole new world of possibilities.

The most powerful of the disulfides—happily, our conquistador might say, called ajoene—inhibits a process called glutathione reduction, which promotes cellular damage; ajoene, an anticoagulant, also seems to burn away serum cholesterol. Ajoene and its congener diallyl sulfide (DAS) may help ward off the chemical PhIP given off by meat cooked at high temperatures, a suspected carcinogen given especially to expressing itself in breast cancer; one medical researcher remarked of an experiment, "We treated human breast epithelial cells with equal amounts of PhIP and DAS separately, and the two together, for periods ranging from three to 24 hours. PhIP induced expression of the cancer-causing enzyme at every stage, up to 40-fold, while DAS completely inhibited the PhIP enzyme from becoming carcinogenic."

As another researcher working on the uses of the compounds admits, their only drawback, commercially, is that they smell strongly of, well, garlic, yet another reason for the olfactorily oversensitive to get over it and embrace this slivered bullet. That pungent, sulfurous smell caused an ancient naturalist, Dioscorides, to recommend garlic as a vermifuge—that is, an agent to expel worms from the body. Too, the great Roman naturalist Pliny the Elder noted, garlic's smell is enough to drive away serpents and snakes, which should be of much interest to those who worry about such things. One test of this might be to comb the low hills bordering the great garlic fields of Gilroy, California, for signs of these creatures, for Gilroy lies at the very heart of American garlic production, its downtown even boasting a couple of shops where you can buy garlic ice cream and other improbable concoctions. Of more ordinary use is a recipe an Iranian doctor once gave me: remove the papery outer skin of enough garlic bulbs to fill a large glass jar. Add the bulbs to the jar, then fill it with balsamic vinegar. Add some chopped chile pepper and a few slices of raw beet, then seal the jar and put it away in a cool, dark corner for six years. Thereafter, he assured me, you will have the most powerful weapon yet known to humankind in the battle against the common cold; when you feel the snuffles coming on, eat a bulb and go to bed, and your troubles will melt away.

Even outside a jar, garlic lasts a long while. In my refrigerator, which suffers from my packrat habits in any event, bits and pieces of it tend to hang around much longer than they should; when you see green shoots emerging from the bulbs, I have since learned, it is time either to plant the old soldier or give it a decent burial. Keep it in the open air, rather than encased in plastic bags or wrap, and it will last still longer—a lesson for all of us.

## ROASTED GARLIC

Pureed garlic makes a fine addition to tomato sauces, bouillabaisse, pilaf, and other dishes, and it can be eaten as a spread on fresh or toasted bread. This simple Spanish recipe yields only half a cup of the stuff, which is enough to last through several dishes, so powerful is it.

3 bulbs white garlic
3 teaspoons olive oil
1 teaspoon sea salt
   Remove skin from garlic bulbs and place in a ramekin or small oven-proof baking dish. Cover halfway with boiling water and add a teaspoon of olive oil. Cover the dish and bake at 375°F for forty-five minutes, adding more boiling water halfway through. Remove from oven to a small glass bowl, add two teaspoons of olive oil and the sea salt, and mash with a pestle or hand-held blender.

## WALNUT-GARLIC SAUCE

This Sardinian sauce, its origins lost in time, accompanies ocean fish such as red snapper, dorado, or monkfish. It is adapted from the adaptation found in Marlena de Blasi's *Regional Foods of Southern Italy*, which contains a lovely recipe for the fish itself.

1 bulb garlic, peeled
1 cup chopped basil leaves
1 cup extra virgin olive oil

2 teaspoons sea salt
black pepper to taste
1/2 cup red wine vinegar
1 cup finely chopped walnuts
1/2 cup pine (or piñon) nuts

Chop garlic into a fine paste. Sauté for just a few seconds in heated olive oil. Mix into a large bowl, and add sea salt, pepper, and vinegar. Add walnuts and pine nuts.

A more elaborate variant of this recipe comes from the 1529 Spanish cookbook *Libro de Guisados,* compiled by Ruperto de Nola, the Italian-born head cook of the Spanish regent of Naples. The proportions are inexact in the original and should be adapted in the modern kitchen to suit the chef's taste—in other words, as with all ancient recipes, think of this as experimental.

Pine-Nut Sauce of Garlic. Take a pound of pine nuts and another of peeled almonds and pound them with mortar and pestle, first separately and then together. Simmer two peeled bulbs of garlic in chicken broth. When it is soft, pound it together with the nut paste. Then add grated cheese, and half a dozen hardboiled eggs, and some more chicken broth, and a spoonful of sugar, and a little vinegar mixed with rosewater, crushed cloves, ginger, cinnamon, and pepper. Cook this slowly until it thickens.

## PARTHIAN LAMB

The Parthian, or Persian, nation was a source of constant wonderment for the Greeks and Romans. Apicius, the Roman cookbook writer, called this recipe "Parthian," and although some of it is garbled—Parthian may be a misunderstanding for pithium, a kind of spice, or pasticum, which means "still nursing"—it makes for an interesting excursion into ancient ideas of deliciousness. The garlic in this recipe is a stand-in for a now-lost related plant called laser pithium, which grew in Central Asia and was probably introduced to North Africa by Phoenician sailors. The story is that the plant was so popular that it was nearly extinct by Nero's time, and when the last known plant was brought to Rome, Nero ate it himself, the better to tune his fiddle with.

5 pounds lamb
1 pound pitted prunes, soaked in water
3 large onions, chopped
1 tablespoon nuoc mam sauce
1/2 cup olive oil
2 tablespoons savory
2 garlic cloves, minced
2 garlic cloves, mashed

1 cup white wine
salt and pepper to taste

Place lamb in a large roasting pan and rub with olive oil, chopped garlic, and salt and pepper. Cook in a preheated oven at 325°F for two hours. Baste with white wine periodically. Sauté the chopped onions in the remaining olive oil over low heat for 15 minutes. Add salt, pepper, savory, prunes, nuoc mam sauce, and mashed garlic cloves. Cook over low heat for 15 minutes. Pour the sauce over lamb and bake for 15 minutes.

## FURTHER READING

Stanley Crawford, *A Garlic Testament: Seasons on a Small New Mexico Farm* (University of New Mexico Press, 1998).

Marlena de Blasi, *Regional Foods of Southern Italy* (Viking, 1999).

Ron L. Engelland, *Growing Great Garlic: The Definitive Guide for Organic Gardeners and Small Farmers* (Filaree, 1991).

Ellen Spector Platt, *Garlic, Onion, & Other Alliums* (Stackpole Books, 2003).

# GRAPE

---

*A vine grew heavy with grapes and leaves. A hungry goat came by and nibbled at it. The vine said, "Why do you injure me without cause? Can't you eat grass? But it doesn't matter. I'll have my revenge soon, for even if you cut me down to the roots and chop off all my leaves, I'll still have wine to offer when you are led to the altar in sacrifice."*

—Aesop

What's purple and lives at the bottom of the ocean?

The answer, of course, is Moby Grape.

If you did not roll with laughter or start in recognition, you probably do not remember much about the 1960s, when grapes and wine enjoyed a renaissance in America, thanks to a handful of California vintners who had steeped themselves in the classics and spent time under tutelage in Italy and other places across wine-dark seas.

But that is all getting ahead of the story, which properly begins in unknown antiquity, somewhere in the Fertile Crescent, where some observant person once noticed that birds and animals fed from wild plants whose ovoid fruits looked good and tasted better. Detached from their hosts, those fruits could be dried and kept indefinitely, always a good thing in times of insecure food supplies. With some coaxing, those fruits could also produce a drink that could send its drinker into communion with the gods.

For in the beginning was the mind, and, it seems, very long ago the mind contemplated itself and decided that it could not stand itself as it

*"Vitis vinifera Linn,"* from J. Plenck, *Icones plantarum medicinalium* (1784). The German artist describes the wine vine, then widespread throughout Eurasia and beginning to enter other parts of the world.

was. And so the mind prompted its mortal possessor to lay aside the quest for food and justice and the philosopher's stone, and instead to seek out the means by which it could be pleasantly altered for a short, sweet, amnesiac spell. Thus, the walls of Jericho, as the archaeological record shows, were built with the fuel of barley beer. Indo-Europeans and Mongols flung themselves throughout the reaches of the world, propelled by fermented mare's milk. The Incas concocted strange brews of coca leaf. The Mayas amused themselves with peyote enemas. The Haidas and Tlingits and Chukchee soared through the vaulted heavens with divine mushrooms. And somewhere in the Zagros Mountains of western Iran, about 7,500 years ago—or so the archaeological record suggests, at least as it now stands—some lucky proto-Hittite or pre-Sumerian happened upon a way to make wine of grapes, a discovery that changed the face of the ancient world, to say nothing of its mind.

In 1990, Patrick McGovern, an archaeologist, and his colleagues Rudolph H. Michel and Virginia R. Badler discovered what was then the earliest known chemical evidence of wine, dating to about 3500–3100 B.C.E., from a site in the Zagros chain called Godin Tepe. A couple of years of analysis followed, whereupon they determined that the very same roomful of ceramic jars contained the earliest chemically confirmed instance of barley beer. Two more years of analysis followed, during which another Neolithic site, Hajji Firuz Tepe, produced evidence of wine some two thousand years earlier than the Godin Tepe material.

All this suggests that some day an even earlier find will turn up, but for the moment wine's pedigree of 7,500 years rests. Fast forward a touch, and the knowledge and use of wine have spread. The Egyptian pharaoh Tutankhamen went to his grave with a plentiful supply of red wine to see him into the afterlife. The Aryan lords of northern India found wine an enjoyable beverage, establishing vast vineyards that would have seemed very alien in the millennia to follow, though now India is seeing a quiet revival of winemaking. In Greece, a great cult was established in honor of the wine god Dionysus, with rites that mixed the copious consumption of wine with spasms of horrifying behavior that even the wildest of celebrants sometimes found shocking—and no wonder, given that naked women would fall upon animals, tear them apart with their nails and teeth, and devour them raw, and given that by at least some archaeological evidence their victims occasionally extended to human children. *In vino veritas,* to be sure, but *in vino violentias* as well; read the headlines, or read the *Bacchae* of Euripides, in the opening lines of which the playwright recounts Dionysus's trajectory with surprising accuracy:

> I've left the fantastically wealthy East,
> lands of Lydians and Phrygians,
> Persia's sun-washed plains, the walled cities of Bactria.
> I've moved across the scrublands of the Medes,
> through rich Arabia, alien lands,
> along the seacoast, through those towns
> with their great strong towers,
> where barbarians and Greeks come together.
> Now I've come to Thebes, this Greek city,
> after teaching those other nations
> to dance in the rituals of my mysteries,
> that let people know of my divinity.

It does not end well, not after the women of Thebes leave the city and tear apart whatever animals—and men—they can find in the forests. Still, the Greeks would not be deterred from drinking wine, and neither would the other peoples of the ancient world.

Marcus Porcius Cato (239–149 B.C.E.), known as Cato the Elder, was the first significant Latin prose writer, and his instructions on farming, *De Agricultura,* tell us much about how growing grapes and making wine were done in the ancient world. For one thing, Cato wrote, farmers offered this prayer to Jupiter, the foremost of the gods:

> O, Jupiter, to the extent that we can,
> we offer you here in my house and among my family
> this cup of wine.

Let this sacrifice
be something that you find of honor to you.

For, if Jupiter were pleased, then the harvest might be good and the farmer might even grow rich. Cato clearly liked his wine, and he offered several remedies for imparting medicinal value to it, some of which may seem to be a little unscientific to us moderns:

> If you wish to make a laxative wine: After vintage, when the vines are trenched, expose the roots of as many wines as you think you will need for the purpose and mark them; isolate and clear the roots. Pound roots of black hellebore in the mortar, and apply around the vines. Cover the roots with old manure, old ashes, and two parts of earth, and cover the whole with earth. Gather these grapes separately; if you wish to keep the wine for some time as a laxative, do not mix it with the other wine. Take a cyathus of this wine, dilute it with water, and drink it before dinner; it will move the bowels with no bad results.

Such instructions were gospel to early winemakers, though, on into the Christian era, when wine retained its practical importance even as the new doctrine borrowed symbolically from the Dionysian cults, absent much of the violence to innocence.

Well before then, though, wine had spread from the Mediterranean into northern Europe. The French, who were beer drinkers, were converted to it by Roman colonists a couple of thousand years ago, and from the descendants of those French converts come much of the vocabulary and mentalities devoted to wine, including the most important of them all: terroir, the idea that somewhere in the world there is an ideal blend of soil, sunshine, climate, and human skill that combines with the grape to make the very best wine of it, a Platonic ideal of Grapeness.

And so it went, as Dionysus traveled. In the year 1007, a European wine connoisseur would have sought fine vintages, as today, in Italy, Germany, and France—but also in England, then a land dotted with flourishing vineyards. In those days, heat-loving beech trees carpeted Europe far into Scandinavia; Viking ships crossed an iceberg-free ocean to ice-free harbors in Greenland and Newfoundland; German farmers enjoyed twice-annual harvests of wheat and other grains; and chroniclers across the continent recorded a succession of long, glorious summers and mild winters.

All that changed in the mid-twelfth century, when a cooling trend set in over the northern hemisphere. The trend reduced the average annual temperature by only a few degrees, but that was enough to change the face of three continents. Over the next three centuries, England lost its storied vineyards to the cold. In central China, orange groves and mulberry trees froze, stilling a citrus- and silk-based economy that had endured for generations. Glaciers in the Alps, the Himalayas, and the Rockies grew by yards, then miles, in just a few years. The Vikings abandoned their colonies in

Greenland and North America when the ground became too hard even to bury the dead, and their seers muttered darkly about the coming of Ragnarok, the legendary time when a great wolf swallowed the sun and the earth was encased in ice.

The effects were disastrous. In a time of reduced crop yields, prices of grain shot up, and for the first time in generations Europe knew famine and malnutrition. The little grain that could be stored developed a cold-tolerant blight called ergot, which, among other effects, produced symptoms of madness—symptoms that were often interpreted as proof of demonic possession. With the gnawing pain of hunger came widespread social unrest, and peasant rebellions and small-scale wars became the norm. At the same time, those powers that could afford the expense mounted expeditions to far-off continents, seeking to establish colonies in warmer climes—and finding, even in the tropics, cold waters and depleted shoals and forests wherever they went.

Better times came in the mid-fifteenth century and the arrival of warmer weather, a time that, not coincidentally, brought the period of economic and cultural expansion we now call the Renaissance. Winemaking never returned to England at quite the same level as it had enjoyed half a millennium before, but wine drinking enjoyed a resurgent popularity, even if it was sometimes viewed as a French (and therefore Catholic) importation and even though the English added a curious twist to the recipe: "Clownes and vulger men only use large drinking of Beere or Ale...but Gentlemen garrawse onely in Wine, with whiche many mix sugar—which I never observed in any other place or kingdom to be used for that purpose," wrote Fynnes Moryson in 1617, describing what might be thought of as an alcoholic soda pop.

Wine traveled onward. Christopher Columbus took vine cuttings along on his first voyage, probably from vineyards in the Azores. They did not take, but on the second voyage vines were planted on the island of Hispaniola. Discouragingly, they soon died in the tropical heat. Hernán Cortés had better luck in Mexico; he brought with him vines from his father's small plot in Estremadura, and they flourished well enough but produced a mediocre wine. With a few exceptions, Mexico's wines remain mediocre to this day (though its brandy is quite good), while the more congenial soil of Chile, Peru, and Argentina yielded excellent vintages almost immediately, threatening the homegrown trade. Spanish growers petitioned the crown to make wine production illegal in the colonies, and once legislation was passed, wine was an art known only to a few, almost all of them connected to the Church. Spain relaxed this rule bit by bit, but one of the hallmarks of the continent-wide wars of independence during the nineteenth century was the revival of secular wine production across South America and Mexico, the latter of which was a gateway to the rich soils of California.

That land saw the realization of Thomas Jefferson's dream that his country would "make as great a variety of wines as are made in Europe, not exactly of the same kinds, but doubtless as good." Wine remained a suspicious subject in Protestant portions of the land ("God loves little boys/Who don't love wine!" was a temperance motto popular in, of all places, New York City, in the 1840s), but predominantly Catholic California remained an island of the winemaker's art throughout the nineteenth and twentieth centuries. During the Prohibition era, the insistence of vintners in places such as Paso Robles and Boonville that they were producing wine only for sacramental purposes helped keep several varietals alive and healthy, even if they were sometimes despised as "dago red" in less enlightened climes. California wines became better and better throughout the postwar years, and particularly in the 1960s, when the back-to-the-land ethic collided with a classically inclined movement toward making bold, organic wines. The crowning achievement came in 1976, when, in Paris, a superb Chateau Montalena 1973 Chardonnay took top prize in a competition between French and California wines, grown in the rich soil of Calistoga, at great remove from the prized terroir of Burgundy or Bordeaux. Still, as George Taber observes in *Judgment of Paris,* his wonderful account of the competition, French and American wines had been sharing tables for generations: it was American rootstock that saved the French wine industry from blight in the nineteenth century, and French grapes that elevated California wines above bathtub plonk. The vintners of that era—among them a Chicago classicist who took up winemaking, a Croatian refugee who helped prove that Zinfandel originated in his homeland, and the children and grandchildren of Italian immigrants who insisted, against the suspicions of their Protestant neighbors, that drinking wine was a good thing—turned American taste around, the modern result being a magnificent and various California wine industry, and a scene much different from that of 1976, in which, as Taber writes, "the dynamic part of the world wine business today is not in Europe, but in the New World—Argentina, Australia, Chile, New Zealand, South Africa, and the United States."

Wine lovers, of course, will not want to forget the red wines of Basilicata and Campagna (viva aglianico!) or the white wines of eastern France and the Mosel Valley or will not want to forgo exploring the pleasures of scarcely known vintages from Bulgaria and Switzerland and other Old World venues; who knows but that some grower in the Zagros Mountains will one day return wine to its roots and produce something wondrous.

In the meanwhile, there are good and healthful reasons to drink wine, with the usual provisos. It is said, for instance, that organic wines do not produce hangovers, and in the interest of science, I have experimented extensively to determine whether it is true; suffice it to say that moderation is best with all things, including, sometimes, moderation itself. I am hopeful that the payoff will come in old age, for according to a study pub-lished in *Neurology* in 2002, wine drinkers have a lower risk of developing dementia, including Alzheimer's disease, probably on account of the anti-oxidant effect of natural compounds called flavonoids. These compounds also likely account for the lower occurrence of stroke and other cerebro-vascular diseases among wine drinkers.

It is worth noting, by the way, that the study was conducted by Danish scientists funded by the Danish government, a Protestant country demon-strably fonder of beer than wine. And it is worth noting, too, that those flavonoids are also present in grape juice, so that one need not consume alcohol to enjoy their benefits. Just so, raisins are known to fight bacteria in the mouth that cause cavities and gum disease, according to researchers at the University of Illinois at Chicago. Five phytochemicals in Thompson seedless raisins—oleanolic acid, oleanolic aldehyde, betulin, betulinic acid, and 5-(hydroxymethyl)-2-furfural—inhibited the growth of two species of oral bacteria, *Streptococcus mutans,* which causes cavities, and *Porphyromo-nas gingivalis,* which causes periodontal disease.

These are all good reasons to keep wine safe from invaders, as did those French and Italian heroes who hid their nation's treasures away when Nazi troops began to cart away thousands of bottles to Germany for the con-querors' enjoyment, even though Hitler did not drink the stuff himself and frowned on anyone else's doing so. Some restaurateurs and collectors hurriedly built false walls to shield better bottles, leaving inferior wines exposed to view; others sprinkled centuries-old carpet dust on cheap young wine to make them taste old, spiriting away the real goods to safety. In many instances, sympathetic Germans played along with the ruse and protected rare vintages, but more often French and Italian citizens paid with their lives. Let us raise a glass in their honor.

## CHEROKEE GRAPE COBBLER

Housed at Columbia University, the John Howard Payne Papers are a repository of thousands of documents of historical and ethnographic importance. Among them are interviews with Cherokee elders, conducted about 1835, that are full of information about traditional ways. One elder describes a grape dessert made by boiling wild grapes (also called possum grapes), mashing them, and then adding corn meal to make a kind of quick cobbler.

1 cup flour
1 1/2 teaspoons baking powder
2 teaspoon sugar
1/4 teaspoon salt
1 tablespoon shortening
1/2 cup grape juice

Mix flour, baking powder, sugar, salt and shortening. Add juice and mix into stiff dough. Roll dough very thin on floured board and cut into strips half an inch wide or roll dough in hands and break off pea-sized bits. Drop into boiling grape juice and cook for ten to fifteen minutes.

## SCUPPERNONG GRAPE WINE

Scuppernong grapes are hard to come by beyond the Appalachians, but they make for a real treat. This recipe, from a collection by Mary Elizabeth Sproull Lanier gathered at about 1880, yields a wine of low alcohol content. As with any recipe for an alcoholic beverage, use this at your own risk.

3–4 gallons Scuppernong grapes
3 pounds sugar
    Remove grapes from stems and wash. Mash them as best you can and press hard. Let juice and hulls stand for forty-eight hours. Drain well to extract all juice. To one gallon of juice add three pounds sugar and stir well. Transfer to fermenting jar and tie linen over jar. Let stand several weeks, ladle into bottles and apply corks. Let it lie a month or two before drinking.

## STUFFED GRAPE LEAVES

This Turkish recipe yields a favorite dish among many Mediterranean peoples.

2 tablespoons olive oil
2 white onions, minced
1 1/2 cups raw white rice
2 tablespoons tomato paste
2 tablespoons raisins
2 tablespoons pine nuts
1 tablespoon cinnamon
1 tablespoon mint leaves
1 tablespoon dill
1 teaspoon allspice
1 teaspoon cumin
8 ounces grape leaves
    In a Dutch oven, heat the oil over moderate heat. Sauté the onions until they are translucent, about five minutes. Add the rice and enough hot water to cover it. Cover and simmer for about ten minutes. Remove the oven from the stove and add all other ingredients except the grape leaves. Allow to cool.
    Rinse grape leaves, then roll them out one at a time on a cutting board, pizza stone, or sheet of wax paper. Spoon a tablespoonful of the rice mixture into the center of the grape leaf, then tuck in the sides and roll the leaf

into a cylinder. Place the grape leaves in a steamer, cover, and cook over low heat for about thirty minutes.

## FURTHER READING

Aesop, *The North Wind and the Sun and Other Fables of Aesop*, translated by Gregory McNamee (Daimon Verlag, 2004).

Andrew Barr, *Drink: A Social History of America* (Carroll & Graf, 1999).

Michael and Ariane Batterberry, *On the Town in New York: The Landmark History of Eating, Drinking, and Entertainments* (Routledge, 1998).

Don and Petie Kladstrup, *Wine & War: The French, the Nazis, and the Battle for France's Greatest Treasure* (Broadway Books, 2001).

Patrick McGovern, *Ancient Wine: The Search for the Origins of Viniculture* (Princeton University Press, 2003).

Ralph Steadman, *Untrodden Grapes* (Harcourt, 2005).

George M. Taber, *Judgment of Paris: California vs. France and the Historic 1976 Paris Tasting That Revolutionized Wine* (Scribner, 2005).

# HONEY

The time is eight thousand years before the present, and out somewhere on the edges of the Pontic Steppe of what is now southern Russia, a man is hiding behind a beech tree, studying the ways of the great brown animal he calls *rkso*. That creature is busily dipping a knife-clawed paw into a fallen log, exciting huge numbers of the creature he calls *bhei*, withdrawing something golden and gummy, delicious enough that the shaggy brown creature is willing to endure a few stings on the snout and between its knuckles. The man silently gives thanks to it, and then, when the creature has left, he dips into the log with his own hands and retrieves the hidden treasure for himself. He now bestows another name on that tutelary spirit of the woods, who has revealed to him and his fellows a new source of sustenance. The name is something like *bhei-ulf*, "the wolf that feeds on bees," and it will resurface thousands of years later, on the coast of southern England, where a Germanic hero named Beowulf will do great things.

Now, there is no direct historical evidence to support the preceding scenario. The earliest discovery of honey probably took place thousands of years earlier, and in some other part of the Old World; indeed, some tantalizing bits of archaeological evidence suggest that Neanderthals might have been beekeepers, and primatologists have long known that nonhuman primates avidly seek and consume honey, which suggests that our pre–*Homo sapiens* ancestors did the same. All the same, linguists surmise that the people we call proto-Indo-Europeans knew about several things very early on in their cultural development. Anadromous salmon were economically important to them. They lived somewhere where the beech, *Fagus sylvaticus,* and the silver birch, *Betula pendula,* grew in abundance. It was a snowy place. They had domesticated the animal they called *ekwos,* the horse, before domesticating any other, and, using it as their chief vehicle, they traveled widely and without hindrance on the great plains north of the Black Sea. They ate apples. And they knew all about bees and honey, drawing on that knowledge to keep hives, to battle infestations of foulbrood and other swarm-killing diseases, and to make and use a variety of apian products, from beeswax to mead, that favorite beverage of Germanic heroes and ordinary Indo-Europeans alike.

We know all these things because the proto-Indo-Europeans shared a common body of words that kept similar shapes when that ancestral people diverged into the many linguistic and cultural groups that would sweep across

Late medieval woodcut of a beehive. The source is unknown, but the style of hive is Swiss or German.

Europe to the west and Central Asia to the east: "bear" is *ursus* in Latin, *arktos* in Greek, *rksah* in Sanskrit; "apple" is something akin to *abel* from Ireland to Sri Lanka; and the words for bee (*bhei, embhi*), honey (*melit*), mead (*medhu*), and beeswax (*wokso*) turn up in languages from Tocharian, in what is now western China, to Hittite, in modern Syria, to Greek, French, Gaelic, and Icelandic.

Honey, then, is one of the earliest foodstuffs known; language history tells us as much. (One datum: one of the earliest Russian family names, transformed by the fortunes of the early tongue, is another name for bear: *medved,* "honey eater.") For hundreds of generations, it was the only sweetener known to humans, though of course only in recent history has the human diet become sickeningly sweet thanks to the overuse of sugar. It is believed that hive apiculture spread from the proto-Indo-European homeland thousands of years ago, as the arts of beekeeping traveled to North Africa and the Nile Valley, to Mesopotamia, to China, and its products turned up in all kinds of contexts, with beeswax used in shipbuilding, honey in medicine, and bees themselves in the symbolism of dozens of cultures, almost always in a positive sense.

It was just in that cultural context, as well as an economic one, that honeybees traveled into the Americas, introduced by the Spanish into the New World; in one sense, the bees were workers for empire, helping sustain the people who cultivated them, but in another—as long as we are being fanciful—*Apis mellifera* helped serve as a kind of psychic anchor, always traveling a bit ahead of Spanish priests and soldiers and reminding them of the things of home in a decidedly different place. The bees served another function for the native peoples of the New World: when they heard them approach, the Indians knew that the Spanish were not far behind, for which reason many indigenous languages refer to bees as "the white men's flies."

For all their buzzing, bees serve quietly and do not often make the news. That changed in the 1980s, when *Saturday Night Live*'s yellow-and-black-clad, machine gun–toting, cigar-chomping "killer bees"—an invading force that invited comparison to Alfonso Bedoya's ruffian gang in *Treasure of the Sierra Madre*—gave way to the real thing. In 1984, when Ronald Reagan warned that Sandinista tanks were a mere three days' drive from the Texas border, abejas bravas—"sturdy bees," let us say—had spread northward from South and Central America into Mexico. Two years later, isolated hives were found in California; "Bee Battalions Mopping Up Killer Bee Invasion," cried the appropriately named *Sacramento Bee,* as the bees were eradicated with cyanide gas.

Those "killer bees," known in scientific parlance as *Apis mellifera scutellata,* are a variety of honeybee first domesticated in the scrub desert of central South Africa. As a rule, although their hives are small, they are more productive than Italian, German, and the other strains of European honeybees to which they are related. They set to work an hour earlier than other bees, are more disease-resistant, lay more eggs, and yield more and better honey for less trouble on a beekeeper's part.

For that very reason, in 1956 the Brazilian government commissioned an émigré professor, an Englishman named Warwick Kerr, to introduce the bees to South America. At the time Brazil ranked forty-seventh among the world's honey-producing countries; with the arrival of the new variety, that country's ranking quickly rose to seventh, and much of the honey eaten around the world now comes from Brazil. Kerr lost favor in 1964, when he protested publicly against the then-military government's excesses, and he spent time in jail for his trouble. In 1969 he was again arrested for dissidence.

To cast doubt on Kerr's credentials as a scientist, the Brazilian government portrayed him as a kind of Frankenstein doctor bent on mayhem, even hinting that Kerr had been training his imported Africans to be killer bees, attacking humans on command. Thanks to the diligence of the military police, the government went on to trumpet, this foreign madman was stopped before he could put his evil drones to work. And thus was the myth of the killer bee born.

In truth, African bees are no more venomous than their European cousins. Neither do they go out of their way to look for targets, human or otherwise. The difference lies in the African bees' defensiveness; when their colonies are attacked or approached, they tend to swarm and sting with abandon, perhaps aware—bees are intelligent creatures, after all—that to do so means death in the defense of their queen. Since their arrival in the Americas, the African purebreds have intermingled with European varieties of honeybee, giving birth to a hybrid, the "Africanized bee." As University of Minnesota professor Marla Spivak, one of the world's leading authorities on Africanized bees, once told me, "For the first five to ten years after they appear in a country, they cause problems, but only because beekeepers find them hard to work with. When you work a defensive colony you have to become a better beekeeper, really pay attention to what they're doing."

It took time for that better beekeeping to come to play across the American industry, and in the meanwhile, thanks to an agricultural-subsidy program initiated under the first President Bush, millions of pounds of honey were imported from China each year at a sale price of forty cents a pound, a full twenty-five cents less than the basic costs an American producer incurs before market. The result was that native honey was driven from the consumer market—until, that is, the largest commercial bee farms in the United States (most in South Dakota) began to introduce strains of Africanized bees into their hives, which improved yield, lowered costs, and helped make American honey competitive against foreign imports—killer bees to the rescue, though at ecological cost, for as they travel, they have displaced native pollinators, with consequences that have yet to be determined but that are unlikely to be positive.

Mainstream consumers of things sweet have taken to preferring sugar—and, much worse, corn syrup—to honey, but there are compelling reasons to incorporate honey into one's diet while eschewing other sweeteners. For one thing, its healthful properties have made honey a favored sweetener for athletes; clinical tests published in 2001 indicate that using honey as a carbohydrate source during intense exercise—bicycle racing, for instance—significantly improved long-term performance and strength, no small consideration for glucose-starved athletes. Honey contains about the same amount of plaque-fighting antioxidants as spinach, apples, bananas, oranges, and strawberries, too. A study conducted at the University of Illinois suggests that a daily dose of mixed honey and water (four tablespoons to a sixteen-ounce glass) has a strong potential to protect against heart disease. Among the honeys tested, arranged from darkest to lightest, were buckwheat, tupelo, soybean, clover, and acacia; the darker the honey, the higher the antioxidant concentrations. Australian scientists have found that honey produced from the nectar of Leptospermum trees has antimicrobial qualities, proving especially effective in fighting *Staphylococcus aureus* (golden staph), with the result that some Antipodean doctors are now using honey to treat wounds and infections. Interestingly, the Illinois study also suggests that honey inhibits the growth of oral pathogenic bacteria such as *Streptococcus mutans,* which can cause tooth decay.

A sweetener to prevent cavities: that is worth pondering. So, too, is another application of honey: according to a paper presented before the United Kingdom's Royal Society of Chemistry, a simple breakfast of toast with honey was as close to a hangover cure as one was likely to find in nature, for honey quickly replenishes alcohol-depleted stores of sodium, potassium, and fructose. This is helpful information for those who are fond of a use of honey deeply appreciated by those ancient proto-Indo-Europeans: namely mead, an alcoholic beverage whose discovery may have been thanks to our friendly bear, stumbling onto a store of fermented nectar and honey in the hollow of a log.

It would be unseemly to close without noting that the bee itself is something to marvel at, and that honey is an against-all-odds, precious thing. A honeybee can wing along its way at up to fifteen miles per hour, covering a good bit of ground for a creature its size, but even so, a single bee would have to fly 55,000 miles and tap the nectar of some two million flowers to produce a single pound of honey. Aristotle observed, twenty-five hundred years ago, that individual bees tend to confine themselves to one flower species at a time when foraging, and he was right, meaning that our pound-producing bee would have to have acres and acres of real estate to himself. In reality, a single bee produces less than one-tenth of a teaspoon of honey in its lifetime, leaving it to us to be thankful for and a little amazed at its gift.

# MEAD

Mead was a favorite of Anglo-Saxon spear-bearers and Parthian archers, but also of settlers along the American colonial frontier. This recipe, adapted from Gertrude Harris's *Manna: Foods of the Frontier,* yields about two and a half gallons of mead. Be warned: any recipe that produces alcohol can be dangerous on several fronts. Use this one at your own risk.

4 pounds raisins
1 teaspoon freshly grated nutmeg
6 cinnamon sticks, broken up
1 clove
1 medium lemon
1 quart honey
2 1/2 gallons soft bottled water
1/2 cup rosewater
    Grind raisins in a food processor with a fine blade. Crush the spices in a mortar or blender. Chop the lemon fine, then peel. Combine the preceding ingredients in a large stoneware or stainless steel bowl and mix in the honey and water. Set aside at room temperature for five days, stirring daily. Drain through cheesecloth to remove sediments, then add rosewater. Bottle and cork tightly.

Other recipes for mead add yeast (particularly ale yeast), which produces a drinkable mead within a week but introduces the danger of exploding bottles. Reducing the proportion of honey and lengthening the fermentation process before bottling lessens that danger somewhat, but plastic soda bottles are probably the best alternative.

# CHICKEN WITH HONEY

It is true: chicken can help alleviate the symptoms of the common cold. This classic example of Jewish comfort food does not require illness for its enjoyment, but it can do wonders for the sniffles.

1 whole chicken
2 tablespoons Dijon mustard
2 tablespoons honey
1/2 teaspoon black pepper
3 apples
1/2 cup water
1/2 cup dry red wine
    Preheat oven to 400°F. Place chicken, spine up, in a greased baking dish, then coat the visible portion with mustard, honey, and pepper mixed together. Cut unpeeled apples into thick slices and place them around the chicken, then add water and wine. Bake at 350°F, uncovered, for one hour.

# FURTHER READING

Stephen L. Buchmann and Gary Nabhan, *The Forgotten Pollinators* (Island Press, 1997).

Carl D. Buck, *A Dictionary of Selected Synonyms in the Principal Indo-European Languages* (University of Chicago Press, 1988).

Gertrude Harris, *Manna: Foods of the Frontier* (101 Productions, 1972).

Tammy Horn, *Bees in America: How the Honey Bee Shaped a Nation* (University Press of Kentucky, 2005).

Sue Hubbell, *A Book of Bees...and How to Keep Them* (Houghton Mifflin, 1988).

National Honey Board, "Antioxidant Capacity of Honey" (Press release, June 21, 2001).

Douglas Whynott, *Following the Bloom: Across America with Migratory Beekeepers* (Beacon Press, 1992).

E.O. Wilson, *The Insect Societies* (Harvard University Press, 1971).

# LETTUCE

The ancient Greeks, by all accounts, were meat-and-potatoes fellows—
well, meat-and-wine fellows, since potatoes would not arrive in Greece
for twenty centuries and more after their time. To trust the descriptions
of the *Odyssey,* they were fond of roasting up an ox or two, even the oxen
belonging to the sun god, Helios, and of devouring fistfuls of olives and
raising a goblet or ten to Dionysus, all while singing and telling ribald
stories.

By the time of Plato's *Symposium,* it appears, the Greeks did not care
much about food at all, for that text is full of ribald stories and wine, with
not a word about what Socrates, Alcibiades, and company ate. If its char-
acters had devoted themselves to talking about their repast, or if Plato
had taken notice of it, one thing is almost certain: the menu would not
have included lettuce, which the Greeks despised as worse than rabbit
food. According to one ancient myth, Adonis, the beautiful seducer of
women and men alike and in every way the antithesis of active jocks like
Herakles, one day decided that he needed to cut a more macho figure.
No wars were then being waged, and so he asked to go along on a hunting
trip. The hunters obliged him, and no sooner were they in the field but did
Adonis find himself cornered by a gigantic wild boar. Adonis immediately
hid himself in a great bed of lettuce, which did not impress the boar;
instead, the boar gored Adonis to death while enjoying a salad to go along
with his treat. Just so, the story concluded, lettuce is "food for corpses."
Worse, ancient Greek physicians continued, lettuce is a plant whose funda-
mental nature is cold and wet, which guarantees that its eater will partake

Lettuce engraving from a late-nineteenth-century American gardening catalog.

of those qualities, sure to cause suffering in bed. Wrote Dioscorides in his *Materia Medica*, "If a man of even less than sixty years of age eats lettuce and then takes a women to bed, he'll just toss and turn all night without being able to do what he wants to, even with a helping hand." Why else would Adonis the lover have died, if not for the shame of lettuce—which, the doctors agreed, could be counteracted only by eating quantities of myrrh, that fabled spice from the Red Sea.

If those doctors were to witness a contemporary American salad bar, with its mounds of iceberg lettuce, they would have just cause to condemn the stuff. Iceberg lettuce, which resembles the tight-as-a-drum cabbage, has no discernible flavor or nutritional value; it is another American invention that, as the food historian Waverley Root complained with respect to apples, seems designed to appeal to people who do not like food. In fact, taste was of secondary consideration to the northern California farmers who developed iceberg lettuce, which took its name from its manner of shipment across the United States, in railroad boxcars packed with ice. Its chief virtue, even today, is its ability to keep refrigerated for up to three weeks without browning, which makes it a great favorite of restaurateurs who would otherwise have to throw lettuce out after a couple of days. (I can attest from experience, by the way, that the town of Dalhart, Texas, does not discard iceberg lettuce even after it is brown and beyond, so strong is the power of local custom.)

In its natural form, lettuce is a weed-like plant that, along with other plants of the so-called *macchia* or *maquis,* sprang up in the Mediterranean and found the hot days and misty dawns to its liking. It was probably first used as a medicine, probably as a tranquilizer rather than a panacea for priapism; Egyptian murals show lettuce plants in medical contexts, and the lactose and latex and other milky substances (in Latin, *lac* means milk) are known to have mildly soporific qualities. Though the Greeks disesteemed *Lactuca sativa*, the Romans enjoyed it; ancient accounts depict Roman meals that closed with a plate of lettuce, presumably to settle the earlier courses, and even modern Roman meals close rather than open with a leafy salad.

Iceberg lettuce continues to dominate the American market, but it no longer enjoys its former stranglehold, which drove a once-thriving garden culture into monoculture. In the 1950s, '60s, and '70s, young Americans who traveled to France and Italy came home with the newfound conviction that it was possible to drink a decent cup of coffee and eat a decent salad. Thanks to their efforts as gardeners, boutique farmers, and consumers, even the most corporate of American supermarkets now offers a variety of lettuces: iceberg, Bibb, and Boston, of course, but also spicier kinds such as Belgian endive, mâche, radicchio, arugula, mesclun, and mizuna, which are both flavorful and comparatively rich in calcium, vitamin A, and potassium.

Those of you old enough to remember the taste of America before the 1980s, let us bow our heads in thanks for deliverance. And as for those of you too young to have such memories, you owe your elders thanks for having fought a brave battle and emerged victoriously.

## ORECCHIETTE WITH ARUGULA AND TOMATOES

The Italian flag is a tricolor of red, white, and green, colors that this Apulian dish proudly bears. Rice or polenta can be substituted for the orecchiette, though it would be a shame to do so, the "little ears" being a distinctive pasta of the southern province of Puglia.

1/2 cup extra-virgin olive oil
2 cloves garlic, minced
1 tablespoon Italian or Chinese parsley
6 Roma tomatoes, peeled and diced
2 tablespoons sea salt
1 tablespoon ground pepper
1 pound orecchiette pasta
1 pound arugula, stems removed
freshly grated parmesan or pecorino cheese to taste

   Heat olive oil in a Dutch oven and add garlic and parsley. Cook until the garlic turns golden, then add tomatoes. Cook uncovered over low heat for fifteen minutes. Add salt and pepper and continue to cook over low heat. In a separate pot, boil six quarts of water. Add orecchiette and cook for six minutes, then add arugula. Cook further until the pasta is done al dente. Drain well and remove the pasta and arugula to a large ceramic bowl. Add cheese and tomato sauce.

## CAESAR SALAD

Cesare Cardini, an Italian restaurateur, opened Caesar's Restaurant in the early 1920s and immediately attracted a crowd of wealthy Californians as his clientele, including some of Hollywood's biggest stars. His restaurant—located in Tijuana, Mexico, where the then-prevailing Prohibition laws could not affect him any way but positively—was known for its innovations, including the owner's famed special salad, which, according to his daughter, was invented to honor the Fourth of July, 1924.

2 large egg yolks
2 garlic cloves, peeled and crushed
1 tablespoon lime juice
2 teaspoons Worcestershire sauce
1 teaspoon dry mustard
8 anchovy fillets, chopped
1 cup olive oil, plus a little extra for frying
freshly ground black pepper
1/2 cup parmesan cheese, coarsely grated, plus another 1/4 cup shaved
1 large head romaine lettuce, washed and torn into pieces
2 cups French bread, crusts removed and cubed

Boil eggs for one minute. When they are cool enough to handle, crack them into a food processor and add garlic, lime juice, Worcestershire sauce, anchovies, and olive oil. Blend thoroughly. Fry bread cubes in olive oil until golden, then drain on paper towels. Place the lettuce in a ceramic or stainless steel bowl, then add dressing, croutons, and cheese. Toss thoroughly and serve.

## ROMAN SALAD

Lucius Junius Moderatus Columella, who lived in the first century C.E., left his native Spain as a young man and moved to Rome. He divided his time between military service and farming, and, usefully, writing about both experiences. His eleven-volume treatise *Res Rustica* (On Agriculture) is the most comprehensive work on the farming practices of the ancient world that we have. He died in Tarentum, in the region of Apulia, where today he would have eaten orecchiette with arugula and tomatoes. Columella offers this recipe for a fresh salad:

Addito in mortarium satureiam, mentam, rutam, coriandrum, apium, porrum sectivum, aut si non erit viridem cepam, folia latucae, folia erucae, thymum viride, vel nepetam, tum etiam viride puleium, et caseum recentem et salsum: ea omnia partier conterito, acetique piperati exiguum, permisceto. Hanc mixturam cum in catillo composurris, oleum superfundito.

Put savory in a mortar with mint, rue, coriander, parsley, a sliced leek (or, if a leek is not available, onion), lettuce and arugula leaves, green thyme, or catmint. Add pennyroyal and salted fresh cheese. Crush this all together and stir in a little peppered vinegar. Put this mixture on a plate and pour olive oil over it.

## FURTHER READING

Marcel Detienne, *The Gardens of Adonis: Spices in Greek Mythology* (Princeton University Press, 1994).

Patrick Faas, *Around the Roman Table: Food and Feasting in Ancient Rome* (University of Chicago Press, 2003).

# OKRA

---

*Ella Mae, woman, come out your house now*
*I got some fresh okra for you*
*Come get my okra, okra,*
*Come get my okra, okra*

—Olu Dara, Mississippi blues singer

It is a curiosity, the eminent French historian Fernand Braudel once noted, that humans have been so incurious about the culinary possibilities of the plant and animal world; of the two million animal species known thirty years ago, when he wrote, only forty-three had been domesticated, while around the world only six hundred plant species, about one percent of the available roster, were under cultivation.

It is another curiosity that Africa, with its vast forested interiors and diverse ecosystems, should have contributed so few plants to that list, and particularly so few that have become popular elsewhere. Even one of the most widespread, okra, is largely confined to the American South and African communities in Central and South America. This is through no particular fault of its own, though even the most stalwart champion will admit that okra is an acquired taste—or, better, an acquired texture.

A member of the mallow family, related to cotton, and the only one eaten as a vegetable, *Hibiscus esculentus* was first cultivated in the region of what the ancient Greeks called "the land of the sunburned people," Ethiopia, which includes that nation and what is now southern Sudan, hot and humid country. From there, likely carried by the caravan trade, okra cultivation spread into the Bantu-speaking regions to the west, where the plant was called *ki ngombo* or *ochinggombo,* the origin of the word "gumbo." Carried even farther west, okra became a staple of the peoples of West Africa, where slavers discovered it as they plucked African people out of their homelands and forcibly resettled them across the ocean.

Slavery brought okra to the Americas, first to Brazil, where it is attested after 1658, then to the north to Dutch Guiana (present-day Surinam), and then to the American South by the late 1680s. Grown in garden plots and small farms, it became a staple of the slave diet, the origin of today's soul food. As with so much slave food, it turned up on the master's table, too,

Woodcut from *Harris Rural Annual* (1893), a source book and catalog for farmers and gardeners.

though it was never so proudly served as would be, say, a dish of green tomatoes or fresh corn. The French Canadians who, forcibly deported from their northern homeland, arrived in Louisiana in the 1750s were not inclined to be ashamed about good food. These Cajuns, as they would come to be known, borrowed the slaves' gumbo, adding to it as a thickener a powder made of sassafras bark called filé whenever okra was not to be had—which would signal hard times indeed. Incidentally, in flush times, Cajun cooks agree, okra and filé should not be mixed, for the gumbo will take on a concrete-like consistency.

Okra arrived in Europe at about the same time that it came to the Americas, but it is not much eaten outside of Spain and southern France, and even there it tends to be a plant for private gardens and private tastes. One particularly industrious grower was Paul Savorgnan de Brazza, the African explorer for whom the old Congo River town of Brazzaville was named, who planted it extensively on various of his properties in the Midi. In part because Cajun cuisine became popular in Europe in the 1980s, the use of okra has increased somewhat in recent years, but not so much as to entice commercial growers there to take up the cause.

It is far better liked in the Middle East and South Asia, where it turns up in all kinds of vegetable stews. There, however, the okra tends not to have the gummy, slimy, mucilaginous quality that makes it such an object of disdain among eaters tender of sensibility (there is the acquired texture business), a quality that results mostly from overcooking, the bane of asparagus, broccoli, and other such vegetables. Middle Eastern chefs often coat okra slices in cornmeal, which keeps it from dissolving into a sticky mess, and to deep-fry it, which keeps it crunchy and brings out its nicely peppery flavor.

There are good reasons to like okra, even to the point of learning how to cook it properly. It is an excellent source of dietary fiber, which gives a stomach a satisfyingly full feeling, thus proving useful to dieters. (It is so fibrous, in fact, that artists use it to make specialty paper.) One of the components of the "Mediterranean diet" is its high reliance on such fibers, and researchers have recently discovered that a diet that incorporates foods naturally rich in soluble fiber—among them cantaloupe, grapefruit, oranges, papayas, raisins, beans, sweet potatoes, winter and zucchini squash, oatmeal, and, of course, okra—are helpful in both averting and controlling type II diabetes. The gooey, gummy stuff of cooked okra, Swiss researchers have found, prevents bacteria such as *Helicobacter pylori* from binding to the stomach lining, giving okra ulcer-fighting powers. Okra contains goodly quantities of protein by weight, too, and of vitamins A, B1, B2, B3, and B6 and of potassium, iron, and calcium, all of which are often insufficiently represented in the diets of older people.

None of us is getting any younger—so come get your okra.

## FISH CALALU

Calalu (or callaloo) is a characteristic dish of West Africa. This variant, from Angola, can be adapted to suit whatever happens to be found in the fishmonger's case.

2 pounds dried fish
2 pounds fresh fish
2 large onions, diced
3 large tomatoes, diced
1 pound okra, sliced
2 pounds spinach
3 cloves garlic
1 cup palm oil or peanut oil
1 pound zucchini
sea salt to taste

1 cup lemon juice
1 cup warm water
    Set dried fish in a large bowl and cover with hot water. Add garlic, salt, and lemon juice. In a large pan or Dutch oven, layer dried fish, fresh fish, onion, tomatoes, spinach, and okra. Add oil and water and simmer on very low heat for an hour.

## CAJUN SUCCOTASH

It is the hot pepper that makes this Cajun, of course.

1 pound fresh or frozen corn kernels
1 pound okra, sliced
1/2 cup warm water
1 cup diced tomatoes
1 large onion, diced
hot pepper sauce to taste
sea salt to taste
    In a large skillet or Dutch oven, combine corn, okra, onion, water, and salt. Bring to a boil. Cover and simmer on low heat for five or ten minutes. Drain. Add tomatoes and bottled hot pepper sauce and heat through for just a minute or two. Serve with rice.

## BHINDI

An Indian favorite, *bhindi* makes judicious use of okra.

1 pound okra, sliced
1 large onion, diced
2 tomatoes, diced
1/2 tablespoon dried turmeric
1/2 cup olive oil or vegetable oil
salt to taste
red pepper to taste
    Add oil to a pan and deep-fry the okra until it is browned on both sides. Add turmeric to the remaining oil, then fry the onion. Layer the okra in a baking dish, then add tomatoes, salt and pepper, and okra. Bake at 250° for fifteen minutes.

## OKRA AND POTATOES

Okra is not widely eaten in much of Europe, but it has found a welcome home in parts of Greece. This recipe is adapted from one that the adventurous food writer Patience Gray recorded on the island of Naxos.

2 pounds okra
1 pound white potatoes
1 large yellow onion

3 tomatoes, diced
1 large onion, diced
2 tablespoons olive oil
1/2 cup red wine
1 teaspoon crushed fennel seeds
salt and pepper to taste

    Trim the okra and cut the potatoes into thick slices, as if for scalloped potatoes. Parboil the potatoes until they are almost cooked through. Slice the onion and layer okra, potatoes, and onion in a large skillet in which olive oil has been heated. Cook on medium heat for 5 minutes. Then add potatoes, wine, fennel seeds, and salt and pepper, reduce heat, and simmer until most of the liquid has cooked down. Drizzle a little more olive oil on the dish and serve.

## FURTHER READING

Fernand Braudel, *On History* (University of Chicago Press, 1980).

John Mack Faragher, *A Great and Noble Scheme: The Expulsion of the French Acadians* (Norton, 2005).

Patience Gray, *Honey from a Weed: Fasting and Feasting in Tuscany, Catalonia, the Cyclades, and Apulia* (North Point Press, 1990).

C. Lengsfeld, F. Titgemeyer, G. Faller, and A. Hensel, "Glycosylated compounds from okra inhibit adhesion of *Helicobacter pylori* to human gastric mucosa," *Journal of Agricultural and Food Chemistry* 52, no. 6 (March 2004): 1495–1503.

National Research Council, *Lost Crops of Africa* (National Academies Press, 1996).

# OLIVE

---

*Wind in the olive trees,*
*wind in the mountains.*

—Federico García Lorca

The absent-minded professor has been with us, as a symbol of intellectual impracticality, for a very long time. It is said that the Greek philosopher Thales (624–550 B.C.E.), for instance, was once so absorbed in studying the night sky that he tripped and fell into a well. He cried for help until a neighbor arrived and called down to him. Learning what had happened, the neighbor said, "Why would you want to know about the heavens when you can't see what's right here beneath your feet?"

Thales probably took a lot of ribbing for that. He got revenge of a kind, though, thanks to his ability to see things in the long term and his understanding of natural processes: judging by rainfall, wind patterns, and the burdened appearance of a grove of olive trees behind his house, he surmised that the year would bring an unusually heavy harvest. Accordingly, he went around the island of Miletus buying up all the olive presses he could find, and when his prediction proved correct he made a fortune making olive oil for his fellow Miletans. For years thereafter, the proverbial reply to anyone who said that eggheads could not make money was, "Oh, yeah? What about Thales?"

When I was a university student in the mid-1970s, I worked over two summers as an archaeological assistant in southern Italy. The small town in which I lived had been noted in antiquity both as the birthplace of the

*The Olive Trees,* by Vincent van Gogh, painted around 1889. Even this black-and-white image shows the dynamism both of van Gogh's brush and of a grove of olives.

poet Horace and as a pleasant stopover along the Appian Way, the object of our survey; its last claim to fame was as the birthplace of one of Mussolini's field marshals. Afterward the town had languished, just another whitewashed village in the shadow of the Apennine Mountains, no place for sophisticates. The town was poor, so poor that the residents of nearby towns called their neighbors *indiani,* as if they were a slice of Calcutta transplanted to Europe.

Yet, as is true all over the Mediterranean, every family had a tiny plot of land on which to grow the basics—tomatoes, lettuces, squash, berries, grapes, sunflowers, sometimes even maize and potatoes, but always shaded by two or three olive trees. I spent much of my free time wandering through the hills among those little gardens, enjoying the coolness and the smells, enjoying the Pleistocene gait of walking. One early morning, while walking among olive orchards that lined a small river, I had the strange perception that I could see straight through the now-shaking trees, that their atoms had somehow disincorporated or that I had suddenly attained X-ray vision like Superman. A few seconds passed until I noticed that the ground below me had momentarily become rubbery. Only then did I realize that I was witnessing an earthquake, that my small corner of the world had indeed flown apart for an instant.

*Olea europaea* is, as anyone who has tried to prune one knows, a sturdy and handsome tree. A relative of the jasmine, lilac, and ash, it appeared along the shores of the Mediterranean untold millennia ago; it is safe to assume that humans who migrated there soon discovered how to domesticate the plant, grafting and improving the working trees to turn out rich yields. The earliest civilizations of the region showed a great talent for doing such work and for sharing the knowledge gained, for domestication quickly spread across the eastern edge of the Mediterranean Basin, eastward into Mesopotamia and Persia, westward to Crete and the islands of Ionia. Domesticated trees came to look quite different from their wild forebear, a thorny bush with a small fruit that is mostly pit and little meat, the opposite qualities of what the orchard keepers were after. The wild relatives bear little oil as well, unlike the domesticated trees, which now produced an essence that Mediterranean peoples found good to eat, good for the skin and hair, good to burn (as was the olive's wood), and, indeed, good for about any use it could be put to.

Small wonder that the olive is so closely tied up with ancient mythologies and religions, for something so good simply had to be from the gods. For the Egyptians it was Osiris. Yahweh took bows in Judea: Noah knew he was finally near land when a dove flew to the ark bearing an olive branch, and it was olive oil that burned miraculously at Hanukkah. The Greeks told a story that Poseidon and Athena once vied for control over Attica, finally agreeing that the one who gave the people the most useful gift would win; Poseidon went first and, being a sea god, brought forth a spring of salt water, while Athena delivered an olive tree, thus winning naming rights over the great city of Athens. In gratitude, the Athenians took care of their olive trees. Solon the Lawgiver decreed that olive trees could be cut down only to serve the polis or the sanctuary of a god, and then only two trees a year from all the groves of Athens, while Aristotle recorded in his Constitution of the Athenians this law: "Anyone who has uprooted or felled an olive tree, the property either of the state or of a private citizen, will be judged in court and, if found guilty, sentenced to death."

As the ancients traveled, they took olive trees with them, and by the dawn of the Roman Republic *Olea europaea* had been introduced along the shoreline of North Africa and in Sicily and southern Italy. Phoenician investors planted vast groves in their colonies at Carthage, Marseilles, and Cartagena in Spain; when Rome defeated Carthage in the Punic Wars and destroyed the city, its sacred and by then ancient olive orchards were the first thing to fall. A huge economy formed around olives and olive oil, perhaps the most prized trade good in the ancient Mediterranean, and one used in abundance; by one modern estimate, the average adult male used some fifteen gallons of olive oil a year. Pliny, the great Roman naturalist, explained matters thus: "Age gives oil an unpleasant taste, which is not so in the case of wine, and oil lasts only a year before it is old. I think of it this way: if wine went bad when it was so new, we would use it all up instead of saving it for its proper use, which is our pleasure. Just so, nature made oil as she did because she wanted us to use it in abundance and quickly, even among the masses."

Olives retained their manifold importance long after the ancient civilizations gave way to new ones. Christian doctrine, drawing on its Judaic origins, anointed priests and the dying with oil and made of the olive branch a symbol of peace. The priests who followed Christopher Columbus's path across the ocean introduced the olive tree to the West Indies and the Americas. Churches around the Mediterranean region kept their own olive orchards to be certain of a steady supply, a custom that traveled with the Spanish to Mexico and California, where every mission even today has at least a few olive trees, and sometimes rich groves. Yet, at first, the Spanish crown forbade the planting of grapevines and olive trees in the New World on any property beyond that of the Church, mostly in an effort to avoid undercutting growers back home in Iberia who were enjoying a revived export trade. Ordinary folk therefore drank wine and ate olive oil imported from Andalusia and other regions of Spain, when they could afford it. The cost of wine caused all but the nobility to find other sources of alcohol, such as tequila, made from distilled agave, while the great expense of olive oil encouraged ordinary cooks to use other fats, especially sheep fat and lard, the latter of which characterizes Mexican cooking to this day. A whole cuisine was thus born of deprivation—and, moreover, deprivation by edict.

Just so, at a secular level competition was fierce for olives. The region around Venice grows few olive trees, for instance, and so Venice took pains to conquer Greek islands where a good supply could be grown; in Tuscany and Liguria, nobles made it obligatory for their serfs to keep healthy orchards in production, and the semifeudal farms of Spanish California followed suit.

The Californian effort helped keep a taste for olive oil alive in North America, and for that we must be thankful, but the best olive oils still come from the Mediterranean. One gauge is this: fresh, extra-virgin oil contains high quantities of a chemical compound called oleocanthal. This compound is unstable, and cooking and age quickly destroy it. Oleocanthal makes for a powerful nonsteroidal anti-inflammatory and pain-relieving agent, another biochemical plus for the thoroughly beneficial Mediterranean diet; researchers reckon that a daily dose of olive oil is the equivalent of a dose of ibuprofen, and much easier on the system. Remarks one scientist, "The Mediterranean diet, of which olive oil is a central component, has long been associated with numerous health benefits, including decreased risk of stroke, heart disease, breast cancer, lung cancer, and some dementias. Similar benefits are associated with . . . aspirin and ibuprofen. Now that we know of oleocanthal's anti-inflammatory properties, it seems plausible that oleocanthal plays a causal role in the health benefits associated with diets where olive oil is the principal source of fat." As it happens, though, the highest concentrations of oleocanthal come from olives grown in Tuscany, while the lowest come from California—which may explain why Berkeley's famed Chez Panisse uses some ten thousand dollars' worth of Tuscan oil every month.

There is plenty of use for California olives yet, for the fruit themselves make fine eating, and one old use of the lees, called *amurca* in Latin, deserves a comeback in an age rightly reluctant to spray chemicals on food. As researchers Allan E. Smith and Diane M. Secoy observe, the Roman writers Cato and Varro recommended that threshing floors be made from soil impregnated with *amurca* to kill weeds, as well as ants and rodents. Columella added that unsalted *amurca*, applied to the furrows of newly plowed fields, would drive away "destructive creatures." Modern science bears the ancients out, for a component of ripe olives, oleic acid, has been proven phytocidal even in small doses.

It is worth trying, and those who live in suitable climes might well try their hand at growing olives and even making oil. The process is as follows: First, wash and clean the olives to remove dirt, twigs, rocks, and the like. Next, grind the olives to a paste on giant stone rollers that you have on hand for the purpose. (An electrical grinder works, but it seems like cheating at the boutique scale.) Next, mix warm water into the olives to coax the oil to form larger droplets, then put the mix into a press to separate the oil and water from the ground olives, called pomace. Place the liquid into a handy centrifuge to separate the oil from the water. Bottle the former. It is just that easy. Once you have found your olive legs, you can practice making extra-virgin oil, which contains 1 percent or less of the free-floating fatty acids such as oleic acid; virgin contains from 2–3 percent, and anything more is a candidate for the lantern.

Actually, making olive oil requires talent and skill, and, as the food writer Patience Gray wisely remarks, "What is the best oil? The oil made from the olives you pick in company with friends, then pressed by a friend in the village olive press, would be my answer." We have an olive tree in our front yard, Crimean by origin, from near the birthplace of *Olea europaea* itself. It is gnarled, weathered by the desert sun. It grudgingly gives off a small yield of bitter olives every couple of years, most of them instantly devoured by dogs, birds, and rabbits. I keep thinking that one day I should do something with the fruit, following Cato and Pliny and all the fine advice of the ancients, perhaps making a fortune like Thales. Or perhaps I will just enjoy the tree's noble shade, glad to have its sturdy presence in a strange world.

## BYZANTINE OLIVE OIL

If a mouse, or any other animal, happens to fall into a vat of olive oil, then, according to the tenth-century Byzantine encyclopedia *Geoponica*, here is how to keep the flavor from spoiling:

Suspend a handful of coriander in the oil. If the unsavory flavor remains, change the coriander. Some people dried the coriander in the shade, then pound it, then throw it in the oil. Others dry fenugreek in the sun and put it in the oil vessel, but it is better overall to take a hot coal of olive wood and drown it in oil. Others take dried seedless grapes and pound them and throw them in, and after ten days they take the grapes out and press them, and put the oil in another container. Others take dried grapes with the seeds left in and pound them with a mortar, then put them in the oil.

On the whole, it is probably better not to let a critter fall in to begin with. Here is a recipe for Spanish oil from the same source:

Pour three measures of water, not too hot, and a little salt pounded and well mixed, into very hot oil from which the amurca has been cleared. Stir it, then let it rest until the water subsides as amurca does. Skim the oil from the surface. Stir warm water into the oil mixture once again. Repeat the process. Then mix in the juice pressed from tender olive leaves.

## SEASONED OLIVES

The Roman writer Marcus Porcius Cato recorded some fine things in *De Agricultura,* among them this concise recipe for spicing up olives.

To season green olives: Bruise the olives before they become black and throw them into water. Change the water often, and when they are well soaked press out and throw into vinegar; add oil, and a half pound of salt to the modius of olives. Make a dressing of fennel and mastic steeped in vinegar, using a separate vessel. If you wish to mix them together they must be served at once. Press them out into an earthenware vessel and take them out with dry hands when you wish to serve them.

## OLIVE PASTE

The best chicken sandwich I ever ate crossed my plate at a little Persian delicatessen called Zand's, on Solano Avenue in Berkeley, California. What made it memorable was its generous use of olive paste atop a fresh baguette; the chicken was simply a bonus. This is my approximation of that magical ingredient.

5 peeled garlic cloves
1 1/2 cups olive oil
2 cups chopped black olives
sea salt and black or red pepper to taste
　　Slice the garlic thin and heat in olive oil until they are nearly translucent. Mix in the chopped olives. Allow to cool. Pack in a small ceramic pot with a lid (available at cookware stores). Refrigerate, then remove excess oil.

## FURTHER READING

Cassianus Bassus, *Geoponika or Agricultural Pursuits,* translated by T. Owen (W. Spilsbury, 1805).

Marcus Publius Cato, *De Agricultura,* translated by W.D. Hooper and H.B. Ash (Loeb Classical Library, 1934).

Diogenes Laertius, *Lives of the Philosophers* (Henry Regnery, 1969).

Mort Rosenblum, *Olives: The Life and Lore of a Noble Fruit* (North Point Press, 1996).

Allan E. Smith and Diane M. Secoy, "Forerunners of Pesticides in Classical Greece and Rome," *Agricultural and Food Chemistry* 23, no. 6 (1975).

Judith M. Taylor, *The Olive in California: History of an Immigrant Tree* (Ten Speed Press, 2000).

# ONION

---

Nature provides its charges with an arsenal of weapons with which to fight off potential predators. The porcupine has its quills, the squid its ink, the rose its thorns, the sea urchin its barbs. To the onion, as to the skunk, nature awarded a supremely effective defense mechanism: a pungent odor that can scare away the toughest of hunters.

You know that smell, that powerful, acrid stench. You know its afteref-fects, too: the burning eyes, the cataract of the tears, part of our own rep-ertoire of defenses to chase noxious chemicals from our eyes and throats. You know it because nature has meant for you to remember what happens when you cut into an onion, rewarded for your trouble by the onion's release of a chemical compound called the lachrymator that mingles with the fluids of your eyes to form nothing less than sulfuric acid.

That lachrymator, when it is cooked, turns sweet—fifty times sweeter, in fact, than refined sugar. Because humans crave their sweets, they have braved the onion's defenses for millennia, making up in taste what they have paid for in tears. For the last seven decades, scientists have been busily developing new hybrids that are high in sugar and water and low in bitter-ness, candies of the vegetable realm, but these sweet onions have yet to conquer the world, and most of the onions consumed even in North America are so-called storage onions, most grown in the inland Pacific Northwest and California.

A native of southwestern Asia, the onion (*Allium cepa*) has been a staple of the Eurasian diet since prehistoric times, as food remains found in Stone Age caves have shown. The onion turns up in an Assyrian text of

2400 B.C.E. commemorating a Babylonian official whose onion patches "were located in the gods' best fields," and it appears in ancient Egyptian tomb paintings depicting commoners' simple meals of bread, onions, and beer. On the strength of such a diet, those ancient Egyptians must have been a tangy lot, which perhaps explains why they were so given to soaking their clothes and hair in perfume. They were also given to stuffing the body cavities and eye sockets of their fallen brethren with onions, in the apparent belief that onions, with their curious ring-within-ring architecture, were symbolic agents of eternity.

That diet of bread and onions was also common in ancient Rome, although Apicius, the author of a cookbook from Nero's day, mentions the onion only as an addition to sauces. The

"Ognon," from Pierre Joseph Redouté (1759–1840), *Les liliacées* (1805–1816).

regimen endured in other European cultures as well, as an eighteenth-century English traveler in Russia attests: "They can make a healthy meal on a piece of black sour bread, some salt, an onion, or garlic."

"*Olla sin cebolla es baile sin tamborín,*" a Spanish proverb remarks—a stew without an onion is like a dance without a tambourine. On that note, a fifteenth-century English cookbook offers this recipe for a simple onion soup that I sometimes whip up when I am in a rush: mince four large onions and sauté them in a quarter of a cup of olive oil on low heat for five minutes. Add the onions and oil to three quarts of vegetable stock and four tablespoons of ground almonds and cook for fifteen minutes. Pour the soup atop a slice of toasted bread, and enjoy: but beware, for there is something oddly addictive about the stuff.

Just ask the monkeys at the village zoo in Bolsherechye, in the Omsk region of Russia, who went out on a hunger strike in the winter of 2005 because, it seems, their keepers were not supplying adequate onions to fuel their addictions. Shunning proffered bananas, kiwis, papayas, and other treats, the monkeys—led by three hamadryads—had become accustomed to being fed onions during the coldest months of the year, as a safeguard against catching flu from human visitors. The monkeys, it seems, had developed something of a ritual in which they peeled a specimen, examined it closely, and then began chewing the onion whole, a torrent of tears in their eyes.

The zookeepers were right to prize onions for their medicinal powers. Like the four-hundred-odd other plants of the genus *Allium,* including chives, garlic, leeks, ramps, and shallots, the onion has a tonic quality on the blood, lowering cholesterol and dissolving blood clots; all contain prostaglandin A1, a fatty acid demonstrated to have therapeutic effects in treating hypertension. The essence of onion is used as well to combat food poisoning from *E. coli* and *salmonella* bacteria, and as an expectorant to relieve bronchial congestion. Pliny the Elder, the compiler of the great ancient compendium called *Natural History,* records more than three dozen medicinal uses for the onion, while in his commonplace book, George Washington recommends eating raw onions to fight off colds, reminding himself and his readers not to spit into the fire in the aftermath. Ancient Greek physicians applied onion-based salves on wounds, noting that the onion extract seemed to have an antiulcerative effect, and medical researchers are now looking at the onion's sulfur compounds, allicin and sulforaphane, as anticancer agents. Mysteriously, those compounds seem to inhibit the growth of beans and peas, so careful gardeners keep those plants widely separated from onions. Just as mysteriously, beets, tomatoes, lettuces, and strawberries seem to enjoy the company of *Allium* in whatever form.

Whatever their medicinal uses, onions contain a moderate amount of vitamin C, folic acid, and vitamins B1 and B6, and lots of potassium— 125 milligrams in half a cup of chopped raw yellow onions—and phosphorus and dietary fiber. Because some of that nutritive value is lost in cooking, food experts recommend that you be brave about adding raw onion to your diet, in salads or as a garnish for cooked vegetables, never mind the possible social consequences. In the South, a traditional favorite meal consists of a "kiss-me-not sandwich," which is simply a slice of Bermuda onion on bread. That elegantly straightforward meal would not have been out of place in Julius Caesar's kitchen—and it certainly lives up to its name.

To combat the tearing that comes from cutting into an onion, by the way, you can try a number of measures. One is to hold a clove of garlic between your teeth as you cut; another is to drape a wet towel around your neck, the idea being that the lachrymator will bind itself to the water molecules in the towel and not in your eyes. Yet another is to hold the onion under running water as you slice it, washing away its evil water-soluble juices before they can rise up to smite you. And yet another is to cut the onion near an open flame, which dilutes the lachrymator gas cloud.

I have tried all these methods, and they are only partly effective. I can say for certain, however, that you can remove the smell of an onion from your hands after cutting it by rubbing them with lemon juice. You will then smell like a lemon, scary to no one, wide open to predators, but perhaps easier to be around. But, all that said, it is good for a body to cry from time to time: we cry because behind the human eye lies a complex system of dozens of secretory and excretory glands bearing such names as "crypts of Henle" and "Wolfring's glands," which combine to produce basal tears that flow into the nasolacrimal duct, which in turn empties into the nose. Under conditions of irritation, emotion, or illness, the glands yield more liquid than the nasolacrimal duct can handle, causing tears to spill out and drain over the eyelids. These tears have a powerful antibiotic quality, removing potentially invasive bacteria from the eyes, mouth, and nose. And in all events, under normal conditions, humans produce only one-tenth to two-tenths of an ounce of tears a day, allowing for all the tears shed in laughing, yawning, coughing, facing brisk winds, chopping onions, and even dealing with an emotion or two. This makes tears practically weightless, so no harm done: long live the onion, provoker of tears, protector of the weak.

## ONION RINGS

Who invented the onion ring? The jury is out: some hold it to be an American invention, while others note the prevalence of onion rings in the cuisine of Central Europe. Call it independent invention, but whoever is responsible, as connoisseurs know, is bucking for sainthood. Here is a sturdy recipe for an all-American version:

Cut six medium onions into quarter-inch-thick slices and separate into rings. Combine one cup plus two tablespoons of all-purpose flour, half a teaspoon of salt, a beaten egg, a cup of buttermilk, and two tablespoons of vegetable oil. Beat with a whisk or fork until the dry ingredients are thoroughly moistened. Drop onion rings in batter and coat on both sides. Fry in hot oil (375 degrees) in a deep skillet or fryer until golden brown; then drain on paper towel and serve.

## ONION SOUP

Adapted from *Le Grand Dictionnaire de Cuisine* (1873) by Alexandre Dumas, this makes a delicious cool weather repast. The instructions are Dumas's.

10–12 large white onions, chopped
1/2 pound butter
2 1/2 quarts milk
1 1/2 quarts chicken stock
2 tablespoons cornstarch, dissolved in 1/2 cup water
6 raw egg yolks
salt and pepper to taste
toasted bread crusts

There are two kinds of onions, the big white Spanish one and the little red Italian one. The Spanish is more nutritious and is therefore chosen to make this soup for hunters and drunkards, two kinds of people who need to recover quickly.

Chop the onions. Put them into a blender and make a purée. Simmer the purée in the butter. Add 1.5 quarts scalded milk and chicken stock and cook for 20 minutes. Bind with dissolved cornstarch. Remove from heat and let cool. Beat egg yolks into remaining milk and add to the soup, stirring. Heat, add salt and pepper and pieces of toasted bread crust. Et voilà.

## CALABRIAN HOT SAUCE

The Calabrian coast near Tropea is a center of Italian onion cultivation, its showcase piece a fiery red onion that is celebrated every August 13 with a spirited festival. This is a lively dish that can take the edge off a summer day by putting a fresh fire in one's mouth.

4 Roma or plum tomatoes, chopped fine
2 red onions, chopped fine
2 cloves garlic, chopped fine
1/2 cup olive oil
1/2 cup roasted red peppers
1 tablespoon red wine vinegar
1 cup water
1/2 cup chopped black olives
1 teaspoon oregano
dash salt

In a medium skillet, sauté onions, tomatoes, and garlic on medium heat for about ten minutes, until the onions have turned a whiter shade of red. Add the black olives and red peppers and cook over low heat for another ten minutes. Add remaining ingredients, stir, and let simmer for thirty minutes, adding water (or vegetable broth) as needed. Serve over pasta with grated parmesan, Romano, or pecorino cheese.

## FURTHER READING

Barbara J. Ciletti, *The Onion Harvest Cookbook* (Taunton Press, 1998).
Thalassa Cruso, *Making Vegetables Grow* (Knopf, 1975).

Jan Dominguez, *The Onion Book* (Broadway, 1996).

Brian Glover, *Onion: The Essential Cook's Guide to Onions, Garlic, Leeks, Scallions, Shallots and Chives* (Lorenz, 2001).

Tom Lutz, *Crying: The Natural and Cultural History of Tears* (Norton, 1999).

N.A. Pavilov, "The Biological Bases of Onion Storage," *Acta Horticulturae* 20 (1971): 53–64.

# ORANGE

The desert city where I live is full of hidden treasures, little out-of-the-way places that escape the guidebooks, that even old-timers do not know about. One of them is gone now: an orange-juice factory, tucked away in a seedy downtown neighborhood alongside the railroad tracks. Truckloads of freshly picked oranges would arrive there each morning from the groves that ring the city, most to be shipped out whole to supermarkets far away, but some to be squeezed on the spot for local stores. If you wandered into the factory, as I did almost daily, you could buy a gallon of fresh juice for under two dollars, an unheard-of bargain.

The place was too much of a hidden treasure, it appears. Even with the scent of oranges hanging in the air as thick as a storm cloud, few people braved the rough downtown streets to find the factory. The owners relocated it to Florida, where the year-round market for citrus pickers is better than Arizona's, and its fresh orange juice became but a memory.

That factory was a wonderful thing, if only because it completed a historical circle within which the orange has traveled from desert to desert across the globe. The orange, *Citrus chinensis,* evolved some twenty million years ago in the tropics of southern China, but archaeological evidence suggests that it first came into heavy cultivation along the desert watercourses of northern India four millennia ago. From there it traveled with Greek and Roman traders to the Mediterranean and was planted in vast groves throughout North Africa—whence the tangerine, the loose-skinned orange of Morocco—and in Spain and southern Italy. Christopher Columbus himself introduced the orange into the Americas, planting

a grove on the island of Hispaniola in 1493. Spanish
missionaries were soon
planting them at desert missions throughout Mexico
and what is now the southwestern United States, recommending them to their
landward charges as being
good for combating *mal
de loanda,* or scurvy, their
name for which contained
the name of the capital of
Portuguese Angola. They
also favored orange juice in
treating typhus, a not
uncommon disease in those
newly conquered lands.

Why the orange, one of
the largest berries on earth,
should take to the deserts
of the world so readily is
no mystery: unlike most
fruits, it loves strong sunlight and disdains abundant
water. Ernestine Hill, an
Australian traveler of days
past, describes an oasis in
the desert of Central Australia made all the happier
by the presence of the tree:
"The first stopping-place
was a hundred miles away
across nothing but stones,

Thomas S. Sinclair (ca. 1805–1881), "Wild orange tree
(*Citrus vulgaris*)," from François André Michaux and
Thomas Nuttall, *The North American Sylva* (1841–1849).

the station of Wellborne Hill, an oasis of comfort and culture, where
Mrs. Ernest Giles is growing larkspurs and lemons, cedars and figs,
oranges and mandarins, on the banks of Henrietta Creek, and nasturtiums
and grape vines and poppies and sweet peas, just to show what the desert
can do." The orange's love of heat and disdain of wet is all to California's
advantage, too, for arid California is the world's leading producer of the
fruit, having given over much of its agricultural land to orange production
in the 1870s with the introduction of navel oranges from Brazil. (Semi-
tropical Florida often outpaces California in bumper-crop years.) The

descendants of those Brazilian navel oranges are the ones you buy in the market today.

As with so many other crops in an industrial agriculture governed by monoculture, consumers have only a few other varieties to choose from apart from the navel. Among them are the tangerine, abundant in winter, and the sweet Parson Brown, Temple, and Valencia varieties. You can also sometimes find bitter Seville oranges on your grocer's shelves, although most Sevilles wind up in sugar-added marmalades.

Oranges are a dieter's dream: a medium navel orange contains only about 64 calories, but the high fiber content is filling enough to give the illusion of having eaten much more. Oranges are also low in starch, which is why they do not continue to ripen after being picked. They are free of fat and cholesterol and low in sodium, full of calcium, potassium, vitamin C, and phosphorus—in short, they are little grenades of health.

For that reason, people who suffer from respiratory-tract allergies like hay fever should include oranges in abundance in their diet; vitamin C opens up capillaries blocked by allergens, just as antihistamines (and the regular practice of Tai Chi, for that matter) do. Some researchers offer still more health-related arguments for eating oranges, maintaining that the flavonoids in oranges inhibit certain carcinogens; citrus pectin, and particularly orange pectin, is now thought to be especially helpful in combating prostate cancer, binding to cells that might otherwise grow malignant. Sailing around the world in 1775 aboard HMS *Resolution,* the ill-fated Captain James Cook also discovered something about oranges that would prove instrumental, if in a small way, in extending the British Empire: he and his crew passed three years under extraordinarily difficult conditions, but, amazingly, only one sailor died, this one by accident. Scurvy, that dread nutritional disease, would have felled many more, but Cook was the first of the sea voyagers of his time to understand the relationship of that disease to lack of vitamin C, or ascorbic acid, even though he did not know quite why. He introduced sauerkraut, a borrowing from Holland that retains ascorbic acid even after pickling, into the crew's diet. He also stocked his holds with malt, salted cabbage, vegetable stock, lemons, oranges, carrots, and marmalades, all highly effective in battling the disease.

In any instance, there is no downside to enjoying a diet full of the fruit the ancient Greeks called "golden apples." Well, perhaps one downside: orange juice can smell awfully strange to a wide range of palates. To some people, the cut or squeezed interior of an orange smells like mothballs, paint thinner, kerosene, and even, shudder, cheesy feet. To others, oranges have happier associations, such as cut grass, roses, and caramel. Some forty natural compounds combine to produce the characteristic smell of orange juice, and some of them can be, well, stinky—but, as a U.S. Department of Agriculture scientist remarks, "necessary to the mix." Oddly, these compounds also tend to disappear rapidly through evaporation when orange juice is concentrated, as so much of it is for the purposes of long-term storage and long-distance transportation. Thus, juice companies are in the habit of using prepackaged "flavor packs" that are added to concentrate when, after a time, it is reconstituted with water to be given new life in someone's refrigerator or on a distant table, as memorialized in a wonderful exchange between John Cleese, as English hotelier Basil Fawlty, and Bruce Boa, as an American visitor clearly used to luxuries Basil can but dream of: "Ah! You'd like freshly squeezed orange juice." "As opposed to freshly unscrewed orange juice, yes."

Fortunately, federal law requires labels to inform consumers whether orange juice is fresh or from concentrate. Unless you live near an orange-juice factory, bet on whatever you have in your refrigerator's being the concentrate-reconstituted variety. And this being a time of micromarketing, niches, and all-around me-firstness, I would not be surprised if in years to come these flavor packs were not tooled to individual sniffers: those of a certain bent could look for the label with the daffodils, while those of another, more pungent bent might look for the label with the buzzing flies.

This could happen some day. For the moment, when you are shopping for oranges in the store, remember that the heavier the orange feels, the more juice it holds. As a rule, too, the thicker the skin, the more arid the orange's place of origin, though regardless of the thickness it will take about six months for the peel to biodegrade under normal environmental conditions. If you were a nice English lady of the Victorian era, you would have been given to selecting lightweight oranges: the gush of orange juice from a ripe fruit seems to have set proper men and women of the time to thinking lascivious thoughts of a kind that only Frank Harris could endorse. For that reason well-bred women withdrew to their rooms to eat oranges in private, far from prying eyes. For whatever it is worth—and it may not be much—both Samuel Johnson and Joseph Conrad collected orange peels, a matter that we are now free to imagine has certain Freudian qualities. Ditto for the fact that orange was Frank Sinatra's favorite color.

Eat them as you wish. In Mexico, oranges are eaten with a dash of vitamin C–rich chile powder, a clear case of coals being brought to Newcastle. This is clearly healthier than the way German children eat oranges, hollowing the stem to make room for a sugar cube that dissolves into the juice, which is then drunk with a straw.

Whether purely healthfully or with an eye toward culinary decadence, there are myriad ways in which oranges and orange juice can be used in cooking. One of the most attractive, to my mind, is a dish I discovered in Turkey and use even now to ward off the heat of the desert summer: a cold salad of black olives, sliced red potatoes, green beans, peppercorns, and oranges drizzled with the tiniest bit of red wine vinegar and olive oil. Another is a specialty of my friend Biagio Quintieri, who lives in a little bit of paradise along southern Italy's Maratea Coast, and who battles the intense summer with a drink called the *tramonto*, or "sundown": blend four parts tonic water with one part each orange juice, lemon juice, and strawberry purée.

Enjoy, and go forth to explore the world scurvy-free and proud— proud, among other things, that after all these years no one has discovered a rhyme for *orange*, a rarity of the tongue in more ways than one.


## LAHM LHALOU

This Algerian dish, which translates to "sweet meat," makes good use of the orange.

2 pounds boneless lamb cut into 1-inch cubes
1 stick cinnamon
1/2 teaspoon salt
1 cup water
2 tablespoons olive oil
4 tablespoons orange juice
1/3 cup blanched almonds
1 1/2 cups pitted prunes
1/2 cup turbinado or organic sugar
   Sprinkle lamb with salt. Cook lamb in medium saucepan in olive oil until lightly browned. Remove lamb from heat and set aside. Add almonds, sugar, and cinnamon to the pan drippings. Stir well. Add water and orange juice. Bring to a boil, stirring constantly. Add lamb, cover, simmer for forty-five minutes. Stir in prunes and cook for another fifteen to thirty minutes. Remove cinnamon stick before serving. Serve with couscous or rice.


## ORANGE OMELET FOR HARLOTS AND RUFFIANS

It pays to know your customer. Johannes Bockenheim, a German, made his living in Rome as a cook for Pope Martin V; on his days off, we presume, he crossed from the sacred to the profane, and in a pleasing little cookbook of his from about 1430 he served up recipes geared to various social classes—including hookers, criminals, and the nobility—and various nationalities alike. The result is a fascinating glimpse at the social life of his time. Bockenheim was proud of an omelet that was as unspecific in its exact makeup as it was delicious, if perhaps unusual to the modern palate: "Take eggs and break them, with oranges, as many as you like; squeeze their juice and add to it the eggs with sugar; then take olive oil or fat, and heat it in the pan and add the eggs. This is for ruffians and brazen harlots."

## BAKED ORANGES

Baking oranges, wrote the Elizabethan cookbook compiler known only as "A.W.," is an easy enough matter:

Faire peele your Orenges, and pick away all the white that is under the peele, and so lay them in fine paste, and put into them Sugar, very little Sinamon or none at all, but a little Ginger and bake them very leisurely.

## ORANGE SAUCE FOR DUCK

Nellie Aldridge, who may have been a Betty Crocker or Aunt Jemima—the figment, in other words, of some manufacturer or trade group's imagination—served up this recipe for visitors to the orange groves of San Bernardino, California, in the 1920s. It works for chicken, too.

juice of 1 orange
juice of 1 lemon
granted rind of 1 orange
grated rind of 1 lemon
1–3 cups corn syrup or sugar
1 tablespoon grated horseradish
2 tablespoons currant jelly
    Strain orange and lemon juice, add the grated orange and lemon rinds, sugar, fresh horseradish, finely grated and currant jelly. Beat thoroughly. Bring to boiling point and serve.

## FURTHER READING

Nellie Aldridge, *Nellie Aldridge's National Orange Show Cookbook* (San Bernardino Growers, 1928).

Ernestine Hill, *The Great Australian Loneliness* (Angus & Robertson, 1940).

Ford Madox Hueffer, *Joseph Conrad: A Personal Remembrance* (Little, Brown, 1924).

John McPhee, *Oranges* (Farrar Straus & Giroux, 1975).

Odile Redon, Françoise Sabban, and Silvano Serventi, *The Medieval Kitchen* (University of Chicago Press, 1998).

A.W., *A Book of Cookrye* (Edward Allde, 1591).

Joel Parker Whitney, *The Orange Tree: Its Planting and Cultivation* (Whitney, 1902).

# PEAR

---

Have you ever seen a pear tree, that beautiful cousin of the rosebush, in blossom? If you live east of the Mississippi River, sadly, the chances are good that you have not. Although *Pyris communis* once covered the East Coast, and although New England was once among the world's greatest producers of its fruit, a blight in the late nineteenth century destroyed millions of pear trees and ruined a once thriving industry.

Now for the good news: pear trees, a familiar sight in the Pacific Northwest, are making a comeback in the East, thanks to the development of disease-resistant hybrids and a significant rise in "boutique farming," where specialty crops, pears among them, are grown for upscale markets.

In the meanwhile, the Northwest produces nearly a million tons of pears each year, enough to satisfy domestic demand, and then some. Most of those pears are Bartletts, a variety developed in 1769 in a small village near Reading, England, by an experimentally minded clergyman named John Stair. The sweet fruit was so popular that Stair's trees were sold throughout England, and their descendants in turn came to Massachusetts, where a farmer named Enoch Bartlett was the first to grow them in commercial quantities. Bartlett named the pear after himself, perhaps unaware of Stair's lineage; to complicate matters, in other parts of the English-speaking world the fruit is called the Williams pear, after the botanist who developed the Bon Chrétien from which Stair's variety sprang. The New Englanders who were the first Americans to migrate to Washington and Oregon took the trees with them, along with a few other varieties that are grown today, among them the Seckel, Bosc, Anjou, and Comice—the last of which connoisseurs of pears hold to be among the most succulent ever developed.

As is true of so many other crops, that handful of varieties represents just a tiny fraction of the breeds that have come and gone throughout history. First domesticated some five thousand years ago in the highlands of what is now Kazakhstan, in Central Asia (the name of Kazakhstan's capital, Almaty, means "father of apples," and the apple and pear are closely related), the cultivated pear spread throughout the ancient world. It turns up as a favorite delicacy in ancient Chinese court documents, in the verses of the Greek poet Homer, and in Sumerian cuneiform tablets, where mashed pear pulp is recommended as a poultice for wounds. Pliny, the Roman naturalist, likewise appears not to have trusted pears as a foodstuff pure and simple, even though his compatriots grew many varieties of them; still, he vouched for their use in healing wounds, a function that the tenth-

"The Beurré Diel Pear," an engraving by Augusta Innes Withers, from John Lindley's *The Pomological Magazine*, vol. 1 (1828).

century Byzantine compilation of earlier Greco-Roman agricultural compendia called the *Geoponika* endorsed, adding, "Wine having pears put in it astringes the body." By the time of the *Geoponika*, pears had spread throughout northern Europe, too; given the bitterness of many apple varieties, it is tempting to think that a line in the Old English religious poem that modern scholars call Genesis B, which reads, "Adam, frea min, þis ofet is swa swete" ("Adam, my husband, this fruit is so sweet)," suggests that at least one Anglo-Saxon monk thought the pear capable of leading humans out of paradise.

It was in China that the thirteenth-century traveler Marco Polo saw "huge pears weighing ten pounds apiece, white as dough inside and very fragrant." The pears grown today seldom reach that size, but China still abounds in sweet, spicy pears that are to Western tastes a bit tough because of their high concentrations of lignin—the little woodlike chunks in pears of all kinds.

On the other side of the ancient world, the Holy Roman Emperor Charlemagne grew nearly two hundred kinds of pears at his capital at Aachen, in what is now Germany. From his gardens came trees whose descendants Thomas Jefferson would plant in his orchards at Monticello, Virginia. (Jefferson's favorite was the beurré, whose French name means "buttery" and refers to the fruit's soft flesh.) And an English gardening manual of the late 1600s lists hundreds of varieties that flourished in the British Isles, among them the Hamden's bergamot, Bon Chrétien, Norwich, black Worcester, Greenfield, Orange, Queen hedge, Lewis, Firth, Arundel, Brunswick, Poppering, Diego, Bing, Bishop, Emperor, Cluster, Rowling, Bezy d'Hery, Evelyn, and Balsam. It verges on crime that of the five thousand or so kinds of pears humans have developed, and of the 2,500 commercially grown around the world, we now eat only five or six. Yet the tiny handful that we have is uniformly delicious. It is also healthful, for pears are high in the insoluble fibers that are so beneficial to the human digestive tract; recent evidence suggests that pears and other fibrous fruit also help combat macular degeneration, a common eye malady of older people. A medium raw pear contains about 100 calories, with no cholesterol or saturated fat, about 18 milligrams each of calcium and phosphorus, nearly 7 milligrams of vitamin C, and goodly amounts of iron, potassium, and vitamin A. Try adding pureed pears to muffins, cakes, and pancakes; apart from adding fiber, you will cut down on the use of sweeteners and, in the bargain, add a delicate, unexpected flavor to baked goods.

Pears are picked before they begin to ripen, for, once their polyphenloxidase compounds—the same substances that so quickly blacken bananas and apples—begin to work, the pear will rot within days. You can slow the action of these compounds somewhat by immersing pears in cold water and then storing them in a cold refrigerator, but, even so, you should eat them within four or five days of purchase. Otherwise, you can always follow the lead of just about every ancient pear-producing culture and make wine of the fermented juice, as an English writer instructed in 1597: "Wine made of the iuce of Peares, called in English Perry, is soluble, purgeth those that are not accustomed to drink thereof; notwithstanding

it is as wholesome a drinke being taken in small quantities as wine; it com-
forteth and warmeth the stomacke, and causeth a good digestion."

When you shop, select pears that are firm to the touch everywhere but at
the neck, where they should be a little soft. Do not mind minor dings or
mild blemishes on the body; deeper blemishes, however, indicate that
the fruit is already ripe and should be eaten immediately.

The Chinese poet Huang Tsun-hsien adds this advice:

Don't buy pears the bees have nibbled.
You can't tell if the core has rotted.
We once shared a pear and formed a bond—
but that bond has turned to separation.

A final word of advice: do not let Huang's sad poem make you associate
pears with melancholy. Pear trees are wonderfully long-lived, lasting for
more than two hundred and fifty years, second only to olives among fruit
trees in staying power. Think of eternity when gazing on one. Think of
Cézanne's joyous still lives of fruit, of Wallace Stevens's resplendent
poems celebrating bowls of pears, of pear trees in blossom long after the
Yuletide partridge has flown away—and enjoy.

## BAKED PEAR

This recipe for a light, easily prepared dessert comes from China.

Cut off the top of the pear to a depth of about one inch. Core the fruit, leaving a deep recess. Fill this with a tablespoon of honey and a dash of cinnamon. Cover with the reserved top and steam or bake at 350º for about
twenty-five minutes. Serve at once.

## PATINA DE PIRIS

Apicius, the Roman cookbook writer, offers a recipe for pear soufflé
that, with a little tinkering, holds up well in a modern kitchen.

2 pounds pears, peeled and cored
6 eggs
4 tablespoons honey
1/2 cup passum (make this by reducing 1 cup of grape juice or wine and
adding a teaspoon of honey)
1 teaspoon olive oil
1/2 teaspoon salt
1/2 teaspoon ground cumin
1/2 teaspoon ground pepper
    Mash pears, pepper, cumin, honey, passum, salt, and oil. Add eggs and
bake in a casserole at 325° for thirty minutes.

## PERRIS IN SYRIPPE

An English manuscript dated to about 1450 gives careful instructions for a treat, pears in syrup, that modern cooks can whip up in less than half an hour:

Take Wardons and cast hem in a fair potte, And boile hem til hei ben tender; and take hem up and pare him. And take powder of Canell, a good quantitite, and cast hit in good red wyne, And cast sugur thereto, and put hit in an erthenpot, ant let boile; And then cast the peris thereto, And late hem boile togidre awhile; take powder of ginger, And a litell saffron to colloure hit with, And loke that hit be poynante and also Doucet

Translated, the recipe is something like this:

4 pears
red wine
1 tablespoon ground cinnamon
3 tablespoons brown sugar
1 teaspoon dried saffron
   Cover pears in water in a pot. Boil until they are soft to the touch. Add enough red wine to cover the pears. Add cinnamon, sugar, and saffron, then boil until the sugar has dissolved. Cut pears lengthwise and serve with whipped cream.

## FURTHER READING

Barbara Flores, *The Great Book of Pears* (Ten Speed Press, 2000).

J. Janick, "The Pear in History, Literature, Popular Culture, and Art," *Acta Horticulturae* 596 (2002): 41–52.

F.A. Roach, *Cultivated Fruits of Britain: Their Origin and History* (Blackwell, 1985).

John Seabrook, "Renaissance Pears," *The New Yorker* (September 5, 2005).

# PINEAPPLE

It is the evening of January 14, 1893, a time that is cold in New England but blustery and humid in the remote Sandwich Islands of the central Pacific Ocean. The lightning-charged sullenness of the weather was an odd sight for the New Englanders who had gathered in Honolulu, but it was appropriate, for they were about to visit the storm of revolution and conquest on the nation that had offered them hospitality.

Earlier in the day, the queen of Hawaii, Liliuokalani, had made a fateful decision: she would issue a revised constitution that gave only Hawaiian citizens the right to vote and, moreover, removed the previous qualification that voters had to own a substantial amount of property. Such conditions had assured power and privilege for the white landowners who had been in Hawaii for only two generations, having arrived as missionaries and evolved into a class of plantation owners growing rich on the production of sugarcane and pineapples.

Liliuokalani was no admirer of the landowners. Neither did she much care for the American soldiers and sailors who now regularly steamed into Pearl Harbor, which her late brother and predecessor had deeded over to the U.S. government in 1887, an event that she recorded in her diary, with an eerily prescient turn of phrase, as "a day of infamy." As American power grew, the queen resisted.

For the *haole* landowners, this was the final insult. Two days later, one of their number, a prominent attorney with strong ties to Washington, wrote a letter to the commander of a conveniently arrived expeditionary force requesting that soldiers be landed "to secure the safety of American life

The first known European depiction of a pineapple, this print is by Jacopo Ligozzi (1547–1626), a member of the Tuscan court, who also painted yuccas, irises, and other plants newly arrived to Europe from the Americas.

and property." The commander obliged, landing 162 marines and sailors in Honolulu. The attorney, Lorrin Thurston, then assembled an antiroyalist Committee of Safety, which picked as its leader a jurist—and, with his brother James, soon to be a pineapple baron—named Sanford Dole. Two days later, the Committee declared the monarchy abrogated and requested annexation to the United States.

It would be America's first imperial act, and one that suggests that the banana has been misapplied as a descriptor of rinky-dink politics, for the phrase "pineapple republic" is just as accurate in describing the power of American fruit companies in making client nations throughout the tropics. As the Chilean poet Pablo Neruda wrote, imagining that the world had been divided up among multinational corporations at the dawn of time,

> The Fruit Company, Inc.,
> took for itself the juiciest lands,
> the central coast of my own country,
> the slender waist of America,

and established a chain of strongman-led client states to preserve their interests, backed always by U.S. Marines.

It was Christopher Columbus himself who brought the pineapple from the Caribbean to Spain, where it was greeted with some puzzlement but immediately planted, thanks to the Admiral of the Ocean Sea's personal assurance that the pineapple was "the most delicious fruit in the world." (George Washington agreed. On a trip to Barbados in 1751 he tasted his first pineapple and declared, "none pleases my taste as does the pine.") Even in the Caribbean, though, the pineapple—a member of the bromeliad family and, technically, an herb—was an import, for it evolved in the lowland interior of southern Brazil and was transported from there along ancient Indian trade routes. The name Columbus knew it by, *anana*, is still widely used in Latin America; our own word for *Ananas comosus* speaks to some bemusement, we might imagine, on the part of the first English speaker to set teeth to one: its insides are firm and crunchy, like an apple, but its exterior is as difficult to break as a pine cone.

The English would not be bemused for long. Charles II, the seventeenth-century English monarch, seems to have regarded the pineapple as a tangible symbol of his far-flung reign, and several official portraits depict him receiving a pineapple as a sign of fealty or standing alongside a specimen, looking contented and pleased. Pineapples were soon traded throughout the English colonies, expensive enough that they were saved for special feast days, particularly Christmas.

The authority of the English crown went with the ill-fated English seafarer Captain James Cook when he introduced the pineapple to Hawaii in 1779, on his third great circumnavigation of the globe. As he traveled —to Easter Island, Tonga, St. Helena, the Society Islands, and elsewhere —Cook planted pineapples and other tropical fruits, work that would save many lives on subsequent ocean voyages. He then returned to England, contemplating retirement to a farm in his native Yorkshire, but he remained ashore for a little less than a year. In June 1776, aboard a ship called *Discovery*, he set out in the hope of discovering the Northwest Passage across North America. He mapped the coast of Alaska, explored a few points farther south, and then turned to Hawaii. There, on the morning of February 14, 1779, he confronted a crowd of natives whom he suspected of stealing a landing craft from his ship. A fight broke out, and Cook was killed. So ended a great life. But, as his fellow seafarer Captain James King remarked, "his death...cannot be reckoned premature, since he lived to finish the great work for which he seems to have been designed."

Cook's introduction would not bear fruit, so to speak, for nearly a hundred years. When it did, under the guidance of those missionaries turned capitalists, the Hawaiian pineapple industry grew quickly. By 1903, James Drummond Dole was canning pineapple commercially and transporting the once-rare fruit to international markets; by 1921, Dole's Hawaiian Pineapple Company was the wealthiest company and largest landowner in the Hawaiian Islands. Other exporters established plantations in South Africa, Mexico, Puerto Rico, Australia, Sri Lanka, Singapore, Ghana, the Ivory Coast, Taiwan, and Thailand. The Dole Company eventually shifted most of its production to the Philippines to avoid the inconveniently high cost of labor in the United States, and by the end of the twentieth century the Hawaiian pineapple industry, which was once the world's largest, produced only 2 percent of the world's pineapples, far behind the three largest producers, Thailand, the Philippines, and Brazil. The final blow came in 2006, when the Del Monte Corporation, the last remaining major producer, announced that it would cease pineapple cultivation in Hawaii altogether after the harvest of 2008. It would be fitting, some might think, to return independence to Hawaii once the pineapple barons are gone.

Pineapple is a good source of potassium, vitamin C, and dietary fiber. Moreover, it contains a proteolytic enzyme called bromelain, an acid so strong that pineapple canners wear heavy gloves and smocks to keep it from contact with their skin. Bromelain is principally used to perform such tasks as tan leather, thin gelatin, and stabilize latex paint, but it also has powerful anti-inflammatory properties, for which reason many doctors are given to recommending a diet of pineapple to promote healing and reduce postoperative swelling. Yet the reason pineapple remains so popular is both simple and powerful: it tastes just as good as Columbus and Washington averred.

Today a couple of dozen varieties of pineapple are grown around the world, though most American consumers see only one or two of them, the Smooth Cayenne and the Hilo. When in Spain and Portugal, you are likelier to enjoy the St. Michael, one of the principal exports of the Azores to Iberia. Elsewhere in Europe, you will encounter the Monte Lirio, Charlotte Rothschild, Mauritius, and Congo Red varieties, all delicious and each with subtle differences. Whatever the breed, to select the best pineapple in the supermarket pyramid, here is a simple trick: tug on a leaf. If it slides from the skin easily, the pineapple is ripe. Now smell where the leaf came out. If the pineapple smells sweet, you have a winner; if it has a slightly rum-like smell, it has begun to ferment and will have a sharp but not necessarily unpleasant taste.

One great mystery surrounds the pineapple, and that is the origin of one of its most familiar expressions, if one that seems to be declining in popularity in recent years: namely, the pineapple upside-down cake. Such a delicious innovation begs to be credited, but no one origin can be pinpointed; as if recapitulating the great Neolithic discovery of grains in different parts of the world, the pineapple upside-down cake seems to have sprung Athena-like from the foreheads of chefs in widely different places sometime in the early twentieth century, at about the time Dole started mass-shipping cans of pineapple into the far interior of the North American continent. From Texas, Utah, and Minnesota we have recipes for "skillet cake," useful for those homesteads without ovens; a similar recipe can be found in the 1943 edition of *The Joy of Cooking*, when wartime rationing encouraged quick-cooking (and thus presumably low fuel-consuming) recipes. The first known recipe to use the "upside-down" phrase as such comes from a Gold Medal flour ad published in November 1925, and by the 1930s other recipes were turning up in the pages of the Sears Roebuck catalog. Champions of the Dole Pineapple Company once claimed the invention as its own, though a popular tourist booklet the company published in 1927, the first known collection of Dole recipes, mentioned no such treat. Other literary sleuths trace the pineapple upside-down cake to a charity cookbook published in Seattle in 1924, and still others to a nationwide radio competition sponsored by Dole in 1925, in which hundreds of nearly identical recipes were submitted for something that looked very much like the current configuration of the delicacy, suggesting that there was a printed source out there in the ether on which all those contestants were drawing. Whatever the case, it appears that the upside-down cake was a twentieth-century invention, one of the few happy outcomes of that long-ago revolution in the Sandwich Islands.

## PINEAPPLE UPSIDE-DOWN CAKE

In 1931, the U.S. Department of Agriculture's Bureau of Home Economics issued a cookbook called *Aunt Sammy's Radio Recipes*, written not by a finger-pointing recruiter but by two accomplished nutritionists, Ruth Van Deman and Fanny Walker Yeatman. For lovers of pineapple upside-down cake, the text has grail-like qualities: it contains one of the very first published mentions of the concoction. Neither author claimed it to be her invention, so the recipe had to have come from somewhere. But where? Therein lies a culinary mystery.

1/2 cup sugar
2 tablespoons butter
2 tablespoons pineapple juice
3 slices pineapple
   Melt the sugar in a skillet over moderate heat, allow it to brown slightly, and stir constantly. Add the butter and pineapple juice and cook until a fairly thick syrup is formed. Place the sections of pineapple in the syrup and cook a few minutes, or until they are light brown, and turn occasionally. Have ready a well-greased heavy baking pan or dish, place the pineapple on the bottom, and pour the syrup over it. Allow this to cool so it will form a semisolid surface, then pour in the following:
1/4 cup butter or other fat
1/2 cup sugar
1 egg
1 teaspoon vanilla
1 1/2 cups sifted soft-wheat flour
2 teaspoons baking powder

1/4 teaspoon salt
1/2 cup milk

Cream the fat, add the sugar, well-beaten egg, and vanilla. Sift the dry ingredients together and add alternately with the milk to the first mixture. Pour this over the pineapple. The batter is rather thick and may need to be smoothed on top with a knife. Bake in a very moderate oven (300–325 degrees F.) for forty-five minutes. Loosen the sides of the cake, turn it out carefully, upside down. If the fruit sticks to the pan, lift it out and place it on the cake. Serve with whipped cream or hard sauce.

## CHICKEN WITH PINEAPPLE

In 1898, a resident of Santa Clara, California, named Encarnación Pinedo published a book called *El cocinero español* (The Spanish Cook). It was noteworthy in its time for the extraordinarily high quality of its recipes, which made ample use of fresh fruits and vegetables, and in ours for having been the first cookbook by a Hispanic author to be published in the United States. A unique compendium of *Californio* cuisine, Pinedo's cookbook offers this recipe, here modernized, for the classically Mexican merging of fruit and meat.

1 large ripe pineapple
2 tablespoons oil
1 slice white bread
2 large cloves garlic, peeled
3/4 pound peeled Roma tomatoes
1 cinnamon stick
6 whole cloves
1 cup warm water
2 teaspoons salt
6 chicken legs with thighs, about 4 pounds

Cut off the top and bottom of the pineapple. Remove the skin and cut the pineapple into quarters. Cut out the center core, then cut the quarters into one-inch slices.

Heat one tablespoon oil in a Dutch oven. Add the slice of bread and cook it for a minute on each side, then remove from the pan. In the same way, roast the garlic until it is browned. Combine the tomatoes, pineapple, browned bread, and garlic in a blender or food processor and blend until smooth.

In a spice grinder or food processor, grind the cinnamon stick and cloves to a powder. Heat the remaining oil in the Dutch oven. Add the pineapple mixture, ground spices, water, and salt. Bring the sauce to a boil, reduce the heat and simmer uncovered for fifteen minutes.

Remove the fat and skin from the chicken legs. Add them to the sauce and simmer, covered, for thirty minutes. Uncover and simmer thirty minutes longer. Serve with rice.

# PIÑA COLADA

Thanks to a demonic tune by Rupert Holmes called, yes, "The Piña Colada Song," the piña colada—the Spanish name means "strained pineapple"—became a beverage of choice among discotheque habitués in the late 1970s. Here is a more or less standard recipe.

1 1/4 ounces rum
splash of cream of coconut juice
splash of pineapple juice
    Combine ingredients over ice in a shaker. Shake, then serve into a large glass. Garnish with a fresh pineapple wedge and maraschino cherry

The drink is often credited to Ramón "Monchito" Marrero, head bartender at the Caribe Hilton in San Juan, Puerto Rico, who claimed that he invented it in 1954. However, a 1922 issue of *Travel* magazine refers to a Cuban piña colada, a drink comprising "the juice of a perfectly ripe pineapple—a delicious drink in itself—rapidly shaken up with ice, sugar, lime and Bacardi rum in delicate proportions." Those who dislike coconut will surely prefer the Ur-drink.

# FURTHER READING

Jean Anderson, *American Century Cookbook: The Most Popular Recipes of the 20th Century* (Gramercy, 2005).

D.P. Bartholomew, R.E. Paull, and K.G. Rohrbach, eds., *The Pineapple: Botany, Production and Uses* (CABI, 2003).

Marion Mason Hale, *The Kingdom That Grew Out of a Little Boy's Garden* (Dole Pineapple Company, 1927).

Steven Kinzer, *Overthrow: America's Century of Regime Change from Hawaii to Iraq* (Times Books, 2006).

Pablo Neruda, "La United Fruit Co.," in *Antología Esencial* (Fondo de Cultúra Económica, 1979).

Encarnación Pinedo, *Encarnación's Kitchen: Recipes from Nineteenth-Century California* (University of California Press, 2003).

Nicholas Thomas, *Cook: The Extraordinary Voyages of Captain James Cook* (Walker & Company, 2003).

# POTATO

As an American of predominantly Irish ancestry, and proud of it, I harbor mixed feelings about the potato. It is delicious, of course, and essential. Still, it was indirectly responsible for the cruel diaspora that nearly emptied the mother country of its people and sent my own family off to America, where, in the words of the lyricist Phillip Chevron, we could "celebrate the land that made us refugees."

Ireland took to the potato late, as such things go, many decades after it was introduced to Europe from South America, but it was not long before *Solanum tuberosum* was revealing itself as both a blessing and a curse. It must have seemed that thousands of years before to the peoples of the central Andes of Peru and Bolivia, particularly the Aymara, who farmed the heights. Long ago, they discovered that certain members of a group of closely related grassy plants, which flourished at elevations between 6,500 and 13,500 feet, produced a tasty tuber over much of the year, adding materially to an otherwise uncertain food supply. The problem was, of the 110 or so species of wild tuber-bearing *Solanum* found in the region, some were extremely poisonous—no surprise, given the toxicity of most members of the vast nightshade family. Others produced mere gastric discomfort, diarrhea, and nausea. Only a few contained low enough levels of glycoalkaloids to be edible straight out of the ground without unpleasant consequences.

Fortunately, those wild *Solanum* were easily hybridized, and the Aymara exercised what turns out to have been a profound practical understanding of plant genetics by identifying the relatively nontoxic strains and putting them to work. Over a period of perhaps six thousand years, they developed an agriculture that boasted dozens of varieties of potatoes, which were traded far afield, with small-scale cultivation extending northward into the highlands of Mexico.

It was in the potato's homeland that the Spanish first encountered it, along about 1530, when one of Francisco Pizarro's lieutenants, Pedro de Cieza de León, described it in his *Chronicle of Peru*. He noted, with evident awe, that the imperial Inca city of Tiahuanaco alone, nested high in the mountains, produced thirty thousand tons of potatoes, though he did not note that by that time homegrown geneticists had developed more than 150 kinds of potatoes. Which one of them was first introduced to Spain is a matter of some speculation,

A calendar entry for the month of December from an Inca codex of the early sixteenth century. The illustration shows a man punching holes in the soil, into which the first woman plants potatoes. The second woman, to the right, will then smooth the soil with a hoe.

though it worked; the potato was firmly rooted in Iberia from the instant it arrived.

At the same time, it came into English hands, probably somewhere in the Caribbean, since the word "potato" derives from the Carib *batata,* "sweet potato," which was similar enough in appearance to permit the confusion. The plant was then introduced to the colony of Virginia, where it flourished in the high, cool region between the Blue Ridge and the Allegheny mountains, so much so that it came to England as the "Virginia potato," with nary a word about its Andean origins. It has long been supposed, without much solid evidence, that the introducer was the English privateer Walter Raleigh, who certainly brought tobacco to England and earned John Lennon's damning "stupid git" for his troubles, to say nothing of being beheaded in a court intrigue in late Elizabethan times. Other sources credit the introduction to another Englishman, Thomas Herriot, in 1586, about the time the English privateer John Hawkins brought it to Ireland.

By that time, the potato was being spread widely throughout continental Europe, received with varying degrees of enthusiasm; the heroes who introduced the crop to the welcoming steppes of Eastern Europe and Russia are unsung, whereas the French agronomist Auguste Parmentier earned a coveted grave in Paris's Père-Lachaise cemetery for his contributions to French cuisine, in which the potato has long enjoyed a cherished place. (The great jazz drummer Gene Krupa kept his internal metronome going by chanting "lyonnaise potatoes and some pork chops" as he played, further honoring France's devotion to *Solanum*.) Having bypassed the Caribbean on the way to continental Europe, the potato had no common name as it marched northward and eastward; the French term *pomme de terre* means "earth apple," while the German and Polish word *Kartoffel* is a garbling of the Italian word *tartufolo*, "truffle," all names that point to the potato's subterranean origin.

The potato became central to the agriculture of vast regions of Europe, helped along, historian William McNeill suggests, by the fact that it could be stored underground until needed—unlike grains, which had a habit of disappearing, being requisitioned by the armies that were crisscrossing Europe in those days. Even so, Italy, no stranger to war, was the slowest to take to it, although the Florentine traveler Francesco Carletti approvingly wrote around 1600 of "certain tubers called 'potatoes' which boiled or roasted under a fire have a delicious taste as pleasant as our chestnuts and which can replace bread." *Solanum tuberosum* was particularly prominent in the economy of Ireland, then a despised colony of England, owned in the main by absentee landlords who converted small truck gardens and orchards into vast fields dedicated to producing potatoes for export. (The busy British army and navy alone consumed huge quantities of them.) When the so-called Potato Famine hit in the 1840s, it did largely because so many Irish farmers were landless and relied on a single crop. That crop was ravaged by a fungus, *Phytophthora infestans,* and with it the island's population: some three million Irish men, women, and children died or emigrated. "God sent the blight," remarked the Irish patriot John Mitchell, "but the British sent the famine," though from far away; by several scientific accounts, the fungus was brought into Europe on shiploads of bat guano from the islands of Peru, an important source of agricultural fertilizers. The blight spread elsewhere in Europe and caused catastrophic damage to other economies, but that experience is little remembered today; only in 1883 was a fungicide finally developed, thanks to the French scientist Alexis Millardet (1838–1902), who had earlier saved the French wine industry from a grape blight. Even with that fungicide, however,

*Phytophthora infestans* persists; in the year 2000 alone, it was responsible for crop losses amounting to $3 billion.

The potato was less central to the economy of the early United States than across the seas in Europe—and in China, which now produces twice as many potatoes as does the United States. As the food historian Waverley Root observes, in 1806 a popular almanac listed but a single variety, but forty years later a hundred and more varieties were being grown across the northern tier from New York to Utah, spread first by German and Scandinavian immigrants, then in large measure by Mormon farmers who saw in *Solanum tuberosum* an easily transportable, durable foodstuff. Mormon farmers were responsible for introducing the potato to the extremely hospitable soil of Idaho, some of the richest farmland in the United States; the Snake River valley is the world's potato breadbasket, so to speak, and the state has proudly used the phrases "Famous Potatoes" and "World Famous Potatoes" on license plates and official correspondence since 1948. For their part, Mormon schoolchildren across the border, in British Columbia and Alberta, introduced the counting rhyme "one potato, two potato, three potato, four" sometime before 1885, when it was first recorded. The Idaho potato of today is different from the varieties those Mormon farmers planted, however; the modern version was developed by the renowned scientist Luther Burbank (1849–1926), who first grew what he called the Russet Burbank potato in his fields in Santa Rosa, California.

Americans are now well versed in matters concerning the potato, and the unversed have been made to suffer. Deak Parsons, the bombardier of the *Enola Gay*, was reminded into old age that he had missed winning the New Mexico spelling bee competition of 1914 by leaving the "e" out of "potatoes," whereas a benighted U.S. vice president named J. Danforth Quayle drew national scorn when he insisted that the "e" belonged in the singular. Mark Twain would have had a field day with that official faux pas, having insulted another grandee, in a letter written but not sent, thus: "Your head wasn't made to put ideas in. It was made to throw potatoes at."

Plenty of nutritionists and dieticians would sooner throw potatoes away than eat them, for potatoes are the supreme starch in an era when starch is little used, even on clothing. A single baked potato delivers a walloping 51 grams of carbohydrate, along with 220 calories, and with not a lot of payback in terms of protein. It is worth remarking, with the food activist Francis Moore Lappé, that the more the poor *Solanum* is processed, the less nutritional worth it has; this is true of all foods, but anyone who has tasted a boutique or heirloom potato knows that its slightly bitter, slightly peppery flavor speaks to everything that we are missing because of our reliance on industrial agriculture.

For all that, potatoes of every commonly eaten variety—russets, golds, Idahos, reds, even purples—carry goodly quantities of dietary fiber, vitamin C, potassium, and niacin, and there is no good reason for anyone but the pathologically inactive to avoid the starch. Surprisingly, though, Americans have eaten fewer and fewer potatoes in the last century or so; Waverley Root records that per capita, Americans ate 200 pounds of potatoes in 1900, but only 120 pounds in 1960, about two-thirds fresh and the rest in processed form. Astonishingly, that figure has fallen to 30 pounds per capita today—nearly half in the form of french fries, a favorite American treat since Thomas Jefferson's day, but one of those breads by which man had better not live every day, lest corpulence ensue. As the food historian Sidney Mintz notes, "carbohydrate consumption in the years 1910 to 1913 was two-thirds potatoes, wheat products, and other such 'starchy' foods, and one-third sugar, the so-called simple carbohydrates." By the 1990s, Mintz adds, sugar had risen to half of that consumption, and "what was left of complex carbohydrate consumption took the form of deep-fried, salted, and sweetened potatoes."

Jefferson walked everywhere, though, and he stayed lean until his dying day; given that regimen, he was allowed to eat as many french-fried potatoes as he cared to. Those more inclined to couch potatodom, which describes the majority of developed-worlders today, are well to curtail their intake, even to the point of avoiding fried spuds altogether. Otherwise, an effective strategy is to avoid eating pasta, bread, and potatoes after 5:00 in the afternoon—and to prefer honey to sugar, and even then in the very smallest of quantities. Those mostly empty calories burn off quickly at active times of the day but can impede the processing of sugars in quiet, un-Jeffersonian moments when the television blazes and the mind grows still, all of which make a recipe for disaster.

## FRENCH FRIED POTATOES

An army marches on its stomach, the adage has it. This recipe for french fries—the french in question coming from a term kindred to julienne, "to cut into thin slices," and not from the nationality—comes from a World War II–era U.S. Army cookbook whose recipes are calculated to serve a hundred hungry GIs at a time. Adjust portions accordingly.

1. Wash potatoes; pare and cut into long narrow strips.
2. Cover with water; allow to stand 30 to 45 minutes. Drain; roll in a cloth to dry.
3. Fry in deep hot fat (350°F) about 4 to 6 minutes or until brown and tender.
4. Drain on absorbent paper. Sprinkle with salt.

# THIOU A LA VIANDE

Numerous carnivores would agree that potatoes are at their best when accompanied by beef, particularly in cold weather. Senegal, in West Africa, seldom gets cold, but no matter: it is a cultural crossroads where French, Saharan, and sub-Saharan African traditions have long met, and beef stew, *thiou,* is a national favorite. This recipe for "chew," as the Senegalese pronounce it, is adapted from Bea Sandler's *African Cookbook.*

1 cup chopped yellow onion
1 tablespoon sea salt
1/2 tablespoon black pepper, freshly ground
1/4 cup canola or safflower oil
1/2 teaspoon ground coriander
1/2 teaspoon dried thyme (or 1 sprig fresh thyme)
2 pounds stew beef, cubed
1 cup tomato paste
2 cups water
1 cup chicken broth
1/3 cup white vinegar
1 pound white potatoes, cut into cubes
1 pound white cabbage
3 cups cooked white rice

In a Dutch oven or deep skillet, sauté onions. Add spices. Then add stew beef and sauté on low heat for twenty minutes. Add tomato paste, broth, water, and vinegar. Cover and simmer on low heat for an hour. Add potatoes and cabbage and simmer for another forty-five minutes. Place rice on platter, then pour stew over it and serve.

# RÖSTI

Rösti, a cake of shredded potatoes rather like hash browns, is a specialty of German Switzerland, its perfect accompaniment a bratwurst from Sankt Gallen, its perfect time a cool afternoon in mid-autumn.

1 pound yellow potatoes
2 tablespoons unsalted butter
1 tablespoon canola or safflower oil

Cover potatoes with salted water and simmer until tender. Drain potatoes in a colander and cool. Remove to a bowl and chill overnight. Peel potatoes, then, with a grater, shred them coarsely. Heat butter and oil in a skillet. Pat potatoes into cakes, then add to skillet. Cook on low heat until both sides are golden brown, about ten minutes for each side. Season with salt and pepper.

## COLCANNON

Colcannon—in Irish, *cál ceannan,* "white-headed cabbage"—is eaten around the year, but especially on feast days such as St. Patrick's Day and Easter. Its only drawback is the necessity of cooking cabbage, which can sometimes be so sulfurous as to make a kitchen smell like a match factory.

    2/3 cup cream
    6 scallions, chopped fine
    1 pound green cabbage
    1 pound yellow potatoes
    1/2 cup butter
        Scald cream briefly, then add chopped scallions. Boil potatoes for thirty
    minutes, then mash with milk and butter to taste. Boil shredded cabbage
    for fifteen minutes, then drain and allow to cool. Chop it very fine. Add cab-
    bage to mashed potatoes. Add butter and salt and pepper to taste.

## FURTHER READING

Pete Hamill, *Piecework* (Little, Brown, 1996).

Timothy Johns, *With Bitter Herbs They Shall Eat It: Chemical Ecology and the Origins of Human Diet and Medicine* (University of Arizona Press, 1990).

Frances Moore Lappé, *Diet for a Small Planet* (Bantam Books, 1973).

Sidney W. Mintz, *Tasting Food, Tasting Freedom: Excursions Into Eating, Culture, and the Past* (Beacon Press, 1996).

Cormac O'Gráda, *Black '47 and Beyond: The Great Irish Famine* (Princeton University Press, 1999).

Bea Sandler, *The African Cookbook* (Carol, 1993).

Raleigh Trevelyan, *Sir Walter Raleigh* (Henry Holt, 2004).

U.S. War Department, *Army Recipes* (War Department Technical Manual TM 10-412, 15 August 1944).

# RICE

___

When I was an undergraduate, way back in the innocent 1970s, scientists of various stripes lived and breathed by chronologies that were inviolate and immovable. The Civil War began in 1861, Vietnam in 1965; humans arrived in the Americas ten thousand years before the present by way of a land bridge across the Bering Strait; Neanderthals died off exactly twenty-five thousand years ago, before the arrival of *Homo sapiens* in Europe; The Beatles broke up in 1970; people stopped speaking Latin along about 1000 C.E.

Scientists these days tend to be a touch less rigid about fixed dates and events, for the most recent historical research suggests that such facts are, if not outright wrong, then in need of qualification. It is more accurate to say, for instance, that the formal military phase of the Civil War began in 1861—not on April 12, when Fort Sumter was shelled, but four months earlier, when Georgia militiamen seized a federal arsenal near Atlanta. Take your pick of years on Vietnam: 1963, 1954, even 1945, perhaps earlier still. Neanderthals and *Homo sapiens* may have lived among each other, possibly intermarried; the chronology of the human arrival in the Americas gets pushed back farther and farther into the past, and it seems likely that the first people to show up came across the sea by kayak. As for The Beatles—well, it depends on whether you are a John or a Paul fan. And as for Latin: well, nonsense. Go to Rome or Tijuana or Paris or Florianopolis, and you will hear it spoken all around you.

All of which is by way of saying, with elaborate evasion, that no one can say with any confidence when humans hit on the idea of domesticating the

A Chinese family sharing a meal of rice; illustration from the *London Illustrated News,* April 11, 1868.

bright green grass that grew wild below the southeastern foothills of the Himalaya Mountains, a grass that spread from there across southern Asia deep in antiquity and that now serves as the single most important foodstuff for fully half of humanity.

For years, archaeologists have posited that other grains preceded *Oryza sativa* in the human larder, arguing that farmers in North China were growing wheat for a millennium before their southern neighbors discovered rice. In 2004, however, other prehistorians turned up a find that, if nothing else, strongly pointed to a conclusion that most scholars have long agreed on, if perhaps uneasily: people have been drinking their grains for as long as they have been eating them.

The find in question was a set of pottery jars unearthed in the Neolithic village of Jiahu, in northern China's Henan province. Within them was a mixed fermented beverage of rice, honey, and fruit dating to at least 7000 B.C.E., about the same time—or so we now think—that barley, wheat, and millet beer and grape wine were first being produced in the Middle East. The remnants provided the first chemical evidence for the knowledge of fermentation in ancient Chinese culture, and they suggested that an early tradition shared by some groups along the Yellow River, namely getting drunk and communing with the ghosts of one's dead relatives, may have had a longer pedigree than had been suspected.

Thus, northern Chinese were drinking rice wine before southern Chinese were supposed to know how to grow it. Never mind: what is most important is that rice was well known to the peoples of East and South Asia thousands of years ago, providing the basis for the beginnings of agricultural intensification, terracing, and irrigation and yielding a genetic stock of at least 100,000 varieties of rice, about 8 percent of which have been thoroughly domesticated. Central Asian traders carried rice westward, and it was known to the ancient Greeks and Romans, though they tended to regard the grain as an exotic and expensive import more useful in medicine than in the kitchen. Thus Romans of his day must have been amazed when Aelian, the naturalist, issued this report about the elephants of India:

> A tame elephant drinks water, but a war elephant drinks wine—but a special wine, made not of grapes but of rice. The elephants go out and

gather flowers, for they love sweet smells and are trained in fragrant meadows. An elephant can be trained to pick flowers. It will fill a basket, then wander off to take a bath, then return, and if its trainer does not return the flowers it will trumpet and refuse food until finally someone brings the flowers the elephant has gathered. Then it scatters the flowers all around its stall, so that it can sleep in all that nice aroma. It seems that the Indian elephants are more than four meters tall and at least two meters wide. The largest are the elephants from Prasia, and the next largest are from Taxila.

Lucky elephants, the Romans must have thought, so pampered as to be fed rice wine in their off hours. Still, rather than follow their lead, the Romans more or less ignored the possibilities of *Oryza sativa*, leaving it to Arab traders to introduce it commercially in the early Middle Ages. By that time, the Arab peoples of the Middle East and Mediterranean had been consuming rice for many generations—it is said that Muhammad's favorite dish was rice, in fact. Those traders took it first to Arab outposts in Spain, where it was planted along the elaborate network of canal-laced irrigated fields that surrounded the great Moorish citadel of Valencia. From there, its cultivation spread to the Italian provinces of Lombardy and Piemonte, where it proved to be fantastically successful, the subalpine climate making a good match for that of the ancestral Himalayas. All rice produces more grain than does wheat, but this fertile region was an embarrassment of riches, and Italian rice was soon being promoted as what was approvingly called "white food" as far away as England, where its consumption was generally confined to the upper classes, mostly because growers along the Po had little to spare for the export market, with the result that rice was fantastically expensive almost everywhere it traveled in Europe.

That began to change, if slowly, with the introduction of rice cultivation in the Americas, a process that took place nearly two hundred years after Europeans first arrived there. No one knows why it took so long to do so, but it is probably not a stretch to suggest that because Europeans had not learned to make and use alcohol from rice, as Asians had done long before, they had not come to prize it properly. Whatever the case, rice cultivation in the New World tended to track the slave economy closely, with plantations established in Brazil and coastal Central America, throughout the West Indies, and along the southern Atlantic coast of British North America, where slaves from Madagascar helped establish a thriving rice agriculture in Charleston, South Carolina. A couple of centuries later, immigrants from Japan and South Asia would help spread rice cultivation to the Pacific coasts of the United States, Mexico, and Central America. In the end, it is a grand historical success story: rice, which tolerates diverse climates and diverse plant neighbors, has spread to every continent save Antarctica and has become a part of the cuisine of nearly every culture, if sometimes as a poor relation to other grains.

Its importance will only grow in the coming years. The first food plant to be completely genetically sequenced, *Oryza sativa* is expected to feed far more people in the future than now; by 2050, demand will likely double, which explains why scientists are now busily working to isolate favorable characteristics such as high yield, drought tolerance, and pest resistance so that future hybrids are assured of success, even in alien growing conditions. Perhaps surprisingly, the rice genome contains 7,500 more genes than the human genome, which suggests that the plant deserves treatment as a highly variable crop, not as a candidate for the monotonous monoculture of industrial agriculture over so much of the world.

Indeed, one scientific study suggests, monoculture would be disastrous, for growing different rice varieties together in a single field increases all of their resistance to disease as well as their yield. This kind of cropping, common in Asia, provides a strong ecological alternative to pesticides, for it was shown that the thousands of Yunnanese fields monitored for the study required no fungicides after two seasons of production, a boon for both health and economy. Though one Chinese scientist warned that "the current world population of over six billion does not allow us to return to agricultural production practices of the past," the rice itself seems to argue otherwise. This is true as well of the cultivation of a cousin, *Oryza glaberrima,* that grows wild along the Niger River and has long been cultivated from Lake Chad westward; it seems to thrive in inclement growing conditions, which may make African rice a crop of increasing importance in the years to come.

For the moment, rice growers face many challenges, not least of them rice stripe virus, carried into fields along the lower Yangtze River valley by a grasshopper-like insect called *Laodelphax striatellus.* The virus takes about 5 to 10 percent of the annual yield there, which is, of course, a huge amount.

There are other Chinese predators to worry about, too. At least, so thought the Red Emperor, Mao Zedong. My Tai Chi master, the late Dr. Wen Zee, was swept aside during the Cultural Revolution; a renowned cardiologist, he was found guilty of the crimes of having gone to an English school and having been born of a bourgeois family and so was forced to carry corpses instead of practicing medicine. Some years earlier, Dr. Zee recalled, an order came to him and to every other Chinese to perform another unusual task. It seems that Mao Zedong had been sitting in his palace courtyard one fall day, and there he saw a sparrow pecking away at the lawn. He ordered that the sparrow be caught and dissected, and in its stomach the inquisitors found four grains of rice. Having done the math on that, Mao decreed that all the sparrows in China be put to death lest they strip the nation of its most important crop and bring on famine, and so Dr. Zee joined his fellow citizens in firing weapons into the sky for days until millions upon millions of birds of all kinds had been killed. Ironically enough, Mao's killing campaign marked the start of the so-called Great Leap Forward. No hungry person felt more full, of course, and the famine continued and worsened, but in the end the exercise was less about food than the Red Emperor's ability to command such great events.

For all that, it is worth noting, as my friend Michael Ableman has, that China's farmers are now feeding nearly a quarter of the world's population on only 7 percent of the planet's arable land, practicing an intense agriculture that has been ongoing for more than seven thousand years. That feat would be impossible were it not for the fact that so much of that farming has been done using organic practices—so that, Michael writes, "fields cultivated during the Han dynasty are still fertile after twenty centuries of continuous use."

It is only fitting, then, that M. F. K. Fisher, the great food writer, should prefer the Asian way of cooking rice to the unfortunate American habit of boiling it until every ounce of nutrient or taste has disappeared:

> One Chinese directive I have says to add two cups of rice slowly to two cups of boiling water, cover the pot tightly, turn heat to medium for ten minutes, to low for ten more, and then off for ten...and "Do not remove the lid at any time." Another instruction...says to wash one cup of rice thoroughly...add it to two cups of fast-boiling water, and stir until it boils again. Then it must be covered tightly, put on an asbestos mat over the lowest possible flame, and "Do not peek!"

Mrs. E. E. Kellogg, the redoubtable Michigander and author of the 1893 classic *Science in the Kitchen*, offers a variant that yields good results, though soaking the rice overnight is an unnecessary extravagance:

> Boiled Rice (Japanese method).—Thoroughly cleanse the rice by washing in several waters, and soak it overnight. In the morning, drain it, and put to cook in an equal quantity of boiling water, that is, a pint of water for a pint of rice. For cooking, a stewpan with tightly fitting cover should be used. Heat the water to boiling, then add the rice, and after stirring, put on the cover, which is not again to be removed during the boiling. At first, as the water boils, steam will puff out freely from under the cover, but when the water has nearly evaporated, which will be in eight to ten minutes, according to the age and quality of the rice, only a faint suggestion of steam will be observed, and the stewpan must then be removed from over the fire to some place on the range, where it will not burn, to swell and dry for fifteen or twenty minutes.
>
> Rice to be boiled in the ordinary manner requires two quarts of boiling water to one cupful of rice. It should be boiled rapidly until tender, then drained at once, and set in a moderate oven to become dry. Picking and

lifting lightly occasionally with a fork will make it more flaky and dry. Care must be taken, however, not to mash the rice grains.

Do not peek, and do not overcook. May the planet hear that last bit as a prayer, for a recent study undertaken in the Philippines suggests that rice yields are negatively affected by rising temperatures. Tropical rice varieties are adapted to a temperature range of 73 to 91 degrees Fahrenheit (23–33 C), while temperate varieties, such as are grown in the highlands of India, require a range of 68 to 86 degrees Fahrenheit (20–30 C). Everywhere temperatures are rising. Rice yields typically decrease by 10 percent for each degree Celsius of increase, which comes as bad news for the three billion and more people for whom rice is a major foodstuff—and, if the worst-case scenario plays out, may yet make rice an expensive exotic once again.

## TEN PRECIOUS RICE

A diet based on rice, a long-term study conducted by the Cornell-China-Oxford Project on Nutrition, Health, and Environment demonstrates, is healthier than one based on wheat. A lead scientist in the study reports that the blood biochemistries of northern Chinese who rely on wheat "resemble those in people with insulin resistance"—in other words, diabetics. That should scare no one from an occasional plate of pasta, but it speaks to the manifold powers of *Oryza sativa*.

This Chinese recipe makes a fine showcase for the grain. Vegetarians can easily adapt it by leaving out the meats; supercarnivores can add other meats to make this a Chinese version of Brazilian *feijoada*. Try shrimp and clams.

1 cup lean pork, sliced
1 cup canned tuna
1/2 cup smoked ham
1/2 cup bamboo shoots
1 whole chicken breast
1/2 cup water chestnuts
pea pods
1/4 cup scallions, chopped fine
4 cups cooked white rice
3 tablespoons soy sauce
2 tablespoons sesame oil
1 cup vegetable stock or broth

Shred chicken breast and tuna with a fork. Heat the oil in a wok and sauté the scallions, then add the meats and cook until the liquid from the chicken runs clear. Add the rice and stock and bring to a boil, then lower the heat and simmer for ten minutes.

## ARROZ DE SABATO

Elias Canetti, the winner of the Nobel Prize in literature in 1980, recalls his boyhood in a riverside town in Bulgaria: "People of the most varied backgrounds lived there; on any one day you could hear seven or eight languages. Aside from the Bulgarians, who often came from the countryside, there were many Turks, who lived in their own neighborhood, and next to it was the neighborhood of the Sephardim, the Spanish Jews—our neighborhood. There were Greeks, Albanians, Armenians, Gypsies. From the opposite side of the Danube came Romanians....There were also Russians here and there." All of those varied peoples had rice in common, and they would have found this Sephardic variation on risotto a pleasure. Saffron distinguishes this "Sabbath rice" as Spanish in origin.

2 1/2 cups long grain white or Arborio rice
3 tablespoons olive oil
1 teaspoon kosher salt
5 cups chicken stock
1 bay leaf
1/4 teaspoon saffron threads, poached in 1/2 cup boiling water
    Preheat oven to 350°F. Over medium heat, heat the olive oil in a casserole. Sauté the rice in the oil until it takes on a golden glow. Sprinkle the salt atop the rice, pour in the stock, and add the bay leaf and saffron threads. Cover tightly and place in the oven. Bake for thirty minutes, then allow to stand for fifteen minutes until all the liquid is absorbed.

## FURTHER READING

Michael Ableman, *From the Good Earth* (Harry N. Abrams, 1993).
Sarah Allan, ed., *The Formation of Chinese Civilization: An Archaeological Perspective* (Yale University Press, 2005).
Board on Science and Technology for International Development, National Research Council, *Lost Crops of Africa,* vol. 1, Grains (National Academy Press, 1996).
Elias Canetti, *The Tongue Set Free* (Seabury Press, 1979).
M.F.K. Fisher, *With Bold Knife & Fork* (Putnam, 1968).
International Rice Genome Sequencing Project, http://rgp.dna.affrc.go.jp/IRGSP.
Mrs. E.E. Kellogg, *Science in the Kitchen* (Bay View Assembly, 1893).

# SPINACH

---

He looked like a walking wart and sounded like an amphetamine-fueled radio-controlled airplane on those unfortunate occasions when he talked, but Popeye the Sailor, that grand and deeply weird child of Depression-era America, descended from noble stock—from, to be more precise, a bloodline founded by the Greco-Roman hero Hercules. Like his legendary ancestor, Popeye drew his strength from the earth, not directly in the manner of Atlas but indirectly through the consumption of a nutritionally supercharged foodstuff. In Hercules's case, that foodstuff was garlic, which—according to a Popeye cartoon of 1954—the hero sniffed in times of need, which occurred to him much more often than they do to the rest of us. Alas, his archfoe Brutus knocked him into a spinach field during one of their frequent brawls, and Hercules chewed the green stuff instead of sniffing the white stuff, and, well, the rest is history, at least of a sort.

It took a hero to convince children of my generation to eat spinach, for, outside of the agricultural belt that ran across the South to California and kitchen gardens kept by mostly southern European people in the temperate North, the only way *Spinacia oleracea* came was sopping wet and near-black, always tasting of the can in which it had been housed. It was nasty stuff, and Popeye had to cajole and lie and keck-keck-keck endlessly in order to make the sale. Even as a child, I inclined toward the view espoused by the inestimable Groucho Marx: "This would be a better world for children if the parents had to eat the spinach." Had I known the famous *New Yorker* cartoon of 1928 penned by Carl Rose and captioned by E.B. White, I would have endorsed it, too: a recalcitrant child, facing a mound of wilted, blackish algal material, cries, "I say it's spinach, and I say the hell with it."

Still, Popeye's detestable ploy worked. In the 1930s, when the cartoon first became popular, spinach consumption increased by a third, and certainly much of the credit has to go to the pugnacious *Thimble Theatre* player. The fact that there was a depression going on and many people could not afford to eat as much meat as before may have had something to do with it, too. No offense to the good people of Crystal City, Texas, who long ago erected a statue to Popeye and declared their town to be the Spinach Capital of the World.

Two millennia ago, the spinach capital of the world lay somewhere on the vast Iranian Plateau, where the plant grew in wild abundance. The people of the

*Spinachia*, illustration from a seventeenth-century German herbal.

region knew a good thing when they saw it, and spinach, which they called *esfenakh, aspanakh,* or *asfanak,* figured prominently in the local cuisine. So highly was Iranian food regarded, then as now, that traders to both the east and the west took seeds as part of their baggage; historical records indicate that spinach was being grown in Nepal in late antiquity, and the plant, introduced into China by Persian merchants, turns up in T'ang dynasty court records and even a poem or two. (For what it is worth, the American poet John Ashbery once wrote a sestina, a difficult medieval form, that made use of the word *spinach* as a line ending a full six times. Try finding six rhymes for it, and you will appreciate his achievement.) In the early Middle Ages, Saracen raiders introduced spinach to Sicily, from which it spread to Malta and Greece; the cooking of the Mediterranean has never been the same since. Italian traders took the plant to France, where it became the *épinard* of culinary fame; the French passed it along to the Germans, English, and other peoples of northern Europe, and it was well established across the continent by the middle of the sixteenth century. For their part, the Spanish planted spinach almost as soon as they landed in the Americas, and in time it was growing in the same profusion as in its Persian homeland, the better to put Crystal City on the map and the rest of us in better health.

And there is no mistaking it; spinach is good for a person, even if its legendarily high iron content was the product of a typographic error. That is to say, in 1870, a German chemist named Erich von Wolf calculated spinach's undeniably high concentration of ferrous oxide, but in transferring his figures from notebook to journal article he located the decimal point in the wrong place, making it seem as if spinach had ten times its true wealth of iron. For the next seven decades, spinach bore the rubric "miracle vegetable" in health manuals in many languages, and not until 1937 did other German chemists realize their colleague's error and correct the figure.

By that time Popeye had been out doing his propaganda work, and few people were inclined to banish spinach from the table on account of a little mistake. As it turns out, spinach is the single best source of folic acid, which is essential to human health, aiding in blood cell production and reducing the incidence of birth defects. Before folic acid was isolated, nutritionists attributed this healthful aspect to chlorophyll; during the First World War, French soldiers suffering from wounds were given wine fortified with spinach juice to raise their production of hemoglobin, and while the wine certainly must have helped their spirits, the spinach did its part, too.

Typo or no, spinach contains goodly quantities of iron, of the aforementioned folic acid, and of potassium, beta-carotene, calcium, and vitamin B6. The food's high concentration of oxalic acid, which has a mildly laxative or diuretic effect in many people, works against this abundance of good things, however, because oxalic acid prevents the body from absorbing iron. The shortcut around this is to eat spinach with lemon juice or tomatoes, the vitamin C in which helps induce iron into the bloodstream.

Spinach also contains rather mysterious flavonoid compounds, technically called methylenedioxyflavonol glucuronides, that have proven antioxidant properties that are of use in fighting various cancers. One long-term study suggests that women who eat ample quantities of spinach experience lower rates of breast cancer than their non-spinach-eating peers, while the same pattern holds true with men and prostate cancer thanks to a carotenoid called neoxanthin. Osteoporosis, heart disease, colon cancer, asthma, arthritis, and even age-related speech and mental disorders seem to be curbed by various other of these flavonoids, and the double whammy of lutein, provided by spinach and more "bioavailably," in the language of food chemists, in eggs, has proven powers of battling age-related macular degeneration, cataracts, and other eye troubles. Have a spinach and mushroom omelet, in other words, and you will be able not only to leap over tall buildings, but also to see right through them.

Spinach does score a couple of demerits, though. Certain of its compounds can interfere with the normal functioning of the thyroid gland, and its high level of purines, which figure in the production of uric acid, can aggravate kidney stones and gout. However, a normal diet with a helping of spinach every couple of days is unlikely to lead to such dire consequences for most people.

So Popeye was onto something after all. And thankfully, with advances in the technology of food preservation, no one need experience the horror of eating spinach from a can ever again, regardless of the behavioral modeling a cartoon character can offer. So what is the best way to eat spinach? Fresh, even frozen, with a squeeze of lemon and, as Popeye would tell you, with olive oil—and maybe some sweet peas and a burger on the side.

## KHORESCHE ESFANAJ

This Iranian recipe highlights two classic ingredients of the region: lamb and spinach.

1/2 cup olive oil
4 pounds lamb shoulder, with bones, cut into stew meat
2 medium yellow onions, chopped finely
1 teaspoon powdered turmeric
1 teaspoon black pepper
1 cup beef stock
1 cup lemon juice
2 pounds spinach leaves, chopped
2 shallots, chopped finely
1/2 cup dried pea beans or black-eyed peas, soaked in cold water overnight
2 tablespoons dill

In a deep casserole, heat two tablespoons of olive oil. Brown the meat and yellow onions, add turmeric and pepper, then pour in beef stock and lemon juice. Cover and simmer on low heat for thirty minutes. In a seasoned cast-iron skillet, cook the spinach and shallots over a low flame without oil. The vegetables should be slightly wilted after about five minutes. Add the remaining oil to the skillet then and sauté the spinach and shallots for another five minutes.

Combine all these ingredients in the casserole and add the beans and dill. Simmer gently for an hour or so until the beans are cooked through. Serve over basmati rice.

## INSALATA DI SPINACI ALLA SICILIANA

This classic salad, many of whose ingredients the island's Arab conquerors introduced into Sicily in the early Middle Ages, makes for a refreshing lunch or supper accompaniment on a summer day.

1 pound baby spinach leaves
1 large yellow grapefruit
1/4 cup wine vinegar
3/4 cup olive oil
1/4 cup black currants or raisins
1/4 cup pine nuts, lightly toasted
sea salt and freshly ground black pepper
    If the spinach is loose, wash and dry it, then place it in a large salad bowl. Chop the grapefruit into bite-sized pieces, pouring any juice into a small bowl. Into this bowl add the oil and vinegar and whip it with a metal whisk. Let the currants or raisins marinate in this mixture for a few minutes. Add the pine nuts to the spinach and toss with the dressing.

## SPINACH DUMPLINGS

Spinach has an agreeably bittersweet flavor that lends itself to use in Chinese dumplings, particularly with a slightly salty accompaniment such as soy sauce or oyster sauce.

1 tablespoon peanut oil
1 tablespoon fresh ginger, peeled and grated
3 cloves crushed garlic, finely chopped
2/3 pound baby spinach, chopped fine
1/2 teaspoon sea salt
20 wonton wrappers
    Heat oil in a wok or deep frying pan over medium heat. Add ginger and garlic and sauté until the garlic begins to brown, a minute or so. Add the spinach and sauté for three or four minutes. Remove from heat and crumble salt over the mixture. Let the mixture cool for an hour. Place wonton wrappers on a dry, clean cutting board and cover them with a damp kitchen towel to keep them from hardening. Take a wonton wrapper and place two teaspoons of the mixture in the center. Using the tip of your index finger, brush the edges of the wrapper with cold water. Twist the edges to seal the wonton, then return it beneath the towel. Fill the remaining wrappers. Then line a bamboo steamer of sufficient size to hold the wrappers with parchment paper. Pour half a cup of water into the wok and suspend the

bamboo steamer above it. Cover and steam for ten minutes, adding water as needed.

## FURTHER READING

Najmieh Batmanglij, *Food of Life: A Book of Ancient Persian and Modern Iranian Cooking and Ceremonies* (Mage, 1990).

Linda Diane Feldt, *Spinach and Beyond: Loving Life and Dark Green Leafy Vegetables* (Moon Field Press, 2003).

Richard Fleischer, *Out of the Inkwell: Max Fleischer and the Animation Revolution* (University Press of Kentucky, 2005).

Fred M. Grandinetti, *Popeye: An Illustrated Cultural History* (McFarland and Co., 2004).

Anna Tasca Lanza, *The Heart of Sicily* (Clarkson Potter, 1993).

# TOMATO

When Europeans first encountered *Lycopersicon esculentum* ("edible wolf-peach," in the scientific neo-Latin), they viewed it with considerable suspicion. For one thing, it was a strange-looking, strange-tasting fruit, bitter and fleshy, one unlike any they had ever seen. For another, the Aztecs who grew it and who gave it the name *jitomatl* were savages in the conquerors' eyes, and anything they favored was likely to be tinged with deviltry.

Spanish eyebrows must have lifted, too, when the newcomers learned of the Aztec belief that the use of tomatoes increased male sexual prowess. The Aztec word, which may have been a borrowing from the Maya, comes from the verb *tomahu,* "to swell." Perhaps some dark magic did indeed lie hidden in the odd fruit, for it became the object of priestly denunciations and, I suspect, not a few secret taste-tests.

The Maya figure because they were intermediaries in the pre-Columbian exchange of the plant from its original homeland in the foothills of the Colombian Andes to points farther north. (The Columbian exchange, a term perhaps more wishful than accurate, refers to the whole New World meets Old World phenomenon; one side got corn, beans, potatoes, and so forth, the other smallpox.) As with other plants of the nightshade family, which includes tobacco and potatoes, the tomato was once borderline poisonous, but some enterprising farmer had sufficient foresight—and perhaps a supply of guinea pigs—to see that, like the potato, this potentially deadly thing had possibilities.

Exotic and potentially erotic, the tomato soon became a staple of the Mediterranean diet, and it spread around the world, entering Persian and Turkish cooking by the early sixteenth century and soon thereafter figuring in Chinese cuisine, in which it was called *fan qié,* literally "barbarian eggplant." (It is indeed related to eggplant, another member of the Solanaceae family.) It was slower to catch on in northern Europe, both because the short growing season did not favor the sun-loving plant and because prim northerners thought that its consumption led to licentiousness and debauchery, qualities they ascribed to their southern neighbors. An Elizabethan traveler reported to his English contemporaries, "In Spaine and those hot regions they use to eat these Apples prepared and boiled with pepper, salt, and oyle; but

"Poma amoris fructa luteo," an engraving of 1613 depicting tomatoes and watermelons by Basil Besler, from *Hortus Eystettensis.*

they yeeld very little nourishment to the body, and the same naught and corrupt." He added, "Likewise, they doe eate the Apples with oile, vinegre and pepper mixed together for sauce to their meat, even as we in these cold countries doe Mustard."

The tomato was similarly slow to catch on in the United States. Thomas Jefferson, brilliant in matters of agriculture as of politics, grew several varieties in his vast gardens at Monticello, and his son-in-law Thomas Randolph recorded the spread of the fruit into the Virginia countryside, farm by farm, in the 1820s. At about that time, a Massachusetts farmer and jurist attempted to dispel his neighbors' lingering suspicions about the tomato, publishing opinion pieces in local newspapers to advocate wider use of the plant; a probably apocryphal story has it that he also ate a basket-ful of them on the steps of the Salem courthouse, and that when he sur-vived a few hardy souls in the neighborhood also took up the tomato habit. Still, little happened until mid-nineteenth-century progressives like Ralph Waldo Emerson, Nathaniel Hawthorne, and Louisa May Alcott (who writes fondly in *Little Women* of the wondrous, sun-ripened toma-toes of her girlhood) championed its use as something other than a door-yard ornamental.

By the turn of the century, the United States Supreme Court had ruled that although the tomato is botanically a fruit—actually, a berry—by federal law it would henceforth be classified as a vegetable. The decision itself bore more on matters of taxation than botany; in those days duties were imposed on vegetables brought in from other states or nations, but fruits passed through duty-free, and there was money to be made in toma-toes. The first of the popular Fanny Farmer cookbooks, published in 1897, included several recipes for the tomato, suggesting that it had been more or less domesticated and accepted in American dooryards and kitch-ens, but even so it was not until World War I, when the government encouraged city-dwellers and rural residents alike to introduce more fruits and vegetables into their diet as a substitute for meat, that *Lycopersicon esculentum* became a common item on American tables.

Today, in terms of sheer volume, the tomato ranks at the head of the fruits and vegetables in the American diet. Low in fats and sodium and high in potassium, and a whole tomato yields about 23 calories, making it an obvious favorite of weight watchers. It used to be that the insipid beefsteak tomato was about the only kind that an American consumer of whatever bent could find in the market, but today dozens of varieties are in circulation—still only a small sampling of the four thousand varieties known to herbarium collectors, but a great improvement over the oppres-sive monoculture of only a generation ago.

The tomato is also rich in fat-soluble carotenoids, some of which the body converts to vitamin A. Those carotenoids, scientists are learning, are of critical importance to our well-being; in fact, one class, lycopenes, is among the best inhibitors of cancer yet discovered; as an antioxidant, lycopene is reckoned to capture twice as many oxygen ions in the body as is beta-carotene. It seems strangely appropriate, too, that a fruit once renowned for its supposed aphrodisiacal powers should help ward off cancer of the prostate. One recent long-range study by Harvard Medical School shows that the incidence of several kinds of digestive-system can-cers is lower in people who eat tomatoes at least once a week; another, by scientists at Johns Hopkins, indicates that the risk of lung cancer is sig-nificantly lower in those who eat tomatoes at least four times a week than in those people who shun them altogether or eat them only occasionally. There is a wrinkle in all of this: cooked tomato sauces seem to be more effective than raw tomatoes, perhaps because cooking dissolves a tomato's cell walls, releasing more lycopene. Transgenic, or genetically modified, tomatoes have been developed that contain nearly three times more lycopene than unmodified varieties, medicine in a very tasty package indeed; other new varieties are not only exceptionally healthful, but also cold tolerant, meaning that the lycopenes may soon enhance the lives of people who live far away from sources of the things.

Tomatoes are a versatile fruit, and there are abundant ways to prepare them. Where I live, in the Southwest, they turn up in the spicy salsas frescas served in Mexican restaurants, and I can think of no better tonic. No matter where you live, you can bring some of the region's flavor to your table by mixing four fresh Roma or plum tomatoes, two roasted japaleño or Anaheim peppers, one cucumber, a sprig of cilantro, and a scallion or two, all finely chopped, with a splash of lemon or lime juice and a dash of cumin.

For a similarly uncomplicated but sublimely pleasant meal, try this quick tomato sauce for pasta: finely chop six Roma or plum tomatoes, one yellow onion, and four cloves of garlic. Saute the onions and garlic in a tablespoon of olive oil just until the garlic begins to crisp; then add the tomatoes, half a cup of red wine or water, and a grated carrot. Add a pinch each of oregano, basil, and pepper; cover and cook on low heat for half an hour, stirring occasionally. For a little more effort—and I find this an oddly satisfying form of relaxation—you can mill the tomatoes in a press, which yields a fine, smooth sauce and removes the seeds, which pack extra acidity and can cause heartburn. I bought my tomato press in Rome a few years ago, but several makes turn up in the cookware catalogs.

You can also go low input, of course, and just carve yourself one of those "heavy slabs of ripe tomatoes" that Thomas Wolfe celebrated so justly in *Look Homeward, Angel*. However you introduce them into your diet, tomatoes will amply reward your devotion, and never mind Jean-Paul Sartre's suspicions about them. Reminded by his partner and sometime collaborator Simone de Beauvoir that vegetables have no consciousness, he agreed, saying, "In all likelihood vegetables have none." He added, weightily, "The cooking of a vegetable is the transformation of a given object without consciousness into another object equally devoid of consciousness. And it is the taking over of the thing by the human world. If it is cooked, a vegetable stops being a vegetable and becomes a thick soup or a cooked salad. Rawness sets it farther apart from us."

Sartre, of course, hated tomatoes, though for reasons that seem independent of the thing itself. A good leftist, he might have considered the tomato's role as a political weapon in the Tomatina, a tomato-throwing festival held each year in Buñol, Spain, where it seems to have been invented as a subtle form of protest against Francisco Franco's fascist government. Even so, Sartre may have been happier about tomatoes if they had been classified as fruit and more widely perceived to be so long ago. So, too, might other diners who still find the tomato to be somehow suspect.

And do the censors need to worry about tomato-induced priapism? Probably not, for the "love apple" trope, it turns out, is based on a misconception: the French *pomme d'amour* is a misapprehension of the Spanish *pomo de moro*, or "Moorish apple," the Arabic world being the source of all things mysterious even when the caravels of Cadiz were known to have been the more immediate point of origin of the golden fruit (which the Italians, also mishearing the phrase, called *pomodoro*). So, as to the aphrodisiacal powers of tomatoes, the jury must remain out. In the meanwhile, I suggest that you do some field-testing of your own—the cooking, I mean, and the other bits as well.

## GAZPACHO

Gazpacho, a cold soup of vegetables and bread, predates the arrival of the tomato to Spain; its name is thought to derive from the Latin word *caspa*, meaning "fragments," or possibly from the Hebrew word *gazaz*, meaning "broken bread." This is a more or less classic version of the dish, a reliably cooling dish for a summer repast.

1 pound Roma or plum tomatoes
1/2 pound green pepper, seeded and chopped fine
1 large cucumber
clove of garlic
5 cilantro leaves
1 tablespoon red chili powder
1 cup yellow onion
1 tablespoon balsamic vinegar
2 tablespoons olive oil
salt and pepper to taste

Remove skin from tomatoes and quarter them. Cut the other vegetables into small pieces, then blend in a blender set on coarse so that the vegetables have separate identity and texture. Add dry ingredients and oil, then chill in refrigerator. Serve cold with crostini (slices of bread fried in olive oil and garlic), broken into small pieces

## GREEN TOMATO PRESERVES

The *Daily American*, Nashville's newspaper of record, offered the following recipe to its readers on November 16, 1883:

Green tomato preserves are in high favor in certain localities, and are entirely unknown in others. Here is a reliable recipe for making them: Take one peck of hard and unripe tomatoes, scald them by pouring boiling water over them, remove the skin and cut them into thin slices; slice also 6 lemons, the skin of the lemon is to be left upon them, but the bitter seeds must be removed; scatter six pounds of brown sugar over the tomatoes and one heaping tablespoonful of ginger; put into a large kettle and let them boil slowly until they are tender; skim them thoroughly; can just as you do any other preserves.

It is just the sort of thing to eat while reading Fannie Flagg's entertaining novel *Fried Green Tomatoes,* a celebration of the essential weirdness of all things Southern.

## FURTHER READING

Andrew F. Smith, *The Tomato in America: Early History, Culture, and Cookery* (University of Illinois Press, 2001).

U.S. Department of Agriculture, "Transgenics for a Better Tomato," www.ars.usda.gov/is/AR/archive/sep00.

Ruben L. Villareal, *Tomatoes in the Tropics* (Westview Press, 1980).

P. Xu et al., "Expression of Antiapoptotic Genes bcl-xL and ced-9 in Tomato Enhances Tolerance to Viral-Induced Necrosis and Abiotic Stress," *Proceedings of the National Academy of Sciences* 101 (November 2, 2004): 15,805–15,810.

# WATERMELON

---

The watermelon (*Citrullus lanatus*) is a well-traveled cucurbit, or gourd, with roots, so to speak, deep in antiquity. Its origins lie in the stabilized sand dune country of the Kalahari Desert of southern Africa, a dry place that is not often forthcoming with abundant food, as this Bushmen story suggests.

When the Bushmen are hungry, they ask the stars to take their hearts and give them their own. For a star is not small. It is large, as if it has just eaten. Therefore, they say, if the stars give them their hearts, the Bushmen will not go hungry.

The stars call out, "Tsau! Tsau!" The Bushmen say that the stars are cursing the springboks' eyes on the Bushmen's behalf. The stars say "Tsau! Tsau!" Summer is the time when they sound.

I would sit with my grandfather in the coolness outside, and he told me that the stars would curse the springboks' eyes for me.

My grandfather used to speak to Canopus, when Canopus had just come out. He said, "Give me your heart, for you sit in plenty. Give me your heart, and take mine, with which I am so desperately hungry. That way I might also be full, like you. I hunger, while you have so much food, for you are not small. Take my stomach and give me yours, so that you will know what it is like to be hungry. Give me your arm and take mine, for mine does not kill. I miss my aim." Then he would shut his mouth and sit down, sharpening his arrows.

For all their hunger, the Bushmen and other peoples of subtropical Africa were at least able to rely on a vine that clung to the ghost trees and hummocks and pointed the way to water twofold—first, because water is likely to be found in proximity to a watermelon patch, and second, because the gourds themselves are full of water, making up more than 90 percent of their weight. Importantly, they also provide vitamins K and C and beta-carotene, the precursor of vitamin A, all of which are in short enough supply in desert climes. The desert people valued the cucurbits accordingly, making several uses of them—not only eating the

*Still Life with Watermelon and Peaches,* a painting of 1828 by Margaretta Angelica Peale (1795–1882), a daughter of the American artist James Peale and niece of the great botanical illustrator Charles Willson Peale. Her own work has recently been rediscovered.

pulpy, water-rich flesh, but also making flour of the seeds and cooking the tendrils and leaves as greens.

When the African explorer David Livingstone first recorded wild watermelons in the Kalahari in 1850, he did not immediately link them to the icebox varieties that are commercially available today, for the *tsamma,* as the Bushmen called the wild melons, could be on the bitterish side; sweet and bitter melons were indistinguishable except by taste, and, Livingston observed, finding a sweet one was a matter of trial and error. So it was with the varieties that spread northward from the Kalahari, leading to a substantial watermelon agriculture along the Nile Valley by 3000 B.C.E. From there, watermelon cultivation spread to Greece and Rome, as well as other parts of the Middle East, though always at a modest level. Strangely, though the plant was known in India and China early on, *Citrullus lanatus* would not be grown widely in either place until about 800 C.E. and 1000 C.E., respectively. North African Arabs, Berbers, and Moors were fond of the melon, but it took a long while to make inroads into Europe; introduced in Spain during the period of the Moorish *conquista,* it began to turn up in private gardens in the Mediterranean region, where a hot, dry climate favored both the plant and its consumption.

The Iberians may not have remembered the watermelon's African origins when they introduced it into the New World at about the same time as the slave trade, but it spread quickly through the Americas once it made land. Indeed, Spanish and French explorers were astonished to find that watermelons preceded them up and down the Mississippi River valley, where it found a welcome reception among native peoples. English colonists brought watermelon to the Massachusetts Bay Colony in 1628, and soon thereafter it was being grown in Indian communities in Virginia and Florida. Francisco Garcés (1738–1781), a Spanish missionary, introduced black-eyed peas, watermelons, and muskmelons to the Indian peoples of the lower Colorado River valley, and it proved so popular that native traders spread seeds along the Pacific coast. (To conserve seeds yourself, put them in a strainer, wash them with a small amount of dishwashing soap to remove the sugar, dry them, and preserve them in a jar.) From the Pacific, early in the nineteenth century, it reached Hawaii, as Washington Irving reports in *Astoria:*

> On the evening of the 12th of February, the *Tonquin* anchored in the bay of Karakakooa, in the island of Owyhee. The surrounding shores were wild and broken, with overhanging cliffs and precipices of black volcanic rock. Beyond these, however, the country was fertile and well cultivated, with inclosures of yams, plantains, sweet potatoes, sugar-canes, and other productions of warm climates and teeming soils; and the numerous habitations of the natives were pleasantly sheltered beneath clumps of cocoanut and bread-fruit trees, which afforded both food and shade. This mingled variety of garden and grove swept gradually up the sides of the mountains, until succeeded by dense forests, which in turn gave place to naked and craggy rocks, until the summits rose into the regions of perpetual snow....
>
> On the morning after her arrival, the ship was surrounded by canoes and pirogues, filled with the islanders of both sexes, bringing off supplies of fruits and vegetables, bananas, plantains, watermelons, yams, cabbages and taro. The captain was desirous, however, of purchasing a number of hogs, but there were none to be had. The trade in pork was a royal monopoly, and no subject of the great Tamaahmaah dared to meddle with it. Such provisions as they could furnish, however, were brought by the natives in abundance, and a lively intercourse was kept up during the day, in which the women mingled in the kindest manner.

And, of course, watermelon became closely identified with the American South, where it was planted in rows along other kinds of crops to refresh slaves in the field. In the early days of the republic, northern newspapers caricatured all southerners as being inordinately addicted to watermelon; only after the Civil War did the idiotic view spread that watermelon sends black people into weird and uncontrollable raptures, but ever since, as Spike Lee so memorably recorded in his film *Bamboozled* (2000), the unfortunate watermelon has become part of a racist vernacular. It should make no one feel any better about the matter to know that watermelon is a favorite treat among desert peoples of Central Asia, a place that ethnic Russians have historically regarded as a savage backwater; some Russians employ *Citrullus lanatus* as an ethnic slur in much the same manner as their ignorant American counterparts do. Even so, it is worth remarking that Russians import watermelons by the trainload from the former Soviet republics of Central Asia, and a common joke is that Aeroflot planes wanting to lift off from Almaty and Tashkent have to order Russian tourists to discard thousands of watermelons from their suitcases before the planes are capable of taking flight.

Naturally, while we are on the subject of ethnic stereotypes, the Russians long ago figured out how to make a kind of beer of watermelons.

Prized though they are by right-thinking people around the world, watermelons were not commercially available in many parts of the United States until the widespread adoption of home refrigeration in the 1930s and '40s; unless kept cold, watermelons, like other melons, tend to spoil rather quickly. At about that time, a government horticulturalist named Charles Andrus developed a hybrid watermelon, the so-called Charleston Gray, that resisted disease and wilting and kept well. It was also, strangely enough, oblong, unlike the round watermelons of old, which made it easy to stack in trucks and railcars without incurring bruising and cracking. That innovation, together with refrigeration, promoted watermelon to a hot-weather favorite nationally, and even brought it popularity in formerly watermelon-bereft parts of the world such as Scandinavia. With the introduction of seedless varieties in recent years, a product of crossing a female tetraploid plant with diploid pollen to make a sterile triploid plant, the watermelon has even emerged as something of a boutique food.

Watermelon contains more of the health-promoting compound lycopene per serving than any other fresh fruit or vegetable, including the tomato; since lycopene is believed to be a powerful antioxidant of benefit in preventing cancer and some age-related diseases, there is a built-in reason to eat watermelon apart from general deliciousness. Whereas in the United States watermelon is usually eaten cold, as a dessert or treat, it sees more inventive uses elsewhere.

In China, for instance, a mixture of powdered watermelon rind and seed is used to treat cold sores and scratches, while the rind is used as a vegetable, stir-fried and pickled. The seeds are a popular snack food, sold roasted and salted, while the oil is used for cooking. So popular is watermelon in China, in fact, that the Chinese Nationalist leader Chiang Kai-shek once demanded that the American general Joseph "Vinegar Joe" Stilwell provide one watermelon for every four Chinese soldiers stationed in Burma before they would deign to fight. And so popular is it that China now produces as much watermelon as does the rest of the world combined, followed by Turkey, Iran, Egypt, the United States, and Israel.

I am very glad to report that a watermelon patch will not, in fact, grow in your stomach if you swallow the seeds, as my grandmother warned would happen. But watermelon is relatively easy to grow, even if it is frost-tender and requires a long growing season. If you are starting from scratch, it helps to have honeybees around for pollinating; otherwise, a carefully tended seed will do. Give the plants good drinks of water from time to time, and they will likely produce. You will know when a watermelon is ripe by its sound; if it is not, it will make a bell-like sound on being thumped, whereas if it is, the sound will be muffled. I leave it to the master, Mark Twain, to sing the praises of a watermelon perfectly picked, chilled, and served:

> I know how a prize watermelon looks when it is sunning its fat rotundity among pumpkin vines and "simblins"; I know how to tell when it is ripe without "plugging" it; I know how inviting it looks when it is cooling itself in a tub of water under the bed, waiting; I know how it looks when it lies on the table in the sheltered great floor space between house and kitchen, and the children gathered for the sacrifice and their mouths watering; I know the crackling sound it makes when the carving knife enters its end, and I can see the split fly along the front of the blade as the knife cleaves its way to the other end; I can see its halves fall apart and display the rich red meat and the black seeds, and the heart standing up, a luxury fit for the elect; I know how a boy looks behind a yard-long slice of that melon, and I know how he feels; for I have been there. I know the taste of the watermelon which has been honestly come by, and I know the taste of the watermelon which has been acquired by art. Both taste good, but the experienced know which tastes best.

To which I can add only a hearty amen, and my thanks to a well-traveled friend.

## SWEET WATERMELON RIND PICKLE

Abby Fisher, a former slave from Mobile, Alabama, found work as a cook in several San Francisco households following the Civil War. The ladies of the city prized her skills, for they bid and outbid one another to hire her. Fisher also regularly won awards at cooking competitions and fairs. Though she could not read or write, she knew her recipes, and in 1881 some enterprising writer recorded them verbatim in the form of the book *What Mrs. Fisher Knows About Old Southern Cooking*, published in San Francisco in 1881.

> Take the melon rind and scrape all the meat from the inside, and then carefully slice all the outside of the rind from the white part of the rind, then lay or cover the white part over with salt. It will have to remain under salt one week before pickling; the rind will keep in salt from year to year. When you want to pickle it, take it from the salt and put into clear water, change the water three times a day—must be changed say every four hours—then

take the rind from the water and dry it with a clean cloth. Have your vinegar boiling, and put the rind into it and let it lay in vinegar four days; then take it from the vinegar, drain, and sprinkle sugar thickly over it and let it remain so one day. To make syrup, take the syrup from the rind and add eight pounds more sugar to it, and put to boil; boil till a thick and clear syrup. Weigh ten pounds of rind to 12 pounds of sugar; cover the rind with four pounds of it and make the syrup with the remaining eight pounds. While the syrup is cooking add one teacupful of white ginger root and the peel of three lemons. When the syrup is cooked, then put the rind into the boiling syrup, and let it cook till you can pass a fork through it with ease, then it is done. When cooled, put in jar or bottles with one pint of vinegar to one quart of syrup, thus the pickles are made. See that they be well covered with vinegar and syrup as directed.

## WATERMELON-TOMATO SALAD

This old Southern favorite has many variations, and it makes a fine weapon with which to fight a hot afternoon.

Enough watermelon to make 3 cups, diced
2 large tomatoes (typically beefsteak), diced
1 small red onion, sliced
Combine ingredients. An old-time dressing would consist of salt and pepper, and perhaps a little buttermilk, but in a modern kitchen we can gussy this simple pleasure up with a little olive oil, fresh basil, and balsamic vinegar.

## FURTHER READING

Wilhelm Bleek and Lucy C. Lloyd, *The Girl Who Made Stars and Other Bushmen Stories,* edited by Gregory McNamee (Daimon Verlag, 2001).

Abby Fisher, *What Mrs. Fisher Knows About Old Southern Cooking* (Women's Cooperative Printing Office, 1881).

Washington Irving, *Astoria, or, Anecdotes of an Enterprise Beyond the Rocky Mountains* (Carey, Lea, and Blanchard, 1836).

H. B. Paksoy, "Identity of Candied Watermelon," lecture delivered at Central European University, Budapest.

Jonathan D. Sauer, *Historical Geography of Crop Plants* (CRC Press, 1993).

Mark Twain, *The Autobiography of Mark Twain* (Harper & Row, 1959).

Donovan Webster, *The Burma Road: The Epic Story of the China-Burma-India Theater in World War II* (Farrar, Straus & Giroux, 2003).

# WHEAT

---

Ten thousand-odd years ago, in the horseshoe-shaped highlands of what are now Iraq, Turkey, Syria, and Israel, Stone Age hunter-gatherers made a fateful discovery: a grass that grew on the mountain slopes grew particularly large seeds that, with some work, could be removed and eaten. What was more, this grass, called einkorn, a variety of wild wheat, yielded easily to cutting with flint blades. Forty years ago, archaeologist Jack Harlan determined that, working with a flint sickle, he alone was capable of harvesting more than two pounds of clean grain every hour, and of a much higher concentration of proteins than the winter wheat grown on the plains of North America now produce.

The work would have required no permanent settlements; a Neolithic family resident in that so-called Fertile Crescent could have traveled into the mountains seasonally and, in the space of weeks, gathered enough einkorn grain to feed themselves for a year and even enjoy some surplus. Thus began the seeds of capitalism. Permanent settlements followed nonetheless, and, beginning in about 7500 B.C.E., the hill country began to sprout sturdy little towns such as Jericho, Beidha, Çatal Hüyük, and Tell Hassuna. Thus the seeds of Western civilization—which may have resulted, geographer Jonathan Sauer speculated in the 1950s, not from the production of bread as a foodstuff per se but of beer. Sauer's guess is helped along by the fact that the oldest known recipe in the world is for beer, found on a 3,800-year-old clay tablet as part of a hymn to Ninkasi, who happened to be the Sumerian goddess of brewing. Sumer and its descendant civilizations were indeed built on beer, so to speak; beer played a central part in ritual, myth, and medicine, and it was a staple of every class of Mesopotamian society. So important was it that the legal code attributed to King Hammurabi, enacted in about 1720 B.C.E., specifies that anyone proved to have overcharged for beer could be put to death by drowning.

Whatever the case, within a few generations of settling down into towns, these now-committed farming people made further discoveries, among them the fact that einkorn (*Triticum boeoticum*) and emmer (*Triticum dicoccoides*) could be modified and improved to reduce the curious habit of these grains' spikes to shatter as soon as they were ripe, which allowed the wild grains to seed themselves more readily. By gaining at least some measure of control over this shattering, the farmers could transport cultivable grains beyond the mountains, and soon wheat was everywhere in the ancient world. The banks of the Nile were thick

Kurt Stüber, "Triticum vulgaris," from Otto Wilhelm Thomé, *Flora von Deutschland, Österreich und die Schweiz* (1885).

with wheat fields. So, too, were the Mediterranean shores of North Africa and southern Europe, making a breadbasket for the rising empires of the Middle East. So, too, was the Indus Valley, even though the warrior lords who ruled the region dismissed it as "food of the barbarians." And so, too, were peninsular Italy and Sicily, long before the rise of Rome; the great Roman historian and scientist Pliny tells us in his *Natural History* that "emmer was the first food of the ancient inhabitants of Latium...[and] emmer porridge was the staple of the Romans for a long period."

Through all this, the farmers continued to experiment, for, as Charles Darwin remarked, "Wheat quickly assumes new habits of life." Those farmers eventually developed what we now call bread wheat, a variety of *Triticum* that did not require a Mediterranean climate of warm summers and mild winters, but instead thrived in cold lands whose summers were overcast and rainy. In time the Pontic steppes of Eurasia sprouted oceans of wheat; *Triticum* varieties had reached as far north as Denmark even in Neolithic times, but gave way there to rye, just as the ancient farmers of what is now France seem to have preferred spelt.

Those holdouts notwithstanding, farmers throughout the Old World adopted the familiar routine of harvesting, threshing, winnowing, thrashing, and grinding, adopted foods such as porridge, bread, and—most important of all in many an ancient civilization—beer. Governments used wheat as a currency; King Solomon himself sent twenty thousand measures of wheat in annual tribute to the Phoenicians, who dominated the ancient eastern Mediterranean. Religions reflected the widespread importance of wheat production, with dying-and-reborning gods and goddesses such as Osiris, Astarte, Demeter, Dagon, and Ceres standing near the head of ancient pantheons.

At the head of my own pantheon of wheat-based foods—and I am far from alone in this prejudice—is pasta, which has been a culinary staple for so long that it is tempting to think those wonderful soft noodles must have grown alongside the apple tree in the Garden of Eden. Pasta is somewhat less ancient than all that, but it enjoys a distinguished history that stretches far back into the ages.

The Chinese have been making noodles for at least four thousand years, and to them goes credit for the discovery that wheat flour and water can make more than homemade glue. (Boil a wheat pasta for too long, though, and that is just what you will get.) Today, most Chinese restaurants sport a variety of *chow mein* and *lo mein* dishes—meaning, respectively, "hard noodles" and "soft noodles"—while the noodle shop is a neighborhood gathering place throughout Asia, as celebrated in Juzo Itami's majestic 1985 film *Tampopo.*

Legend has it that Marco Polo, the great Venetian adventurer, introduced the Chinese staple dish to Italy upon returning from his travels in the Far East early in the fourteenth century. It is a fine story, but, as with so much received wisdom from history, it is not quite true, and in all events Marco Polo was famed—or, better, defamed—in his day with the nickname *il milione,* referring not to a million adventures or miles crossed but myriad fibs told. In fact, southern Italians had been thriving on pasta dishes for several centuries, courtesy of the Arab conquerors who ruled the lower peninsula in Polo's time and before. The Arabs, in turn, had borrowed noodles from the Chinese, one of the many goods that traveled the long trade routes between their worlds.

Marco Polo aside, pasta became the single most important element of the Italian diet over the centuries, and today dozens of varieties are made there, differing from one region to the next. Their names are affectionate culinary poems: some of the better-known ones are vermicelli (little worms), penne (feathers), spaghetti (little twigs), and linguine (little tongues). The best pasta still comes from Italy, where purist food laws prohibit the addition of soft wheat (farina) to hard wheat (durum), ensuring a flavorful and chewy product. In recent years, though, as many Italian pasta makers are naturally reluctant to admit, much of the highest-quality wheat is imported from Australia as farmlands in fertile Italy get turned into housing developments and shopping centers.

Macaroni dishes have been part of the American diet for more than four hundred years, imported as part of basic British cuisine. British travelers to Italy had long since brought back the recipe for that old stalwart, macaroni and cheese, which in time came to be associated not with world-traveling sophisticates but instead with the daily food of the lower classes. The British song "Yankee Doodle"—"doodle" being a Cockney rhyming synonym for "noodle"—was thus meant to be an insult to Americans, who, it was presumed, could afford nothing fancier; their lords in London ate finer things than wheat noodles, and their own prejudices were widespread. The taunt backfired, though, when early patriots gladly adopted the song as a marching tune, content enough with their simple diet of baked macaroni and "hasty pudding," itself a concoction of wheat flour and tapioca in the British Isles but, in America, often a kind of corn porridge.

With the arrival of five million Italian immigrants in the last decades of the nineteenth century, Americans began to enjoy a wider variety of pasta dishes than simple macaroni and cheese. Americans, in fact, have made spaghetti an everyday, stand-alone meal, a departure from the Italian custom of putting just the barest amount of sauce on pasta, the opening plate in a multicourse meal. Sadly, as modern Italians get busier, integrated into the buzz and strife of the world economy, those meals are becoming ever more hurried, whence the arrival in Italy of some of the world's biggest consumers of wheat—namely, American fast-food restaurants.

Today macaroni accounts for a sizable portion of our diet. Per capita consumption of noodles in the United States now stands at just over eleven pounds a year. This is barely 15 percent of the Italian average, so Yankee Doodles have a lot of catching up to do, but Americans increasingly partake of another wheat-rich diet, namely that of Mexico and, more specifically, northern Mexico, where growing conditions are just right for Mediterranean-style wheat, chiles, and beef, the classic makings of a burrito.

Not all people are fond of wheat, of course, and those who suffer from celiac disease, which impedes the absorption of the protein gluten, have the unenviable task of having to filter through hundreds of processed foods that contain wheat in one form or another, from canned soups to hot dogs and even to ice cream. For those people, the Mayo Clinic recommends substituting one of the following for a cup of wheat flour:

    3/4 cup plain cornmeal, coarse
    1 cup plain cornmeal, fine
    5/8 cup potato flour
    3/4 cup rice flour

Those who can and do eat wheat flour, wheat bran, wheat germ, and kindred foods know well that nothing else quite has wheat's laxative, innard-scrubbing power, the application of which has been proven to be of critical importance in battling cancers of the digestive tract.

This leads to the greatest health food of them all, the pizza, that perfect marriage of wheat flour, cheese, lycopene-rich tomatoes, and such meats and vegetables as one wishes to add, with due respect and moderation, of course. One of the best pizzas I have ever eaten, in Guadalajara, Mexico, made judicious use of ham and pineapples, an unlikely but perfectly delicious combination. The single best one, at an outdoor restaurant in Fiesole, Italy, was nothing more than a brushload's smearing of tomato sauce and olive oil atop a thin disk of wheat flour, topped with a sprinkling of buffalo mozzarella, fresh basil, and mushrooms freshly picked in the nearby forest. That thin bread is key, for although some standard Italian dictionaries protest that the origin of the word is unknown, speakers of the Calabrian dialect, which is full of Greek words, know better: pizza is a southern Italian pronunciation of *pita,* the Greek flatbread that is itself becoming well known to American consumers.

Absent the tomato, that treat could have been very much like the one given to the famished Aeneas and his party of fugitive Trojans on their arrival to Italy. Aeneas had said that he was so hungry that he would eat the *mensa,* the table itself. Amazingly enough, the locals distributed disks of flatbread that they called *mensae,* which doubled as tables and plates; two diners shared a loaf, thereby giving rise to the biological term *commensalism,* using it as a platform on which to pile roasted meats, vegetables, cheese, and other treats. The *mensa* itself, now soaked in the juices of these foods, was saved for last: pizza for dessert, a health food and brain food, perhaps the perfect food above all others, period.

## GAZELLE STEW AND BABYLONIAN BREAD

The earliest known cookbook is about thirty-five centuries old. The best preserved page—actually a thin clay tablet bound to other tablets with leather thongs—contains Babylonian recipes for such artery-clogging delights as gazelle stew, with the entire animal soaked in various oils and fats, and served with a gravy of beer and wheat flour. Modern cooks should take note that for best results, the gazelle's head, tail, and legs should be singed before stewing.

If gazelle is not available at your local market, goat will do. Giraffe will work in a pinch, too. You may just want to bake a loaf of bread à la Babylon, following this recipe, based on one reconstructed from Akkadian sources by scholars at the University of Chicago's Oriental Institute Museum. An ancient would have eaten this bread with a raw onion, but a slice of apple or cheese does nicely, too.

14 ounces wheat flour
1 cup water
1/2 teaspoon salt
    Mix the water, flour, and salt together slowly. Then knead the dough and form it into flat round patties. Cover the dough with a cloth and let it sit overnight. The next day, bake it in an oven at 350°F for thirty minutes.

## ANGRY FEATHERS

A favorite comfort food of central Italy, *penne all'arrabiata* makes a perfect bone-warming meal for a cold day.

Cook one large minced onion and three cloves of garlic in two tablespoons of olive oil until the mixture is a deep golden color. Add two tbsp crushed red pepper flakes and two sixteen-ounce cans of tomatoes or two pounds fresh tomatoes. If the tomatoes are canned, add one small grated carrot to remove the acidic taste. Cook over low heat for two hours. Boil sixteen ounces of penne (macaroni cut on the diagonal) until cooked al dente, firm to the bite. Cover noodles with sauce and grated parmesan or Romano cheese.

## MACARONI AND CHEESE

The American classic—a northern European invention of unknown but deep antiquity—remains at the top of many modern people's list of comfort foods, too. Call it a cold-climate rejoinder to *penne all'arrabiata.*

Boil sixteen ounces of small elbow noodles for eight minutes or until done. Drain in colander. Place noodles in buttered, ovenproof casserole dish with lid. In a saucepan, melt two cups grated mild cheddar cheese in one cup milk or light cream. Add a dash each of ground black pepper and dry mustard, and pour mixture over noodles. Sprinkle the top with dry bread crumbs and a quarter cup of grated cheddar. Cover and bake at 350° for 45 minutes.

# FURTHER READING

Alain P. Bonjean and William J. Angus, eds., *The World Wheat Book: A History of Wheat Breeding* (Lavoisier, 2001).

Samuel Copland, *Wheat: Its History, Characteristics, Chemical Composition and Nutritive Properties* (Houlston and Wright, 1937).

Peter T. Dondlinger, *The Book of Wheat: An Economic History and Practical Manual of the Wheat Industry* (Scholarly Resources, 1973).

Bette Hagman, *Everyday Gluten Free Cooking: Living Well Without Wheat* (Blake Books, 2002).

Jonathan Norton Leonard, *The First Farmers* (Time-Life Books, 1973).

M. M. Postan, ed., *The Cambridge Economic History of Europe* (Cambridge University Press, 1966).

Marshall Sahlins, *Stone Age Economics* (Aldine, 1972).

E. H. Satorre and G. A. Slafer, *Wheat: Ecology and Physiology of Yield Determination* (Haworth Press, 1999).

# INDEX

Ableman, Michael, 159
Adam and Eve, 13, 32, 58, 137–38
Adonis, 107, 108
Aelian, 156
Aeneas, 184
Aesop, 7, 91
Afghanistan, 55, 85
Africa, 3, 9, 14, 20, 32, 35, 39, 40, 57, 89, 96, 102, 112, 130, 131, 143, 153, 158, 174, 175
African rice, 158
age-related illnesses, 52, 57, 138, 165, 177
Alcott, Louisa May, 170
*alegría,* 11
alfalfa, 9, 43
Algeria, 70, 134
Almaty (Alma-Ata), 13, 137, 177
almond, 1–6, 17, 36, 89, 125, 134
Alvarado, Pedro de, 8
Alzheimer's disease, 46, 97
amaranth, 7–12
amaranth pasta, 11
amaranth tortillas, 11
*American Cookery,* 17, 30, 58

amino acids, 9, 28
*amurca,* 120–21, 122
Anatolia, x, 44, 90, 124, 180. *See also* Fertile Crescent; Turkey
anchovy, 46, 47, 110
Andalusia, 29, 120
Andrus, Charles, 177
Angola, 114, 131
anticarcinogens, 46, 52, 87, 132, 170. *See also* cancer
anti-inflammatory properties, 40, 75, 120, 144
antioxidants, 16, 45, 52, 76, 82, 97, 104, 164, 170, 177
aphrodisiacal properties, 21, 57, 169, 172
Apicius, xi, xii, 89, 125, 139
apple, 6, 13–19, 32, 35, 57–58, 77, 78, 81, 101, 104, 105, 108, 137, 138, 143, 150, 182, 185
apple and orange tart, 17
apple butter, 18–19
apple kuchen, 18
apple pudding, 17
Apulia. *See* Puglia
Arab world, 3, 4, 20, 21, 23, 29, 32,

## ABOUT THE AUTHOR

**GREGORY MCNAMEE** is a writer, editor, photographer, publisher, and publishing consultant who makes his home in Tucson, Arizona. He is the author or editor of more than twenty-five books, among them *Blue Mountains Far Away: Journeys Into the American Wilderness, The Mountain World: A Literary Journey,* and *Gila: The Life and Death of an American River.* He is also the author of the texts for several books of photographs, including *In the Presence of Wolves* (with Art Wolfe) and *American Byzantium: The New Las Vegas* (with Virgil Hancock).

McNamee's work has appeared in such journals and online publications as *Science News, The Nation, Modern Maturity, Newsday, Discovery,* the *Los Angeles Times, Salon,* and the *Washington Post.* He is a contributing editor to *The Bloomsbury Review,* a regular reviewer for *Kirkus Reviews,* and the literary critic and books columnist for *The Hollywood Reporter.* McNamee is also a consultant in world geography to the *Encyclopaedia Britannica* and a regular contributor to it and its online adjunct, Britannica.com.

Please visit www.gregorymcnamee.com for more information. For news about this book, please visit http://moveable-feasts.blogspot.com.

HEALTH LEARNING CENTER
Northwestern Memorial Hospital
Galter 3-304
Chicago, IL